E

7
3

D1124866

Restructuring American Foreign Policy

JOHN D. STEINBRUNER
EDITOR

LIBRARY
FLORIDA KEYS COMMUNITY COLLEGE
5901 West Junior College Road
Key West, Florida 33040

THE BROOKINGS INSTITUTION
WASHINGTON, D.C.

Copyright © 1989 by
THE BROOKINGS INSTITUTION
1775 Massachusetts Avenue, N.W., Washington, D.C. 20036

Library of Congress Cataloging-in-Publication data

Restructuring American foreign policy / John D. Steinbruner, editor.
   p.   cm.
  Includes index.
  ISBN 0-8157-8144-X (alk. paper)   —ISBN 0-8157-8143-1
(pbk. : alk. paper)
  1. United States—Foreign relations—1981– 2. World
politics—1985–1995.   I. Steinbruner, John D., 1941–
II. Brookings Institution.
E876.R47   1989
327.73—do19

9 8 7 6 5 4 3 2 1

The paper used in this publication meets the minimum requirements
of the American National Standard for Information Sciences—
Permanence of Paper for Printed Library Materials,
ANSI Z39.48-1984.

Set in Linotron Sabon

Composition by Monotype Composition Co.
  Baltimore, Maryland

Printing by R. R. Donnelley and Sons Co.
  Harrisonburg, Virginia

THE BROOKINGS INSTITUTION

The Brookings Institution is an independent organization devoted to nonpartisan research, education, and publication in economics, government, foreign policy, and the social sciences generally. Its principal purposes are to aid in the development of sound public policies and to promote public understanding of issues of national importance.

The Institution was founded on December 8, 1927, to merge the activities of the Institute for Government Research, founded in 1916, the Institute of Economics, founded in 1922, and the Robert Brookings Graduate School of Economics and Government, founded in 1924.

The Board of Trustees is responsible for the general administration of the Institution, while the immediate direction of the policies, program, and staff is vested in the President, assisted by an advisory committee of the officers and staff. The by-laws of the Institution state: "It is the function of the Trustees to make possible the conduct of scientific research, and publication, under the most favorable conditions, and to safeguard the independence of the research staff in the pursuit of their studies and in the publication of the results of such studies. It is not a part of their function to determine, control, or influence the conduct of particular investigations or the conclusions reached."

The President bears final responsibility for the decision to publish a manuscript as a Brookings book. In reaching his judgment on the competence, accuracy, and objectivity of each study, the President is advised by the director of the appropriate research program and weighs the views of a panel of expert outside readers who report to him in confidence on the quality of the work. Publication of a work signifies that it is deemed a competent treatment worthy of public consideration but does not imply endorsement of conclusions or recommendations.

The Institution maintains its position of neutrality on issues of public policy in order to safeguard the intellectual freedom of the staff. Hence interpretations or conclusions in Brookings publications should be understood to be solely those of the authors and should not be attributed to the Institution, to its trustees, officers, or other staff members, or to the organizations that support its research.

Board of Trustees

Louis W. Cabot
Chairman

Ralph S. Saul
Vice Chairman

Elizabeth E. Bailey
Rex J. Bates
A. W. Clausen
William T. Coleman, Jr.
Kenneth W. Dam
D. Ronald Daniel

Richard G. Darman
Walter Y. Elisha
Robert F. Erburu
Robert D. Haas
Pamela C. Harriman
B. R. Inman
Vernon E. Jordan, Jr.
James A. Joseph
Thomas G. Labrecque
Donald F. McHenry
Bruce K. MacLaury
Mary Patterson McPherson

Maconda Brown O'Connor
Donald S. Perkins
J. Woodward Redmond
James D. Robinson III
Howard D. Samuel
B. Francis Saul II
Henry B. Schacht
Howard R. Swearer
Morris Tanenbaum
James D. Wolfensohn
Ezra K. Zilkha
Charles J. Zwick

Honorary Trustees

Vincent M. Barnett, Jr.
Barton M. Biggs
Eugene R. Black
Robert D. Calkins
Edward W. Carter
Frank T. Cary
Lloyd N. Cutler
Bruce B. Dayton
Douglas Dillon

Charles W. Duncan, Jr.
Huntington Harris
Andrew Heiskell
Roger W. Heyns
Roy M. Huffington
John E. Lockwood
James T. Lynn
William McC. Martin, Jr.

Robert S. McNamara
Arjay Miller
Charles W. Robinson
Robert V. Roosa
H. Chapman Rose
Gerard C. Smith
Robert Brookings Smith
Sydney Stein, Jr.
Phyllis A. Wallace

Foreword

In some respects, the United States is struggling these days with the consequences of its own success. In the aftermath of World War II, we underwrote reconstruction and encouraged expansion in Germany and Japan, and now feel the challenge of their extraordinary economic performance. We promoted open markets that permitted smaller countries to emerge as significant industrial competitors as well. We built military forces to contain deliberate aggression, and succeeded to an extent that strongly limits the use of military power as an instrument of policy for all governments, including our own.

These accomplishments have dramatically improved American living standards and have prevented global war for four decades. They have also thrust our nation irreversibly into a leadership role in worldwide events, but with diminishing leverage. With the largest economy, the most extensive technological base, and the most capable military establishment, the United States can hardly avoid the concomitant expectations and responsibilities. But it cannot work its will as readily as once seemed possible. Continued leadership in the decades ahead will almost certainly require new ideas, new objectives, and new methods of pursuing them—that is, a redesign of American foreign policy. It will also require some hard political decisions to make a redesigned policy effective.

In this book the authors identify the principal issues that appear to make this restructuring necessary. They describe the changes that have occurred in the economy, in security, and in the policies of important countries and analyze the general implications of those changes. In this overview they draw upon detailed research that has been published in several recent Brookings publications. The authors share the conviction that our foreign policy cannot be altered without extensive public discussion and eventual consensus. Their primary goal in this book is to stimulate and focus that discussion.

The editor of this volume, John D. Steinbruner, is the director of the Brookings Foreign Policy Studies program. Kenneth Flamm, Harry Harding, Ed A. Hewett, Edward J. Lincoln, and Thomas L. McNaugher are senior fellows in that program. Barry P. Bosworth and Robert Z. Lawrence are senior fellows in the Brookings Economic Studies program. William W. Kaufmann is a consultant at Brookings and a faculty member of the John F. Kennedy School of Government at Harvard University. Harold H. Saunders is a visiting fellow at Brookings.

The authors wish to thank Ashton B. Carter, Abram Chayes, Richard Kaufman, Robert Molander, and John Tillson for their comments on the manuscript; Phyllis A. Arthur, Ethan Gutmann, and Amy S. Salsbury for research assistance; Charlotte Brady, Judy G. Buckelew, Kathryn Ho, Susan E. Nichols, Louise F. Skillings, Susan L. Woollen, Kathleen Elliott Yinug, and Ann M. Ziegler for preparing the manuscript; and Kathryn Ho for her assistance in managing the project. Caroline Lalire, Jeanette Morrison, and James R. Schneider edited the manuscript; Phyllis A. Arthur, Susanne E. Lane, Patricia A. Nelson, Andrew Portocarrero, Andrew C. Scobell, and Amy R. Waychoff verified it; and Grace D. Egan prepared the index.

Brookings is grateful to the Carnegie Corporation of New York and to the John D. and Catherine T. MacArthur Foundation both for financial support and for the encouragement to undertake the effort.

The views expressed in this book are solely those of the individual authors and should not be attributed to the Brookings Institution, to its trustees, officers, or other staff members, or to the organizations that support its research.

BRUCE K. MACLAURY
President

November 1988
Washington, D.C.

Contents

Tables

Figures

CHAPTER ONE

Introduction

JOHN D. STEINBRUNER

In the final decade of an eventful century, the United States faces the probable necessity of altering the basic objectives and operating principles of its foreign policy—a formidable problem in a large democracy. The imperative is created by changes in the economy, in security conditions, and in the substance of international politics too extensive to be assimilated into the habits of mind and domestic consensus formed in the aftermath of World War II. The adjustment required is largely constructive, with opportunity providing as strong a motive as danger. It will nonetheless be difficult because it is compelled more by force of circumstance than by trend of opinion. Ideas that have dominated American perceptions and organized American policy for two generations will have to be reformulated. Some hard political choices will have to be made, whether by design or by default.

The matters at stake are certainly important enough to inspire new lines of thought and sharp political decisions. The prosperity of the next generation of Americans is in question. For those who care about their children or about themselves at a later time, there is strong reason to pay attention now. National investment needs to be increased and redirected, and the reasons for doing so need to be absorbed. The security of the next generation of Americans is also much more in question than the current national consciousness would realize or admit. The recognized danger—deliberate aggression—has been powerfully contained, but a distinct possibility of uncontrollable catastrophe lurks in the configuration of current military forces. The reasons why this is so must also be absorbed before actual experience makes it obvious. It is tragic enough to lose a space shuttle before we take seriously the effects of cold weather on the design of missile boosters. To destroy the country out of neglect of subtle but dangerous interactions between military establishments would exceed tragedy. But neither the demands of prosperity nor the threats to security are dramatically displayed in the pattern of immediate events, and that is part of their special difficulty. It has never been easy to act on problems that lie beyond the horizon.

The necessity for American leadership is not in question. The United States is irretrievably engaged on a global scale. A major retrenchment of international commitments is simply not feasible. There is no other country in a better position to lead the management of prosperity and security, and both do require effective management. Leadership will have to be pursued on a very different basis, however, from that of past decades. Economic wealth and military capacity have diffused. Accurate information and sound judgment have acquired greater significance than sheer power. Unilateral action is insufficient for the most demanding problems, and international collaboration is indispensable.

THE CENTRAL EVENTS

The most compelling of the events that are forcing changes in policy is the scale of international economic development. The American economy is no longer a national bastion and automatic source of worldwide authority. In fulfillment of our own expressed intentions, economic capacity has developed globally and has been irreversibly internationalized, bringing the United States greater absolute prosperity but less relative advantage and more international influence over our domestic economic performance than we are yet prepared to handle. In 1945 the United States produced half the economic product in a world severely retarded by the destruction of war. It wielded the overriding authority of an occupying power in West Germany and Japan and projected the type of influence on other European countries, whose empires were still nominally intact, that a magnetic field has on metallic particles. By 1985 the United States was producing less than a fifth of a world economic product that has increased fivefold since 1945. Though political influence is less measurable than economic power, it undoubtedly has been diluted even more as nations everywhere have established their independence. It is a better world on the whole, but one much less spontaneously responsive to the actions of the United States or of any other national government.

Containing an expansionist communist bloc is no longer the dominant security problem for similar reasons. The prominence of that particular objective has been superseded by the consequences of the methods used to achieve it. Existing strategic forces impose a deterrent that is powerful beyond question against a calculated attack, and existing conventional forces establish direct barriers to invasion which are reasonably adequate against the assaults that could realistically be mounted against them. Neither fact, however, guarantees the prevention of war—inevitably the central commitment of policy. The two opposing alliance systems continuously operate large, technically advanced establishments. Extensive, sophisticated, globally dispersed military interactions have been created whose manageability under crisis conditions is very much in question. Effective containment and compelling deterrence have spawned secondary security problems not yet fully recognized or mastered.

The familiar conceptions of political threat that were crystallized into national purpose during the cold war are also being transformed by evolving events, most notably by the internal policy changes initiated first in China and more recently in the Soviet Union. Both countries are now implicitly acknowledging that they do not have a viable independent model for the international economy and must integrate into the existing industrial order if they are to prosper internally. Both countries face impressive obstacles in overcoming their isolation and in adjusting their central planning mechanisms to market conditions. Neither is likely to accomplish these aspirations quickly. The potential is nonetheless strong enough to reshape international politics. China and the Soviet Union are large, underdeveloped economies whose internal inefficiencies present, in principle, marked opportunities for productive investment. They are attempting to open to the outside world at a moment when most nations are projecting sluggish economic growth and are therefore inherently receptive to new market opportunities. Even the vision of these opportunities can carry international relationships beyond the bounds of traditional alliance and adversarial arrangements.

THE POLITICAL PROCESS

The American political system has difficulty in reacting to trends of this magnitude for reasons inherent in its fundamental design. The Constitution effectively protects against concentrations of power that might be the incubator for tyranny and in doing so disperses practical authority. Coordinating action across agencies and over time cannot be achieved without underlying consensus, and consensus in a diverse society is not readily created. Many ideas are expressed and advocated— virtually the full range of human opinion. Very few are taken seriously enough to be acted on; and ironically, those that are may not be clearly articulated. In a bureaucracy organized to control the power of decision, obfuscation and ambiguity are frequent by-products of internal compromise.

Moreover, though a strong rhetorical aspiration for leadership exists in the United States, the larger political process works more effectively to contain leaders than to encourage them. Elections always evoke some promise of initiative but far more powerfully impose a contract of reassurance. Successful candidates are disciplined to honor prevailing commitments of opinion and interest. As a rule, they do not seek and are not granted a mandate for radical departure.

So configured, the American system produces political stability and protects individual rights and is justifiably revered for those reasons. It does so, however, at some cost to the coherence and adaptability of policy. If one speaks of the effective substance of policy and excludes nominally authoritative declarations, such policy is not neatly determined by regular procedure or predictable schedules. It evolves by accretion over time and occasionally by the catalytic action of dramatic events. At any given moment it is incomplete and imperfectly consistent, but those elements that are truly established are not easily redirected.

It is practical to assume, therefore, that a reformulation of American foreign policy compelled by external circumstance will not be an orderly or readily observable process. It is undoubtedly well under way already even if its ultimate character cannot yet be clearly identified. It is not likely to be completed in the course of a single election or governmental transition. It almost certainly will not be the sole accomplishment of an individual leader, a political party, or a prestigious committee. Policy adjustments of the scope required depend on changes in prevailing ideas—the assumptions and attitudes that guide an entire society. The primary, unavoidable method is simply the continuous process of debate and public discussion through which common beliefs are formed.

It is also practical to assume that the process of reformulation will depend on a set of illustrative, organizing issues. It is the fundamentals of American policy more than the specifics that are in question, but fundamental assumptions cannot be engaged without some defining context. General assertions of principle come to have an enduring effect only when they are connected to precedent-setting actions.

There is considerable, even intractable, uncertainty involved in recognizing in advance which specific decisions will play this formative role. The determination of policy is attempted or asserted more often than it is achieved. There is less mystery, however, about the type of decisions involved, since the American government operates in well-known channels. It sets budgets, levies taxes, and regulates financial flows; in doing so it establishes conceptions about the economy. It purchases military equipment and operates military forces and in doing so forms conceptions of security. Increasingly it negotiates with the Soviet Union as an assumed adversary and thereby encounters the question of how to relate the result of such negotiations to the purchase and operation of weapons. It communicates with other governments and thereby defines American purposes. The reformulation of policy will necessarily involve these principal channels of operation. The results will clearly be molded by impending domestic financial pressures. They will be tempered, most predictably, by the deliberate reform efforts in the Soviet Union and China, by the more spontaneous evolution of new political relationships in Asia, and by the chronic crisis of the existing order centered in the Middle East.

THE FORMATIVE DECISIONS

It is evident that conditions in the American economy are not in stable harmony with the international markets and that major adjustment is unavoidable. In recent years the United States has been consuming more than it produces and investing more than it saves. The foreign capital flows necessary to finance these domestic imbalances cannot be indefinitely sustained, and the process of adjustment will involve some element of political and economic pain. A temporary reduction in American standards of living is likely to occur; the question is how severe and how enduring.

This adjustment could be imposed by additional declines in the value of the dollar. That method avoids the difficulty of explicit political choice but promises a more lasting disruption of the economic performance in the form of renewed inflation, high interest rates, and retarded investment. Alternatively, the adjustment could be managed by reducing the internal budget deficit by about $30–$50 billion a year (accurately calculated) over a five-year period. That method would enhance longer-term economic performance and would provide some portion of the credibility necessary for American leadership in the emerging international economic order. But it would require unpopular decisions—a combination of raising taxes and cutting expenditures.

The economic imperative to reduce the fiscal deficit and the political difficulty in doing so have been recognized by virtually everyone who follows American policy, but the international implications have been less clearly appreciated. As detailed in chapter 2, the radical change in the status of the United States in the international economy has also changed the role that economic considerations must play in American foreign policy. Rather than being an implicit source of leverage useful for pursuing political objectives, the American economy now imposes its own objective, and it is one of overriding importance. If the domestic economic adjustment is to be managed successfully without a cycle of renewed inflation and severe recession, American exports will have to be expanded considerably. In support of that requirement, American foreign policy will have to defend and in fact to increase the openness of the international trading system. To do that, the United States must not only conquer its own political and conceptual instincts for protectionism but also establish the credibility necessary to resist those instincts in other countries. It must not only remove formal barriers but also assertively promote expanded trade against the ubiquitous human tendency to restrict competition. And all this must be done under conditions where sheer leverage is not sufficient.

The consequence of this new imperative will undoubtedly be felt in security policy. Any feasible outcome of the impending economic adjustment will constrain the defense budget to levels, as a practical likelihood, no greater than their current ones in real terms. These levels, already roughly 10 percent below the historic peak in 1985, are containing an unprecedented surge in defense budget authority that averaged about 9 percent annual growth from fiscal 1981 through 1985 and that was allocated in the fiscal 1986 five-year defense plan as if it would continue at an annual growth rate of nearly 7 percent for five more years.[1] Since the increases were disproportionately directed to major weapons procurement, the surge implicitly increased the projected rate of replacement of military equipment from an average of twenty years, reflecting standard weapons design assumptions and life cycle experiences, to a rate substantially faster. That more rapid rate cannot be sustained. Quite apart from fiscal constraints and the apparent moderation of threat, it is increasingly evident that the technical design process cannot support such an acceleration. The time required to master the sophisticated designs of contemporary weapons, in particular to make them work in

---

1. Calculation of current and historical defense budget authority is based on constant 1988 dollars. See *Historical Tables: Budget of the United States Government, Fiscal Year 1989*, p. 97; and Office of the Assistant Secretary of Defense (Comptroller), *National Defense Budget Estimates for FY 1988/1989* (May 1987), pp. 92–94. The 1986 five-year defense plan is based on constant 1986 dollars. See *Department of Defense Annual Report, Fiscal Year 1986*, pp. 71, 78.

actual military operations, cannot be compressed to that extent, at least not at a feasible cost. The initial models of new weapons designs almost always have important design defects that cannot be discovered and corrected until operational experience has accumulated. Forcing full-scale production at the outset of deployment propagates design errors and forces military users either to tolerate these defects, at a cost to their potential performance, or to undergo retrofit programs whose cost regularly swamps whatever economies of scale were achieved in the initial production runs. The rate of weapons replacement in the United States has been seriously out of line with economic, technical, and military realities, and again a substantial adjustment appears inevitable.

Alternative ways to ensure American security could be adopted to meet these circumstances. As described in chapter 3, it is possible, even with fiscally constrained defense budgets, to preserve traditional international commitments under traditional conceptions of threat, but not with domestic politics as usual. There would have to be much greater discipline imposed on the internal allocation of resources and on the resulting configurations of missions and forces than has been achieved in recent years. Major weapons procurement programs would have to be extended over longer periods of time, and some would have to be cancelled, particularly those that duplicate mission capability already reasonably well established. Some important but chronically neglected areas—reserve equipment, sea and air transport, and close air support, for example—would have to be protected. In the process, established political commitments to individual weapons programs, to the accelerated rate of procurement, to particular service missions, and to several other individual components of the defense effort would have to be subordinated to an efficient design of an overall security posture. Unpleasant as the fact may be, the fiscal austerity does have the virtue of forcing managerial efficiency; in that sense it is an opportunity as well as a problem.

There is a larger opportunity, however, both to relieve the burdens of achieving a more efficient allocation of the defense effort and to establish a more stable military balance by means of international agreement. As detailed in chapter 4, measures that would accomplish these results have been outlined in recent arms control negotiations and have apparently emerged as the principal thrust of a significantly revised Soviet security policy. The measures include reductions of nuclear and conventional weapons and associated restraints on technical modernization and operational practices. They are designed to diminish the capacity for performing rapid, potentially preemptive offensive missions.

Their implementation would not diminish the basic deterrent power of
the opposing military establishments but would render their crisis
interactions much less volatile and inherently more manageable. This
latter effect provides a security incentive that strongly complements
economic considerations in motivating a restructuring of the prevailing
military balance.

Though the financial magnitudes are smaller and the triggering effects
of impending fiscal austerity therefore less powerful, the process of
adjustment would logically include as well a restructuring of national
technical investment. As reviewed in chapter 5, the United States implicitly
used the occasion of World War II and the competition in military
development that followed to organize and finance a critical level of
technological development intermediate between fundamental science on
the one hand and specific commercial and military applications on the
other. This type of investment requires a public subsidy—and hence a
justifying rationale—since the risks are too large, the uncertainty too
great, and the rewards too remote for it to be sustained by normal
market forces. Beginning in World War II, the national defense effort
provided much of the rationale and the subsidy for this investment in
the United States, with productive results both for the military establishment and for the economy generally during the ensuing decades.
Computers and aircraft technology are the most prominent and significant
historical examples; superconducting materials perhaps the most significant emerging instance. But the circumstances that made defense-oriented
technical investment a productive pattern for the United States have
changed substantially. Technology has diffused internationally, and
commercial markets have developed more impetus and capacity. In a
number of other countries, particularly Japan, a more commercially
oriented pattern of technical investment has been strikingly successful.
Moreover, conditions for making productive investments in military
technology have also evolved to the point where marginal improvements
are far more expensive, more time consuming, and more dependent on
the opponent's reaction. A substantial adjustment in the American pattern
of technical investment seems necessary in part to generalize its rationale
and purpose and in part to make the defense component more consistent
with contemporary security requirements.

THE TEMPERING CONDITIONS

As noted, the same imperatives that appear to compel a restructuring
of American economic and security policy have already inspired drasti-

cally different formulations of policy in the centrally planned economies, where the need for adjustment has been even greater. In fact, Mikhail S. Gorbachev has made the Russian term, *perestroika,* very nearly a universal household word and in doing so has successfully implanted the idea of changes so fundamental that the basic objectives and operating principles of the state would be altered and its actions pervasively affected. The idea of *perestroika* and the international resonance the word has enjoyed are an expression and also conceivably a catalytic agent of radical change. That is the stuff out of which new eras of history are made, and to the extent that such thoughts are taken seriously, the United States can hardly expect to conduct business as usual.

The content and prospects of reform in the centrally planned economies are reviewed in chapter 6, providing the larger context for the new Soviet security conception discussed in chapter 4. Chapter 6 documents a vision of reform seriously enough presented and powerfully enough motivated to preclude summary dismissal. Both China and the Soviet Union are pursuing a redesign of their economies and their social order. Improved economic performance is the central objective, and in pursuit of it central controls are to be loosened, the power of decision dispersed, material incentives increased for normal workers and consumers, and inevitably economic security decreased. These reforms amount to the outline of a new social contract in which the foremost welfare states of the world are proposing to expose themselves and their constituents to increased risk and market discipline in order to motivate an improvement in their own performance. China has already "normalized" many of its external political relationships in support of that process, a phrase that understates the significance of the change in its relationship with the United States in particular. The Soviet Union is now articulating commensurate intentions, and from a base of far more extensive military engagement than China's is explicitly attempting to stabilize its external relationships. The intention has been authoritatively formulated, but the implications are only minimally defined and not yet implemented. Those implications are a major preoccupation both for the Soviet Union and for the rest of the world.

As deliberate efforts proceed to embody the ideas of normalization and stabilization in actual practice, they are likely to be guided by spontaneous developments in Asia that appear to offer an experimental model. The remarkable surge in many of the Asian economies has generated new patterns of economic relationships to which political attitudes are rapidly adjusting. The increased importance of Japan is unmistakable as is the regional significance of an emerging China. But the larger story is the networking among many centers of power that is producing a different form of international order. That process is also accompanied by domestic political transformations in several countries that have successfully used highly authoritarian systems to direct economic development and by incipient crisis in several other countries that have attempted to do so with unfortunate results. Conceptual understanding appears to lag well behind the pace of events in Asia, which do not march to anyone's clear design. The future of international politics nonetheless appears to be forming there, and the spontaneous patterns are likely to have a strong effect on America's efforts to reformulate the fundamentals of its policy. Chapter 7 reviews the Asian experience with this in mind.

But the promise of the future is not the only prevailing influence. The weight of the past in the form of unavoidable and unresolved problems can also be expected to affect the process of reformulation. The balance between these influences is probably most compellingly and poignantly present in the Middle East, where the past and the emotions it generates are powerful, where traditional designs of policy are obviously in deep trouble, and where the spontaneous evolution of social relationships seems to be giving more impetus to politics than economic interest or strategic calculation does. This difficult subject is explored in chapter 8, which in considering the recent events and inherent policy problems of the Middle East reconceptualizes how international diplomacy is most effectively conducted. The focus of that analysis is more on the process than on the substance of policy, recognizing that it is much easier in the Middle East to identify imaginable outcomes than to devise realistic methods for achieving them.

IMPLICATIONS

The formative issues and background political developments discussed in this book obviously do not present a comprehensive review of all the matters that impinge on the United States. Many other problems of seminal importance are likely to affect a reformulation of policy, such as the handling of international debt, the increasing necessity of global environmental management, the control of civil violence, the enabling of economic development, and the graceful recognition of suppressed national identities. There are many areas of the world not directly discussed that will also be important. The analysis presented here is not inclusive enough to provide a complete redesign of American foreign policy.

Some selective attention is almost certainly a practical requirement, however, for working out new principles of policy. Without conceptual focus, effective comprehension is likely to be overwhelmed by the pace and scope of international events. Though not sufficient to establish final conclusions, the issues discussed here are urgent and central enough to compel focused attention and to initiate new lines of thought. That beginning is important even if the end is not yet in sight.

Nor are the ultimate implications completely mysterious. The realignment of the American economy, the reallocation of the defense effort, the pursuit of cooperative security, and the reconfiguration of technical investment are true imperatives. They are objectives whose importance cannot be reasonably denied, and the degree of success in achieving them will affect all other issues. In procedural terms, moreover, it is equally undeniable that the United States must eventually develop a more interactive, less unilateral style of action. Habitual reliance on what is believed to provide bargaining leverage will have to be reduced in pursuit of greater effectiveness. Both the lure of financial subsidy and the threat of economic sanction or military coercion are increasingly unreliable instruments unless set in a legitimizing context. As emphasized particularly in chapter 8, results are now achieved or denied as a consequence of continuing international relationships in which the principles of reason and equity are, over time, more powerful and more stable determinants than submission to superior leverage or clever maneuver. For the most practical of reasons it is necessary for the United States to develop refined principles of diplomacy and to promote internationally the central feature of its political system—the rule of law.

All this can be accomplished only if the United States develops a more extensive and more penetrating public discussion of the need to do so. The promotion of that discussion is the central purpose of this book.

CHAPTER TWO

America's Global Role: From Dominance to Interdependence

BARRY P. BOSWORTH
ROBERT Z. LAWRENCE

For much of the period after the Second World War, the United States dominated the world economy. Richly endowed with natural resources, it had the world's most highly educated and trained work force, the most modern plant and equipment, and the latest technologies in almost every industry. Combining these factors with the economies of scale in a huge and rich domestic market in the 1950s, the United States produced about twice as much per worker as its wealthiest European counterpart and its citizens enjoyed the world's highest standard of living.

The relationship between America and the rest of the world was asymmetric. The value of the United States to the world economy flowed from its unparalleled productive base. It was often the only source of the products based on new technologies that emerged after the war. New products and technologies were usually introduced in the United States and then diffused abroad. Foreigners depended on the U.S. dollar for an international medium of exchange and on U.S. leadership for maintaining and expanding the global trading institutions and rules. But America still determined its economic fate at home. Trade was only a small share of economic activity, foreign capital flows were a small share of financial activity, and economic policy was based on domestic considerations.

America faced the rest of the world with confidence. Sure of their economic advantage, U.S. business and labor leaders agreed that free trade was in the nation's interest and that prosperity abroad was good for America. American foreign policy focused on political rather than economic goals—often trading economic advantage, such as access to U.S. markets or technology, for political gains—driven by the perception that America's greatest threat was a political one from the Soviet Union.

The nation's international economic policies were based on the principle of multilateralism: the notion that international economic policies should be used not only to increase American power but also to open markets for all. This concept is most clearly embodied in the basic principle of the General Agreement on Tariffs and Trade (GATT)— most-favored-nation treatment.

By the late 1970s much had changed. In several respects the United States was no longer clearly preeminent. The postwar economic recovery in other industrial countries brought their standards of living much closer to that of the United States. The United States offered little that was unique on the production side: American workers did not always have the best skills or work with the most modern equipment. Increasingly, American management appeared to fail to maintain quality, motivate its work force, and make decisions for the long term. Instead, the importance of the United States rested on the sheer size of its markets and the defense umbrella it provided. It continued to support a large research base, but new technologies were often introduced faster in other countries.

In addition, the channels linking the United States to the global economy had grown deep and wide, so the effects of change were now felt in both directions. Trade had grown to account for almost 20 percent of gross national product, and the United States was no longer self-sufficient in natural resources. Most of the barriers to international capital flows had been removed, and vast electronic networks integrated American financial markets into a global system. Financial capital and technology could move relatively freely across national borders—it had become a far more open, competitive economic system.

In an earlier era of limits on exchange rates, communications, and transportation, comparative advantage in trade was heavily based on national endowments and evolved only slowly over time. Today, trade competition between developed countries is based more and more on ephemeral advantages in technology, and production facilities can be readily moved from country to country in response to changes in exchange rates and costs. And, while a large world market has increased the rewards of success, so too has it raised the costs of failure. The results are an increased vulnerability to fluid competitive conditions and a greater potential for dislocation of communities and work forces.

This opening of world markets was actively promoted by the United States, but Americans were slow to recognize the significance of the changes. Open financial markets, combined with flexible exchange rates, provide a mechanism by which changes in fiscal-monetary policy are quickly felt in other countries. The effects of policy changes can rebound on the originating country in ways that were not fully anticipated. In such a world, a nation's fiscal and monetary policies are more constrained than in the past by the discipline of international capital markets and the competitive pressures that exchange rate changes exert. Even measures undertaken for purely domestic considerations, such as taxes, safety regulations, and antitrust laws, will influence international trade and investment flows.

It was remarkable that, despite these changes in America's global position, the Reagan economic program in its early years was based entirely on a domestic perspective. The goals were to reduce inflation and to stimulate growth. The tools were monetary restraint and tax cuts. The importance of global economic relations and the increase in international interdependence were not part of the policy debate. Indeed, the administration's policymakers differed from their predecessors on three basic principles: they were skeptical of efforts to coordinate national economic policies, they actively disavowed any intention to monitor or control exchange rates, and they were highly distrustful of international organizations.

At first the international linkages facilitated the policy. Monetary restraint pushed U.S. interest rates to record levels. High interest rates became a magnet for capital inflows from other countries, driving up the demand for dollars and thus the exchange rate. The resulting fall of import prices reinforced high unemployment in pushing down the rate of inflation. Other countries were forced to undertake contractionary policies to offset the inflation shock of their depreciating currencies. The ultimate easing of American monetary policy in the face of huge tax cuts stimulated the expansion of demand and economic recovery.

Over the medium term, however, the dynamic altered. Once they had absorbed the inflationary effect of the appreciating dollar, foreign economies felt the stimulus of the surge in American imports and the withdrawal of American exports from world markets. The U.S. trade deficit grew and forced a restructuring of domestic industry as capacity and employment in tradable goods industries shrank to be replaced by an expansion of industries oriented toward the domestic market. Pressures for protection mounted, and the administration responded by restricting imports in more and more industries. The excess of imports over exports left world markets with a rapidly growing supply of dollar liabilities to be absorbed. The dollar began to fall in 1985 as the increased supply of dollars was coupled with reduced demand—private investors feared the potential losses from future declines in the dollar's value. Initially acting in concert, the U.S. and other governments aided the decline. Later, foreign governments in particular, while calling on the United States to reduce its budget deficit, intervened in exchange markets to slow the dollar's fall and protect their exports.

The Reagan administration was forced to reverse its approach to international economic policy. It expanded the role of the International Monetary Fund and World Bank when the debt crisis erupted, and it joined in efforts to influence the dollar's value and coordinate national economic policies. Interdependence reemerged as a theme of American international economic policy.

Today America finds itself in a new situation. Confidence in the beneficial effects of an open international system and in itself has been shaken. It no longer has hegemony over the world economy. Instead, its position might be described as "first among equals." U.S. foreign economic policy can no longer be used solely to achieve political goals: it has become crucial to domestic economic well-being. The nation's freedom to control its own destiny is more constrained by its position as a debtor country, forced to dance to the tune of its creditors.

Over the next decade the United States will face continued pressures from the world economy. It will ultimately be forced to adjust to the decline in its net foreign asset position and the costs of financing its debts, accepting reduced growth of domestic spending and further depreciation of the dollar. It will become even more concerned about foreign industrial and trade practices as it struggles to recover lost export markets. Even if it chooses to delay adjustment, it will have to respond to the concerns of foreign investors by offering higher interest rate premiums on U.S. securities or borrowing in foreign currencies. As foreign debt and interest payments grow, it will have to borrow more or begin to reduce the deficit in the trade account. Delay places great pressure on monetary policy in the short run and ensures that, when adjustment does occur, the required shifts in economic structure and spending patterns will be even greater.

As convenient as it is to blame the rest of the world for the problems of the U.S. economy and the threat to future living standards, those problems primarily reflect failings in U.S. domestic policies. The growth of an open international economy alters the symptoms of those policy failings and complicates the recovery, but does not change the prescription for recovery: increase national saving and productivity growth. To repeat, the international economy is not the source of U.S. problems. The United States is not disadvantaged by economic growth abroad, it is not the innocent victim of unfair trade practices by others, and its tradable goods industries do not suffer from a fundamental inability to compete.

The options for American economic policy and the implications of its role in the international economy are discussed in greater detail in the following sections. First we analyze the domestic imbalances in saving and investment that triggered the reliance on foreign borrowing and the corrective measures that will be needed to reduce it. Next we look at the issues that have surfaced under the general heading of "competitiveness." How well has the U.S. performed in world markets, and what does the change in its position vis-à-vis other economies mean for U.S. welfare and power? In the final section we examine policy responses to the domestic imbalances and America's changed international position.

DOMESTIC IMBALANCES

In the 1980s the U.S. economy has been on an enormous consumption binge, selling assets and borrowing heavily both domestically and abroad. Consumption (public plus private) per capita has expanded since 1980 about 50 percent faster than domestic production. The experience for many Americans has been pleasurable: tax cuts have bolstered their spending power, cheap imported goods have cut the rate of inflation, and unemployment has fallen to levels last reached in the early 1970s.

The spending spree, however, has been at the cost of a sharp decline in national saving. The net national saving rate averaged only 2 percent of net national product in 1986–87. The country has been spending more than it produces, importing more than it exports, and borrowing from abroad at an annual rate of $150 billion. The resulting trade deficit has caused a wrenching realignment of American industry as many firms found themselves priced out of world markets by the sharp rise in the dollar exchange rate during the first half of the decade. Increasingly, the pleasures of the spending binge are being tempered by a recognition of its costs: a loss of world markets and the burden of debt placed on future generations.

The implications of this situation for the future can be most simply addressed by examining the options that American policymakers face. If nothing is done, how long could the United States continue to borrow from abroad to support its consumption? What events would bring the process to an end? If, instead, the United States brings its spending levels

Table 2-1. *Net Saving and Investment as a Share of Net National Product, United States, 1951–87*[a]
Percent

Item	1951– 1960	1961– 1970	1971– 1980	1981– 1985	1986	1987
Net saving						
Private saving[b]	8.7	9.4	9.7	8.2	7.2	6.1
Government saving	−0.7	−1.0	−2.0	−4.5	−5.2	−4.1
Net investment						
Net foreign investment	0.3	0.7	0.3	−1.3	−3.8	−3.8
Net domestic investment	7.7	7.7	7.5	5.0	5.7	5.8
Total national saving-investment	8.0	8.4	7.7	3.6	2.0	2.0

Source: U.S. Department of Commerce, Bureau of Economic Analysis, *United States National Income and Product Accounts*, table 5-1. Figures are rounded.
a. Net saving and investment equal the gross flow minus capital consumption allowances (the depreciation of existing capital). Net national product equals gross national product minus capital consumption allowances.
b. Defined as business and household saving. Employee pension funds of state and local governments are allocated to household saving to match the treatment of private pension funds.

back in line with production, what budget actions will be needed and what economic impact will they have?

The Saving-Investment Balance

The pattern of excessive consumption is illustrated in table 2-1, which summarizes recent trends in saving and investment. Despite the tax incentives enacted in the 1980s, the private sector is responsible for much of the decline in saving. The private saving rate fell from an average of 9.7 in the 1970s to 6.7 percent in 1986–87.[1] The principal blame for the decline in national saving, however, lies with the budget policies of the federal government. The budget deficit ballooned from 1 percent of national income in the 1960s to 2 percent in the 1970s and then to 4.5 percent in the 1980s. In 1987 the deficit absorbed two-thirds of private saving. Because little of the current budget deficit can be attributed to cyclical factors in the economy, it largely reflects a structural imbalance between taxes and expenditure.

On the investment side, domestic capital formation has been below

1. Three partial explanations for the decline in private saving can be mentioned. First, more investment in short-lived capital has raised capital consumption allowances relative to GNP (the gross private saving rate fell by 2 percent of GNP compared with the 3 percentage point fall in the net). Second, large capital gains on private wealth promoted greater consumption in the 1980s. Third, the rise in the rate of return on financial assets led employers to contribute less to private pension funds.

the rates of earlier decades. Even at the current rate of 6 percent of national income, though, it still exceeds the nation's rate of saving—hence the need to borrow abroad. In 1987, for example, the United States saved 2 percent of its income, invested 6 percent, and borrowed the difference from other countries by running a current account deficit equal to 4 percent of national income.[2] The low rate of domestic investment shows that the infusion of foreign capital was not merely a response to new investment opportunities in a revitalized American economy. Clearly, the borrowing is financing more consumption, not investment.

An accounting identity equates the difference between domestic saving and investment with the current account balance. The discussion so far has focused on the domestic side of that identity. In theory, the impetus for the trade deficit could have come from other countries: an inflow of foreign capital could have driven up the value of the dollar, causing the trade deficit. But if the trade deficit were being forced on the United States by other countries, one would expect to see a domestic economy beset by high unemployment and interest rates lower than those in the rest of the world. Just the opposite occurred in the United States when the trade deficit emerged: total demand and employment were expanding very rapidly. By the same token, claims that trade eliminated millions of American jobs seem absurd, since unemployment fell throughout the period of rising trade deficits. There was a major restructuring, however, as workers were moved from tradable goods industries to nontradables (where foreign production could not help meet the surge in consumption demand).

The trade deficit is also often blamed on the unfair trade practices of other countries or cited as evidence of decline in the competitiveness of the U.S. economy. More accurately, however, it is a symptom of an extravagant domestic consumption. Without the trade deficit, the U.S. economy would be facing too much demand for its productive capacity. Either inflation would accelerate sharply or, if the Federal Reserve attempted to restrain demand, interest rates would rise steeply.

The large trade deficit was not anticipated when the current economic program was enacted in 1981. Many observers did foresee that the combination of large tax cuts, a defense buildup, and a restrictive

---

2. "Net foreign investment" in the national income accounts is equivalent to the concept of the current account in balance of payments accounting. In 1987 the current account deficit was $158.2 billion. The corresponding figure for net foreign investment was −$160.6 billion. *Survey of Current Business*, vol. 68 (July 1988), p. 69.

Figure 2-1. *Exchange Value of the U.S. Dollar, 1970–88*

1980–82 average = 100

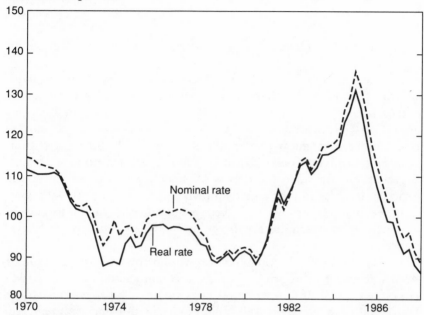

Source: Morgan Guaranty Trust Company of New York, International Economics Department, *World Financial Markets*, various issues.

monetary policy would drive up domestic interest rates. In previous episodes, however, that policy mix had crowded out domestic investment—particularly housing—and created domestic political pressures to reverse the policies. The new factor in the 1980s was investors' willingness and ability to move capital across national borders in response to higher interest rates in the United States. The increase in foreign investors' demand for dollars led to a sharp rise in the exchange rate and a net inflow of foreign resources (lower exports, higher imports) sufficient to finance the surge of consumption plus a near-normal level of investment.

Because there are lags in the response of trade to exchange rate changes, the whole process overshot. By 1986 the United States was actually borrowing more than it needed to finance domestic demand, and interest rates and the exchange rate plummeted (figure 2-1). But there are limits to how far this process can go in reverse because the United States still needs a substantial current account deficit to balance saving and investment at current interest rates. Efforts to expand exports over the long term will be constrained by the limits of productive capacity, adding to inflation. Any sustained decline in the current account deficit must await a reduction of the budget deficit and a recovery of the national saving rate.

The Limits of Debt Finance

The current account deficit has financed a rise in American living standards in the 1980s that would have been impossible if the nation had been forced to live within the limits of its own production. Reducing growth in U.S. consumption—private and public—enough to balance trade will be economically and politically painful. Thus there is a strong political incentive to delay adjustment and blame the policies of other countries for the trade imbalance. Ultimately, Americans will adjust, either in the short run through their own efforts to raise national saving, or in the long run through a reduced rate of domestic capital formation, as American interest rates are driven up by the effort to attract foreign financing.

During the 1980s the United States will borrow at least $800 billion from foreigners, transforming it from a creditor nation to the world's largest net debtor. If future interest rates are near 10 percent, the United States will have to export $80 billion more than it imports every year simply to meet the interest payments on the debt of a single decade. The process is cumulative: each year of continued current account deficit means more debt and larger interest payments in the future. For the nation to achieve the trade surplus needed to make these interest payments, the real exchange rate will have to fall. The price of American goods in world markets will fall and the price of imports will rise— lowering the growth of American standards of living until consumption is forced back in line with production. This gradual process could extend many years into the future while the debt continues to grow. The United States currently borrows from abroad about 3–4 percent of its income yearly. Because it is a wealthy country, it may be able to continue to do so for years to come. The policy may be foolish, but foreign investors might support the process as long as voters are willing to pass the costs onto future generations.

Alternatively, a crisis in financial markets is possible. To attract foreign capital the United States must offer a rate of return above that in other countries and high enough to offset the fears of investors that interest rate gains will be wiped out by a future exchange rate decline. Fears that the financing cannot be maintained and that the exchange rate will decline can lead to a sudden outflow of private capital and an abrupt self-fulfilling fall in the dollar. Such a precipitous fall was avoided in 1987 only because foreign governments stepped in to support the dollar when confidence waned.

But governments cannot accumulate dollar assets on a large scale indefinitely. The United States will have to offer higher interest rates to attract private capital and maintain the dollar's value. If it does not, a lower dollar and a recovery of exports, without a comparable reduction in domestic spending, will strain U.S. industrial capacity, pushing up the rate of inflation. Ultimately, voter dissatisfaction with either rising inflation or interest rates may shift national sentiment in favor of the harsh actions needed to cut back domestic consumption.

Prospects for the Budget Deficit

In the long term, decisions about the proper size of the budget surplus or deficit must be based on its implications for national saving and capital formation.[3] At the beginning of the 1980s, supply-side economics was sold as a means to raise national saving above its historic rate of about 8 percent of net national product. Instead, the saving rate has plummeted to 2 percent—a shift for which there is no economic justification. The rate of return to capital has not declined, and retirement saving should be higher because the U.S. population is aging.

Furthermore, except in times of surging domestic investment, a highly developed country like the United States should normally be an international creditor, rather than a debtor. The achievement of that goal would require a minimal increase in the national saving rate of 3.8 percent of net national product (see table 2-1).

Reducing the federal budget deficit is a basic step in the effort to raise the national saving rate.[4] Short of coercive action, government can do little to raise private saving. Tax incentives in the early 1980s failed to raise private saving. Many taxpayers rearranged their finances to take

3. The budget deficit will, of necessity, fluctuate on a year-to-year basis to offset cyclical fluctuations in private demand and concerns about inflation and unemployment. Comparisons of American budget deficits with those of other nations, with sharply different patterns of private saving and investment, are not sufficient to evaluate the full balance of saving and investment.

4. For a further discussion of the relationship between the budget deficit and national saving, see Lawrence H. Summers, "The Results Are in on the Deficit Experiment," paper presented at a conference sponsored by Americans for Generational Equity, Washington, D.C., September 10, 1987.

Table 2-2. *Federal Budget Deficit with and without Retirement Trust Funds, Selected Fiscal Years, 1980–93*
Billions of dollars

Item	1980	1987	1988	1989	1993	Change, 1980–93
GRH targets[a]	...	− 144	− 144	− 136	0	...
Total federal deficit	− 74	− 150	− 155	− 148	− 121	− 47
Less surplus in social security[b] (off-budget)	− 1	20	39	52	99	100
On-budget deficit (unified)	− 73	− 170	− 194	− 200	− 220	− 147
Less surplus in medicare[c]	1	12	16	20	15	14
Less surplus in federal employee retirement	10	31	34	37	44	34
General fund nonretirement deficit	− 84	− 213	− 244	− 257	− 279	− 195

Source: Numbers for 1980 and 1987 are from *Historical Tables: Budget of the United States Government, Fiscal Year 1989*, pp. 16, 313, 317; *Budget of the United States Government: Appendix, Fiscal Year 1982*, p. I-V118; and *Appendix, Fiscal Year 1989*, pp. I-H13, I-W5. Numbers for 1988 through 1993 are from U.S. Congress, Congressional Budget Office, *The Economic and Budget Outlook: An Update* (Washington, D.C.: CBO, August 1988), p. 60.
a. Gramm-Rudman-Hollings balanced budget law.
b. Old age, survivors, and disability insurance.
c. Health insurance.

advantage of the tax benefits, such as individual retirement accounts, without increasing their overall rate of saving. The loss of tax revenue increased federal borrowing while the private saving rate actually fell.

Some analysts expect the private saving rate to recover from the abnormally low levels of the mid-1980s when the large baby-boom generation moves into the age brackets in which saving should be high. The influence of demographics is a weak peg on which to hang expectations of higher future saving: they have had small effect on past trends in the saving rate, and they cannot account for the decline in the 1980s.

Current government projections of the budget deficit for the next five years provide the basis for the argument that it is on a declining path. After reaching a peak of $221 billion in fiscal 1986, the deficit did decline to an estimated $155 billion in fiscal 1988. It is projected to fall further, to $121 billion in fiscal 1993 (see row 2 of table 2-2). The $121 billion would represent 1.8 percent of GNP, which compares favorably with the average of 2.1 percent in 1978–79, and less so with the 1.2 percent in 1972–74, comparable years of cyclical expansion.

Yet it is important to understand that these figures are merely projections of the current services budget. On the spending side, they allow for no new programs. The costs of defense and other annual appropriation programs are increased only to cover inflation. As a result, expenditures are always projected to fall as a share of GNP (in this case, by about 1 percentage point over five years) even though actual expenditures have increased by about 1 percent of GNP for each decade since the 1950s. Revenues are projected on the basis of current law and remain a constant or slowly rising share of GNP. Thus projections of this sort almost invariably show the deficit to be falling over time.[5]

Second, the total budget, which is most often cited, includes the revenue and expenditure of the social security trust fund. That fund had a surplus of $39 billion in fiscal 1988, and it is projected to grow to an annual surplus of $99 billion by fiscal 1993. The social security surplus was intended to offset some of the cost of that program when the baby-boom generation retires. Under current budget practices the federal government will simply borrow the surplus to finance consumption-type expenditures in the rest of the budget. As shown in table 2-2, if the social security surplus is excluded, the deficit in the unified budget was $194 billion in fiscal 1988 and will grow (even under current services assumptions) to $220 billion by fiscal 1993. If we exclude the other retirement accounts as well (medicare and federal employee retirement), the deficit rises to $279 billion by fiscal 1993. Exclusive of the trust funds, the budget deficit problem is getting worse, not better.

Currently the Balanced Budget Reaffirmation Act of 1987 calls for eliminating the deficit in the overall budget (including social security) by 1993. Unless the private saving rate rises in the meantime, the United States will still be left with a national saving rate below that of the 1970s, but the change from 1987 would raise national saving by an amount large enough to eliminate foreign borrowing (the current account deficit). In addition, because the target includes the social security surplus, it reflects a substantial shift in tax burden. The surplus in the retirement program, financed by a tax on annual wages below $45,000, would be used to pay for general fund expenditures.

If the budget deficit targets were revised to exclude the social security surplus—aiming for balance in the on-budget accounts—the national saving rate would be boosted an additional 1.5 percentage points in the mid-1990s. Assuming that the private saving rate stays at the 1986–87 average of 6.7 percent, the national saving rate would return to the average of the preceding three decades. This policy would require a mix of tax increases and expenditure reductions of $220 billion annually by 1993, or about $1,000 per capita. Such a substantial scaling back of the

5. U.S. Congress, Congressional Budget Office, *The Economic and Budget Outlook: An Update* (Washington, D.C.: CBO, August 1988), p. 51.

recent growth rates of living standards will be particularly hard at a time when the public pressure for new social programs—day care, medical care, education—seems to be increasing, though unmatched by comparable support for tax increases to pay for them.

Adjusting to Smaller Deficits

The long-run target for the budget deficit may be of academic interest only, however, since it could not and should not be achieved overnight. Although a major reduction is necessary, it must be achieved in a series of yearly steps. A more practical question is the speed with which the adjustment could be made without seriously disrupting the economy.

A restrictive fiscal policy (lower public spending or higher taxes) will tend to depress economic activity, but it can be offset by an easing of monetary policy to promote compensatory increases in private spending. One principal effect of smaller budget deficits should be lower interest rates and higher domestic investment. Another more significant response should be a decline in the U.S. exchange rate and an improvement in the net trade position. Production will move away from products for domestic consumption toward exportables and increased investment—a reversal of the restructuring that occurred in the early 1980s.

The deficit targets of the balanced budget law (Gramm-Rudman-Hollings act) specified yearly reductions of $30 billion to $40 billion, or about 0.75 percent of GNP, which seem well within the ability of the economy to adjust to without recession. The economy has adjusted successfully to similar annual changes in the deficit in the past three decades. The projected decline in the current account deficit that accompanies those targets should cause less disruption than the increases in the 1981–86 period, because it proceeds at a slower pace. Finally, the large reserve of untapped business investment projects could be undertaken quickly when credit conditions ease, helping to offset reduced government demand.

The change in U.S. policy would affect the world economy dramatically. During much of the 1980s, the U.S. trade deficit allowed other countries to sustain production and employment through exports. If the United States does not have a deficit, the rest of the world cannot in the aggregate have surpluses. They too will face difficult adjustments, because they must redirect their economies away from exports to greater reliance on domestic demand.[6]

6. The process is already evident in Japan, where the government has acted in

The adjustment is likely to trigger more intense international disputes over trade policy. After seeking to restrict trade in the early part of the decade, the United States will have a strong interest in a more open trading system when it tries to regain the market shares lost in earlier years.

THE ISSUE OF COMPETITIVENESS

Many believe that American policies toward the global economy must be radically altered. These concerns have reached a fever pitch in the national debate over competitiveness. Some advocate reducing the links between the United States and the rest of the world; others suggest that industrial and trade policies need to be restructured.[7] A common theme is that the United States must abandon its multilateral approach to international economic issues and pursue its own national advantage. Some even suggest a system of managed trade in which the United States uses the lure of access to its large market to extract larger concessions from major trading partners.

The discussion is often confusing, however, because the term competitiveness is not well defined. It is important to distinguish between arguments about how well the United States performs in world markets (particularly, the argument that the trade deficit of the 1980s is a symptom of America's inability to compete) and the issues that arise out of the changed relative position of the United States in the world economy.

Trade Performance

The trade deficit of the 1980s, as we argued earlier, reflects the domestic imbalance of saving and investment: nations that spend more than they produce will have a deficit in their transactions with other countries. In a world where exchange rates are determined by market forces, those exchange rates will alter the relative prices of exports and imports to generate a current account balance consistent with domestic

---

anticipation of the adjustments that must be made. Domestic demand has been expanding rapidly and the current account surplus has begun to shrink.

7. See, for example, David M. Gordon, "Do We Need to Be No. 1?" *Atlantic Monthly*, vol. 257 (April 1986), pp. 100–08. He argues that "we should begin . . . to work toward greater independence from the world economy, seeking self-sufficiency" (p. 100).

Figure 2-2. *U.S. Terms of Trade, 1960–88*

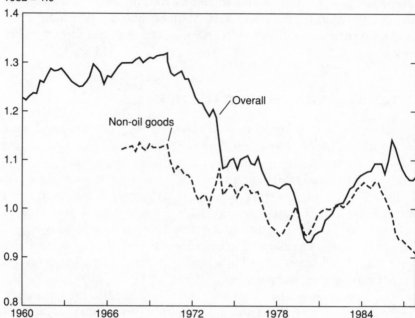

Source: U.S. Department of Commerce, Bureau of Economic Analysis, *United States National Income and Product Accounts*, tables 4-3, 4-4; and *Survey of Current Business*, various issues.

saving and investment. In the short run, exchange rates may be influenced by more temporary speculative forces, but those episodes have consistently been of short duration since the United States abandoned a fixed rate system in 1971.

A measure of performance more relevant than the change in the trade balance is the *price* of U.S. products required to maintain any given trade balance. A loss of competitiveness implies that the prices of American goods in world markets must fall to finance imports. A decline in the terms of trade (a fall in the price of American exports relative to the price of imports) adversely affects the living standards of Americans because they must give up more resources to obtain a given amount of imports. If the terms of trade must fall to maintain a constant trade balance, the United States suffers a loss of trade competitiveness.

As shown in figure 2-2, the terms of trade were roughly constant in the 1960s but fell sharply after 1971. That decline can be traced largely to the rise in the price of oil, which is a major imported good. Exclusive of oil, the decline is smaller. Most of this decline is attributable to a shift from a balance in non-oil trade in 1972 to a surplus of $57 billion in 1980.[8] Thus much of the decline was required to earn the foreign exchange to pay for oil imports. Since 1980 the terms of trade have increased slightly, but against the backdrop of a large increase in the overall trade deficit. Today the elimination of the trade deficit would require terms of trade below those of 1980.

Empirical studies have found evidence of a long-term tendency for the terms of trade, adjusted for variations in the trade balance, to move against the United States. That phenomenon has been explained by assertions that American products are gradually being replaced in world markets by superior foreign products.[9] If growth in the United States proceeds at the same rate as in other countries, U.S. tradable goods prices must fall relative to those of other countries to maintain a given balance of trade.[10] The required long-term decline in the U.S. real exchange rate, however, appears to be small—about 0.5 percent a year.[11] Such a decline is important, but it would have little effect on the growth in American living standards.

Those who believe that U.S. competitiveness has suffered advance two major arguments. The first is that American workers cannot compete against workers in low-wage countries. Given the international mobility of capital and technology, they reason, production will go where labor is cheapest. Economists argue that the spread of technology will bring about a convergence of world living standards as wage rates in other countries rise to the U.S. level. American workers, however, fear that the convergence process is for them one of regression toward the mean.

The second argument is that the multilateral world that has defined past American trade policy is a myth. The real world is dominated by nationalistic policies that systematically discriminate against imports

8. If non-oil merchandise trade had been balanced in 1980, assuming that price elasticities of exports and imports are about unity, the terms of trade would have been about 25 percent higher in 1980.

9. Declining terms of trade are most often attributed to loss of market share, but they could occur for two other reasons: if income growth in the United States matched that of other countries but had a higher propensity to import—a higher income elasticity; or if the United States consistently grew more rapidly than other countries.

10. An early example of this argument is provided in Hendrik S. Houthakker and Stephen P. Magee, "Income and Price Elasticities in World Trade," *Review of Economics and Statistics,* vol. 51 (May 1969), pp. 111–15. More recently, see Paul R. Krugman and Richard E. Baldwin, "The Persistence of the U.S. Trade Deficit," *Brookings Papers on Economic Activity, 1:1987,* pp. 1–55 (hereafter BPEA).

11. Robert Z. Lawrence, "The International Dimension," in Robert Z. Lawrence and Robert E. Litan, eds., *American Living Standards: Threats and Challenges* (Brookings, forthcoming). The impact on living standards is the percentage decline in the terms of trade times the share of trade in GNP, which is about 10 percent.

(through trade protection and selective procurement policies) and target major markets in the United States. The United States should act like other countries and manage trade to its advantage.

LOW WAGE COUNTRIES. The first argument has little empirical support. Imports into the United States are not coming more and more from low-wage countries. In 1960 two-thirds of American imports came from countries with wages less than half the U.S. level. By 1986 their share had fallen to less than one-third.[12] The emergence of a trade deficit in the 1980s does not support the argument, because the United States lost ground with every major trading area of the world, not just with low-wage countries. Furthermore, the argument ignores the fact that growth in low-income countries expands the market for American exports. In 1987 less developed countries accounted for 34 percent of American exports and 37 percent of imports.[13]

Those who believe that low-wage countries are hurting U.S. competitiveness assume that high American wages can be maintained only by preventing the flow of technology abroad. In fact, American workers are paid high wages not because they have a monopoly on technology, but because of their own high productivity, which in turn is based on their education, skills, capital, and technical knowledge. American productivity and living standards are not diminished by improvements abroad. Only about 10 percent of U.S. production, on which those living standards are based, is traded with other nations. Future improvements in American living standards will depend, as they have in the past, on productivity improvements in the American economy. The welfare of Americans does not depend on the maintenance of poverty abroad.

UNFAIR TRADE. Could the trade deficit be the result of the sudden introduction of more trade restrictions by other countries? If so, there was a massive well-coordinated conspiracy. The United States now has a deficit with every major region of the world, and the increase in the deficit between 1980 and 1987 is roughly proportionate to the volume of trade with each region (see table 2-3). The United States has also increased the share of its imports covered by nontariff barriers more than other countries have.[14]

12. Robert Z. Lawrence and Robert E. Litan, " The Protectionist Prescription: Errors in Diagnosis and Cure," BPEA, *1:1987*, p. 292.

13. *Survey of Current Business*, vol. 68 (June 1988), pp. 46–48.

14. Bela Balassa and Carol Balassa, "Industrial Protection in the Developed Countries," *World Economy*, vol. 7 (June 1984), pp. 179–96.

Table 2-3. *U.S. Merchandise Trade Balance, by Region, 1980, 1987*
Billions of dollars unless otherwise specified

Region or country	1980	1987	Change	1980 share of total trade (percent)
Canada	−1.3	−12.6	−11.3	18
Japan	−10.4	−56.9	−46.5	11
Western Europe	20.4	−27.5	−47.9	24
Latin America	1.3	−12.3	−13.6	16
Newly industrialized economies[a]	−3.6	−34.8	−31.2	7
Other countries	−31.9	−16.2	15.7	24
Total	−25.5	−160.3	−134.8	100
Addendum[b]				
OPEC countries	−38.2	−13.7	24.5	15
Industrialized countries	9.3	−94.9	−104.2	56
Other countries	4.7	−51.7	−56.4	29

Source: *Survey of Current Business*, vol. 68 (June 1988), pp. 46, 48. Numbers are rounded.
a. Includes Hong Kong, South Korea, Singapore, and Taiwan.
b. Values for 1980 do not sum to total because of discrepancies in the allocation of balance of payments data for years before 1984. See *Survey of Current Business*, note on p. 67.

Such a sudden deterioration of the trade balance with every region of the globe suggests not worldwide conspiracy, but a change here at home. That leads us back to the collapse of domestic saving and the increase in foreign borrowing to support an excessive level of consumption.

To recap: there is little support for the contention that the United States is damaged by competition from low-wage countries. Nor is there compelling evidence that the trade deficit reflects unfair trade practices of other countries. Some of the benefits of international trade are lost because of national trade restrictions, but the United States has also been guilty of such measures. If other countries successfully promote their own exports to or restrict imports from the United States, American terms of trade would decline: it would be necessary to lower the price of American exports to offset these actions. Yet as we have already mentioned, the decline in our terms of trade has been surprisingly small. If the playing field is unlevel, the slope is not very steep.

Relative Economic Performance

The relative economic decline of the United States is clear. Its share of world gross domestic product (GDP) has fallen from 27 percent in

Table 2-4. *Relative Levels of Gross Domestic Product and Productivity, "Group of Seven" Countries, Selected Years, 1950–87*
U.S. GDP = 100.0

Country	1950	1960	1970	1980	1987
	Gross domestic product				
United States	100.0	100.0	100.0	100.0	100.0
Canada	6.4	7.2	8.2	9.9	10.0
Japan	8.8	14.8	28.1	33.9	36.1
France	11.8	13.3	15.8	17.3	15.9
West Germany	11.1	18.7	20.1	20.1	18.3
Italy	10.4	13.1	15.8	16.4	15.6
United Kingdom	20.1	19.2	17.5	16.2	15.7
Addendum: U.S. share[a]	59.3	53.7	48.7	46.8	47.3
	GDP per employed person				
United States	100.0	100.0	100.0	100.0	100.0
Canada	77.1	80.1	84.2	92.8	95.5
Japan	15.2	23.2	45.7	62.6	70.7
France	36.8	46.0	61.7	80.1	85.3
West Germany	32.4	49.1	61.8	77.4	81.1
Italy	30.8	43.9	66.4	80.9	85.5
United Kingdom	53.9	54.3	58.0	65.9	71.9

Source: U.S. Department of Labor, Bureau of Labor Statistics, Office of Productivity and Technology, "Comparative Real Gross Domestic Product, Real GDP per Capita, and Real GDP per Employed Person: Thirteen Countries, 1950–1987," unpublished data, pp. 9–10, 13–14.
a. Percentage share of the total output of the seven countries listed.

1950 to 18 percent in recent years.[15] During that period all six of the other leading industrial countries posted GDP gains relative to the United States (see table 2-4). Japan's GDP grew from only 9 percent of U.S. GDP in 1950 to 36 percent in 1987. Similar gains have been recorded by the other countries. Output per worker in Japan expanded from only 15 percent of that of the United States to 71 percent. The change in relative size, however, does not reflect a failure on the part of the United States. Rather, it reflects its success in rebuilding the world economy after World War II. The United States has been joined by many nations with similar technologies, productivity, and standards of living—a return to the situation that existed before World War I. The period after World War II has seen an unparalleled expansion of the world economy, due in part to the opening of world trade and economic relations.

Furthermore, the United States continues to have unique attributes that make it the world's key economic actor. It is the world's largest

15. Robert E. Lipsey and Irving B. Kravis, *Saving and Economic Growth: Is the United States Really Falling Behind?* Conference Board Research Report 901 (New York: Conference Board, 1987), pp. 6, 24.

economy and most important trader. In 1986 almost 30 percent of all world trade involved an American as a buyer or seller—a figure not very different from what it was in 1960. Although Europe has extensive relations with Asia and Africa, and Japan with other Pacific nations, the United States is unique in the extent of its global relations with other major actors. For example, U.S. trade with Europe or Japan far outweighs their trade with each other, and U.S. trade with developing nations is as great as that of the European Community.

Given that reconstructing the world economy was the avowed objective of U.S. policy, its success should hardly be taken as a sign of American failure. U.S. foreign policy failed only if its goal was to maintain American superiority. If the goal was to maximize the welfare of Americans, which is enhanced by rapid foreign growth, relative decline is neither unexpected nor undesirable.

The relative decline of the United States has differing implications for American power and for American living standards. The "power" of a nation flows from its relative economic capacity—the economic performance of the United States compared with that of other nations, particularly its adversaries.[16] In this sense the power of the United States declines in a richer world economy. Conversely, the welfare of a nation's citizens is largely a function of its absolute economic capacity: living standards are primarily based on the nation's productivity, which is promoted, not reduced, by trade. Productivity is also raised when increased innovation abroad provides U.S. manufacturers more opportunities to emulate foreign products and processes. When we evaluate the relative economic performance of the United States, the perspective matters greatly: the United States is made less powerful when others do well, but the welfare of its citizens is improved.

RELATIVE INCOME AND PRODUCTIVITY GROWTH. Concern about the relative decline of the economic power of the United States has surfaced at a strange time. The U.S. share of the GDP of the large industrial countries fell far more before the 1980s than during the 1980s (see table 2-4). It dropped from 59 percent in 1950 to 49 percent in 1970. In the 1980s, by contrast, GDP grew as rapidly in the United States as in the rest of the world. U.S. industrial production rose 5 percent faster than the average of all market economies, and the U.S. share of GDP in the

---

16. The term "power" is ambiguous, but we employ a political science concept of power that implies an ability to induce other nations to take actions that they would not do of their own volition.

Table 2-5. Annual Rates of Growth of Gross Domestic Product per
Employed Person, "Group of Seven" Countries, 1951–87

Country	1951–60	1961–73	1974–79	1980–87
United States	2.0	1.9	0.0	0.8
Canada	2.4	2.6	1.3	1.0
Japan	6.5	8.2	2.9	2.8
France	4.4	4.9	2.7	1.9
West Germany	5.7	4.1	2.9	1.5
Italy	5.7	5.8	1.7	1.9
United Kingdom	2.1	2.9	1.3	1.8

Source: Department of Labor, "Comparative Real Gross Domestic Product," pp. 17–18.

"Group of Seven" countries actually increased.[17] While Japan continued to gain, growth in Europe faltered and the world economy as a whole performed poorly.

Relative economic growth, however, offers no insight into the more important measure of economic performance—the absolute gain in American living standards. Much of the recent U.S. economic growth is simply the result of rapid growth in the labor force. Except for Canada, labor force growth is much lower in the other industrial countries. Growth in the total economy may be relevant to measures of economic power, but it has little relation to improvements in standards of living.

The comparison with other countries is less favorable if the focus is on the growth in productivity, which is closely related to living standards. Since 1950 growth in GDP per worker in the United States has been consistently below that of other countries, and the rate of improvement has been especially low since 1973 (see table 2-5).

A comparison of productivity growth rates is distorted by the low starting point in other countries. The difference in levels of output per worker between the United States and other countries remains surprisingly large in America's favor.[18] In 1987 the average French, German, and Japanese worker produced 14.7, 18.9, and 29.3 percent less than his American counterpart (see table 2-4).[19]

17. United Nations, Monthly Bulletin of Statistics, vol. 42 (August 1988), pp. 28, 258. The G-7 countries are Canada, France, West Germany, the United Kingdom, Italy, Japan, and the United States.

18. These comparisons of GDP and GDP per worker are based on purchasing-power-parity exchange rates. The exchange rates have been adjusted to reflect equivalent purchasing power of each country's currency.

19. According to an alternative study by Summers and Heston, in 1985 per capita incomes were 14.1, 15.0 and 28.8 percent lower in Germany, France, and Japan than in

Table 2-6. *Comparisons of Productivity Growth, United States,*
OECD, and Japan, before and after 1973
Percent

| | United States vs. OECD | | United States vs. Japan | |
Period	Total factor productivity	Labor productivity	Total factor productivity	Labor productivity
Pre-1973	−1.4	−1.9	−4.8	−6.6
1973–79	−0.8	−1.3	−1.9	−2.9
1979–85	−0.5	−0.8	−2.0	−2.5

Source: Organization for Economic Cooperation and Development, *Economic Outlook*, vol. 42 (December 1987), p. 41; and authors' calculations.

Because it is far easier to copy than to innovate, there is connection between initial productivity levels and growth rates.[20] In the past foreigners were able to increase productivity by adopting U.S. technologies, while productivity gains in the United States came from pushing out the frontiers of knowledge. As other countries have moved closer to the United States, their rates of productivity growth have tended to decline. The difference between productivity growth in the United States and in the countries of the Organization for Economic Cooperation and Development has narrowed since 1973 (see table 2-6). The difference for total factor productivity growth (output per unit of capital plus labor) declined from 1.4 percent a year before 1973 to 0.5 percent during 1979–85. The differential with Japan narrowed in the same way.

Not all of the difference in productivity growth between the United States and the other major industrial countries reflects catch-up. Although U.S. productivity in total manufacturing remains the world's highest, in some industries (automobiles, steel) productivity levels in Japan have surpassed those in the United States. In part, that is because foreign economies have been accumulating capital per worker at a more rapid pace than the United States has.

Foreigners are also shifting from copying to innovating. The share of sales spent on research and development by German and Japanese manufacturing firms is now similar to that of American firms. In the past the product cycle originated in the United States and moved abroad. Now, innovations cross the Atlantic and Pacific in both directions. In

---

the United States. See Robert Summers and Alan Heston, "A New Set of International Comparisons of Real Product and Price Levels Estimates for 130 Countries, 1950–1985," *Review of Income and Wealth*, series 34, no. 1 (March 1988), pp. 1–25.

20. William J. Baumol and Edward N. Wolff, "Is International Productivity Convergence Illusory?" Research Report 87-38 (New York University, C.V. Starr Center for Applied Economics, September 1987).

1970 the United States granted eighteen and eleven patents to Americans for every one granted to Japanese and German nationals, respectively. By 1985 the ratios had declined to three and six.[21]

RELATIVE PRODUCTIVITY GROWTH AND TRADE PERFORMANCE. Since 1973 the growth of U.S. productivity (output per labor hour) has slowed significantly, and the real earnings of American workers have stagnated. Over the same period, the United States suffered numerous shocks from the world economy, including the emergence of a large trade deficit after 1981.

Given the current infatuation with "competitiveness," it is tempting to see causal links between these problems. Many blame the sluggish growth in U.S. productivity and earnings on the changed international environment and argue that unfair trade practices of other countries reduce American productivity and living standards. Others use what they call a decline in U.S. trade competitiveness to justify greater efforts to raise productivity growth. The apparent link between trade performance and productivity, however, is misleading for two reasons. First, U.S. productivity growth has slumped mainly in sectors that do not engage in international trade. Although it is difficult to measure productivity growth in individual sectors, productivity growth in U.S. manufacturing seems to have *accelerated* in the 1980s.[22] Second, relatively faster productivity growth abroad will not diminish U.S. living standards. During the period before 1973, when foreign economic growth exceeded that of the United States by a wide margin, American living standards grew faster than at almost any time in U.S. history.[23] Lester Thurow has argued that the U.S. dollar must fall to offset differences in productivity growth between the United States and its industrial competitors.[24] In fact, Thurow confuses changes in nominal exchange rates (which have no effect on living standards) with changes in real exchange rates. If

21. National Science Board, *Science and Engineering Indicators* (Government Printing Office, 1987), p. 302.

22. U.S. Department of Labor, Bureau of Labor Statistics, *Multifactor Productivity Measures, 1986* (Washington, D.C.: BLS, October 13, 1987).

23. Lipsey and Kravis, *Saving and Economic Growth*, pp. 8–10.

24. According to Thurow: "If American productivity grows at 1 percent per year and the productivity of our industrial competitors grows at 4 percent per year, the American dollar must fall by approximately 3 percent per year to maintain a balance in America's balance of trade. With 12 percent of GNP imported . . . this . . . causes American standards of living to fall by [about] 0.4 percent (.12 x .03) per year forever." Lester C. Thurow, *The Zero-Sum Solution: Building a World-Class American Economy* (Simon and Schuster, 1985), pp. 93–94.

higher productivity growth abroad is absorbed by higher wages and profits abroad, prices will not change, and devaluation will not be necessary. If higher productivity abroad is passed forward into lower prices of foreign products in their domestic currencies, a *nominal* decline in the dollar (or fall in U.S. price level) might be required to maintain trade balance. This decrease, though, would not raise import prices relative to domestic prices in the United States and would thus leave absolute U.S. living standards unaffected.

It is true that when productivity growth abroad is concentrated in industries that compete head on with U.S. export- or import-competing firms, real exchange rates could be affected. But uniform productivity growth (the case implicitly considered by Thurow) need have no such effect. In fact, in the simplest case higher productivity increases a country's income, and it imports more. The *foreign* (not the U.S.) real exchange rate and terms of trade would actually have to fall to induce a compensatory increase in demand by the rest of the world for its exports.[25]

INTERNATIONAL BUYING POWER. Differences in the structure of expenditures and the relative prices of the goods and services produced in different countries make it difficult to compare real productivity and welfare between nations. Our earlier comparisons of relative GDP, which attempted to adjust for price differences between the United States and other countries, suggest that American standards of living are still substantially higher than those of other industrial countries. Yet simple comparisons based on 1987 market exchange rates imply that GDP per employed person was 11.1, 5.2, and 4.3 percent higher in Germany, France, and Japan, respectively.[26]

These differences arise because the other major industrial countries lag far behind the United States in their ability to provide nontradables, primarily in the distribution, food, and services sectors. These gaps continue, despite the fact that several countries have nearly matched

25. This relationship between productivity and the terms of trade was examined many years ago, when it was Great Britain that was worried about rapid American productivity growth. See, in particular, J. R. Hicks, "An Inaugural Lecture," *Oxford Economic Papers*, vol. 5 (June 1953), pp. 117–35. Later articles have pointed out that, in general, the result is more indeterminant. A survey is provided in Richard E. Caves, *Trade and Economic Structure* (Harvard University Press, 1963), pp. 152–60.

26. U.S. Department of Labor, Bureau of Labor Statistics, Office of Productivity and Technology, "Comparative Real Gross Domestic Product, Real GDP per Capita, and Real GDP per Employed Person: Thirteen Countries, 1950–1987," unpublished data, p. 51.

U.S. efficiency in the production of tradable goods. Their standards of living would be much higher if they could buy nontradable goods from the United States, rather than at home. In effect, these nations, particularly Japan, have much lower standards of living than their efficiency in the production of tradable goods would suggest.[27]

Critics of American economic performance often focus on the manufacturing sector—a proxy for tradable goods. But an improvement in productivity in the tradable goods industries is not necessarily better than one in nontradables.[28] Ninety percent of the goods and services consumed by Americans are produced by Americans. As in the past, Americans' future standard of living will depend on the gains in the economy as a whole.

MILITARY SPENDING AND ECONOMIC GROWTH. Some allege that the burden of military spending has been a chief cause of America's relative economic decline.[29] But we believe the link between economic performance and military power is not strong, because, apart from the direct impact of the resources they use, military expenditures simply do not exert a significant influence, positive or negative, on economic growth. Beyond a certain level of GDP, military spending will reduce a nation's growth only if the nation is unwilling to tax itself and reduce consumption to finance it. In a rich economy like the United States, the financing of military outlays is constrained far more by politics—how much a nation

27. In 1987, for example, the market exchange rate for the Japanese yen was 144.5 per dollar. The corresponding purchasing-power-parity exchange rate was 213.7. Ibid., pp. 41, 53.

28. One exception is provided by arguments that industries can earn rents by creating monopoly-like conditions. Governments have no incentive to help firms create this condition in nontradables because the rents would be paid by their own citizens. Some rents earned by export industries, however, will be extracted from foreigners. Thus governments of small economies might have an incentive to help their industries dominate a few markets where rents might be extracted. It is a less attractive policy for the United States, though, because the ratio of foreign-to-domestic demand is low in almost all markets. Issues of this type are illustrated in Paul R. Krugman, ed., *Strategic Trade Policy and the New International Economics*, 2d ed. (MIT Press, 1987).

29. See, for example, Paul Kennedy, *The Rise and Fall of the Great Powers: Economic Change and Military Conflict from 1500 to 2000* (Random House, 1987). The reverse causal link, between relative economic power and relative military power, must also be made with caution. The key distinction here is between U.S. allies and U.S. adversaries. The nations that have developed very rapidly, like Japan and Korea, are firm U.S. allies. Their economic development has not increased U.S. military burdens, although they now pay less for their defense than many would like. An increase in their defense, however, would not necessarily reduce U.S. defense burdens—Japanese efforts to defend Japan are not a perfect substitute for American efforts to defend the United States.

is willing to pay—than economics. Military outlays, if deficit financed, can dampen growth by crowding out domestic investment, but so can all forms of government expenditures.[30]

Until the 1980s, changes in U.S. military spending made little difference to the budget deficit. Taxes were raised to cover higher defense spending in both the Korean and Vietnam wars, and the deficit did not shrink during the long intervening periods when defense spending declined as a share of GDP. The budget deficit and defense spending did go up together in the 1980s, but the relationship is complicated by the enactment of a large tax cut in 1981.

If the United States, like Japan, spent only 1 percent of its GNP on defense, and if it invested the remaining 5 percent, the economy would grow faster and the nation would be richer. But on the basis of past fluctuations in defense spending, it is more realistic to believe that the United States would spend any dividend from reduced defense spending in about the same proportion as the rest of its income, consuming 94 percent and investing 6 percent.[31]

Economics cannot determine the appropriate level of defense spending for the United States. It can simply suggest that, at least in peacetime, voters pay for defense through taxes and reduced consumption, not through deficits and reduced investment—an argument true not only for defense, but also for most forms of government spending.

POLICY OPTIONS

Although the United States no longer dominates all areas of the global economy, its ability to raise the living standards of its citizens is not thereby diminished. In a more pluralistic world, there may be less scope for the United States to exercise its will at the expense of others and less room to enjoy rents from monopolies, but economic growth abroad brings with it important benefits to the United States, including a productivity boost from the technological innovations of others, access to larger markets as a producer, and greater variety as a consumer.

---

30. We assume that taxes fall more heavily on consumption, while investment is affected more than consumption by variations in interest rates.

31. Defense does absorb scarce scientific and intellectual resources that would otherwise be employed in the civilian sector. In the long run, however, the supply of scientists will respond to the demand, so this problem is most severe when defense efforts fluctuate in the short run.

Moreover, while the United States is less than dominant, no other country will soon rival its importance to the world economy.

Over the next decade, the foremost challenge for U.S. economic policy at home is to boost living standards by raising national saving and productivity. The principal task of U.S. economic policy abroad is to provide an international environment supportive of the adjustments in spending patterns needed to achieve that task. In this section, we consider the adjustments in domestic policy and the options for international economic policy that are most likely to aid it. In the final section, we draw some implications for U.S. foreign policy more broadly.

Productivity Growth

As we argued earlier, the growth in American living standards has slowed because U.S. productivity growth has fallen. One key to future growth in living standards is higher productivity. Although improvements in productivity may improve competitiveness and U.S. trade performance, their primary importance is as a source of gains in overall standards of living. They are beneficial regardless of whether the nation engages in trade. Moreover, they are of approximately equal value in industries that do and do not engage in trade.

Although much of the post-1973 slowdown in U.S. productivity growth remains a puzzle, existing studies do agree on a partial agenda of actions that the government could take to reverse the trend. It could encourage a higher rate of private capital formation; it could increase its own investments in the social infrastructure (for example, transportation); it could expand research and development outlays; and it could improve the quantity and quality of education. Government has traditionally played a role in all these areas, but that role has cost money. To finance these efforts, Americans must be willing to reduce their current level of public or private consumption. In a country already faced with large deficits on its government budget and heavy overseas borrowing, greater spending in these areas will be very difficult to achieve.

None of the actions, moreover, will have large immediate effects on economic growth. They do not, as is sometimes suggested, provide a means for the United States to grow out of its second major economic problem, the budget deficit.

Increased Saving

In the immediate future, the dominant issue for American economic policy is how to cut the growth of consumption, both to eliminate the need to borrow abroad and to provide the investment resources to improve U.S. living standards in the future. From a political perspective, slower consumption growth is a dismal prospect, and the extent to which political debate seeks to redirect public attention to the international arena and to blame the policies of other countries should not be a surprise. If the United States lowers its budget deficit, however, it will increase the national rate of saving, and market forces, supported by an easier monetary policy, will translate that saving into a lower trade deficit and a higher rate of domestic investment. Once it has reestablished a balance between its current government programs and the taxes to finance them, the country will be able to engage in a rational debate over the merits of spending more money to foster productivity growth.

A balanced U.S. budget would change U.S. policies toward the international economy in two major ways. First, the United States would discover a strong interest in promoting a more open trading system—a turn away from protectionism—as it sought to recover its export markets. Second, it would have a strong interest in opposing efforts to fix exchange rates.

Trade Policy

Much of the public discussion of the trade deficit implies that it is the result of a sudden flood of imports into the United States. Yet the rise in imports, as a share of GNP, is completely in line with a long historical trend (see figure 2-3). Most industrial countries have seen a similar long-run trend associated with lower trade barriers and transportation costs and improved communication. In the past, however, this rising trend of U.S. imports was matched by a similar growth of exports. The change in the 1980s was in the collapse of exports, as the rise in the real exchange rate priced American goods out of world markets.[32]

32. The response of American exporters in the early 1980s seems to contrast markedly with that of Japanese firms presented with a similar situation in 1987–88. The American

Figure 2-3. *Nonagricultural Exports and Non-oil Imports as Share of GNP, 1970–88*[a]

Percent of GNP

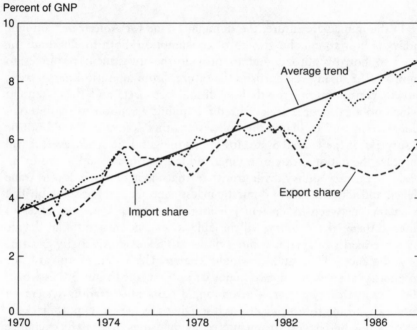

Source: Same as figure 2-2, table 4-3; and *Survey of Current Business,* various issues.
a. The least-squares trend is the average of exports plus imports for 1970–80.

The recent return of the real exchange rate to 1980 levels will lead to an improvement in the trade balance, but the gains will be on the export, not the import, side of the account. The dollar value of expenditures on imports will be largely unaffected: higher prices will reduce the volume of imports, but Americans will pay more for them. The same is not true of exports, for which there is no offsetting decline in the dollar price as the volume goes up.[33] Given the importance of recapturing lost export

firms, faced with a booming domestic market, simply gave up and withdrew from overseas markets or moved their production facilities abroad. Japanese producers, on the other hand, engaged in a vigorous round of cost cutting, productivity soared in the export industries, and the rise in prices was far less than the change in the real exchange rate.

33. Recent empirical studies have uniformly found that the price elasticity of U.S. import demand is near unity, meaning that a 1 percent rise in price will reduce the volume of imports by 1 percent, leaving expenditures unchanged. There is the potential for secondary income effects; but, given the targeting of monetary policy on maintaining a growth of the domestic economy in line with that of potential output, any income effects are largely neutralized. In addition, because of lags in adjusting to price changes, the effect on expenditure on imports may actually be perverse in the period immediately after a rise in import prices.

markets, it is surprising that some urge U.S. policymakers to pursue trade restrictions. After all, closing our markets would give other countries an excuse to close theirs to American exporters.[34] Again, the failure to understand the changed international situation has led to the consideration of policies that are contrary to America's interests.

Trade policy has three primary dimensions: ensuring that foreign markets are open to American firms; ensuring that other nations' trade policies do not harm U.S. interests; and helping domestic firms and workers adjust to international competition. In the near term, given the improved price competitiveness of U.S. exports that follows from a lower exchange rate, American policy should concentrate on the first.[35] If the United States is to sustain domestic economic growth despite budget tightening, reduce its foreign borrowing, and service its international debt, it must enjoy rapid export growth. If American exports rise because of growth and liberalization, there will be no need to stimulate sales by lowering the prices of U.S. products and reducing U.S. living standards. An open expanding global economy seems to us to be strongly in America's economic interest.

But there is a growing view that the United States' trade policy goals and objectives should shift to reflect its decline in global preeminence. In the 1950s and 1960s, advocates of such a shift suggest, it was appropriate for the United States to fashion its trade policies primarily for the benefit of others and to keep its market open while turning a blind eye to protectionist policies abroad. At that time, they argue, it was correct for the United States to aim for a system with liberal rules and norms achieved through application of the most-favored-nation principle, under which concessions granted to one country were extended to all.[36] But today, the striving for an open international trading system under the GATT rules represents the triumph of ideology over the national interest. Instead, they contend, the United States should aim for a system of managed international trade, which best serves American national interests by exploiting U.S. leverage to obtain reciprocal advantage.

Advocates of this view stress that the weaknesses of U.S. policies have

34. By the first quarter of 1988, U.S. merchandise exports were up 28 percent from their level a year earlier. *Survey of Current Business*, vol. 68 (July 1988), p. 70.

35. For discussions of unfair trade and trade adjustment, see Robert Z. Lawrence, *Can America Compete?* (Brookings, 1984), pp. 117–45; and Robert Z. Lawrence and Robert E. Litan, *Saving Free Trade: A Pragmatic Approach* (Brookings, 1986).

36. Robert O. Keohane, "Reciprocity in International Relations," *International Organization*, vol. 40 (Winter 1986), pp. 1–27.

become most apparent in trade relations with Japan. The Japanese government allegedly takes advantage of the openness of the U.S. market while reserving local markets for domestic firms. In the past it carried out this mercantilist policy through such formal protectionist measures as tariffs and quotas. Today it uses administrative guidance, discriminatory standards and regulations, selective government procurement, the official organization of firms into cartels, and weak enforcement of antitrust laws. Imports into Japan are also discouraged by unofficial practices: the strong relationships between local suppliers and buyers, "just-in-time" inventory practices that give nearby suppliers an edge, and an unusually complex distribution system that creates substantial barriers for newcomers. The barriers to foreign investment in Japan are also high: while Japanese firms may freely acquire U.S. firms, Japanese strictures on hostile takeovers prevent similar actions by Americans seeking to acquire Japanese businesses.

The U.S. approach has been to pressure Japan to remove trade barriers in a series of piecemeal negotiations. That policy has engendered much friction between the two nations, and many find the results disappointing. As Clyde Prestowitz describes it, for an American an open market implies that everything is allowed unless it is expressly prohibited; for the Japanese, however, nothing is allowed unless it is expressly permitted.[37] After tough negotiations, Americans often obtain concessions only to find that other barriers remain.

Because interpretations differ so radically over the meaning of the rules, the solution, according to Prestowitz and others, is to bargain over results.[38] Essentially this implies a regime in which the emphasis shifts toward more managed trade and less free trade.

Several concrete suggestions about how to implement this new approach have been made. Lester Thurow, for example, argues that the United States should determine the largest trade deficit it could afford to run with Japan and then each quarter auction off import licenses "in the appropriate amount."[39] Henry Kissinger and Cyrus Vance recommend similar approaches.[40] Prestowitz suggests that U.S. trade in particular

---

37. Clyde V. Prestowitz, Jr., *Trading Places: How We Allowed Japan to Take the Lead* (Basic Books, 1988), pp. 80–81.

38. See also Pat Choate and J. K. Linger, *The High-Flex Society: Shaping America's Economic Future* (Alfred A. Knopf, 1986), pp. 63–77.

39. Thurow, *Zero-Sum Solution*, pp. 360–63.

40. Henry Kissinger and Cyrus Vance, "Bipartisan Objectives for American Foreign Policy," *Foreign Affairs*, vol. 66 (Summer 1988), pp. 899–921.

sectors be allocated along the lines of the international airline cartel. Just as airlines from different nations divide up the traffic between them, so firms from the United States and other nations could divide up the business in any sector.[41]

Stephen Krasner argues that a system of managed trade based on "specific" reciprocity, if used to govern global trade relations, would offer important advantages.[42] Instead of unrealistically assuming nations can be induced to follow liberal practices, it would permit acceptance of the diversity of values and institutional structures in the international system. It would also restore congruence between American interests and capabilities. Indeed, as the nation with the world's largest market, the United States should have the greatest leverage.[43]

In fact, the United States already engages in some managed trade. Examples include the voluntary restraint arrangements with the Japanese in textiles, steel, and automobiles; the multifiber agreement; and the Japan–United States cartel arrangement embodied in the 1986 semiconductor agreement. But would the widespread application of these principles actually improve the system for the United States?

A managed trade system will afford the greatest benefits to those governments best able to control trade. Aside from the inefficiencies inherent in managed trade, it will not necessarily lead to improved trading conditions for the United States. Managed trade generally involves setting quotas. By limiting the quantity or dollar value of the products or services a nation can sell in the United States, we encourage that nation to charge us as high a price as possible. If foreign governments can limit competition for quotas among their firms, they can act like monopolists, maximizing the rents (or benefits) to their nation.

Japan, in particular, would reap great benefits under such a system. Given a particular dollar value for its U.S. sales, Japan would undoubtedly select products in which it enjoyed either the greatest current benefits (because profit margins were highest) or future benefits (because the

---

41. Prestowitz, *Trading Places*, p. 324.

42. Stephen D. Krasner, "A Trade Strategy for the United States," *Ethics and International Affairs*, vol. 2 (1988), pp. 17–35; and *Asymmetries in Japanese-American Trade: The Case for Specific Reciprocity*, Policy Papers in International Affairs 32 (Berkeley: Institute for International Studies, 1987).

43. As Krasner puts it, "American national interest would be better served by a policy based on specific reciprocity, a policy that paid more attention to short-term payoffs, outcomes rather than procedures, and differences in the domestic institutional arrangements of major economic partners." Krasner, "Trade Strategy," p. 34.

products were perceived as high-tech or strategic). Given the ability of the Japanese Ministry of International Trade and Industry (MITI) to guide its firms, Japanese strategies would be effectively implemented.

Facing similar restrictions the United States would be much less likely to allocate its products strategically and more likely to do so on political grounds. Many advocates of a managed trading system believe it would reconcile the differences in national economic systems. In fact, it would expose their contradictions.

A managed trade system reinforces precisely the differences between the United States and other nations that exacerbate trade tensions. When the United States persuades Japan to "volunteer" to limit its sales of automobiles, it vastly increases the power of MITI to influence the Japanese automobile industry. Indeed, it is the United States rather than Japan that becomes the proponent of Japanese industrial policy.

A managed trade system will have extremely damaging effects on some other nations. It will severely inhibit the trade of smaller and poorer nations with limited bargaining power. Yet these are precisely the nations that reap the greatest relative benefits from the economies of scale that trade provides. Bilateral negotiations based on power would severely restrict their ability to raise their incomes through specialization. The result would be a more sluggish global economy—a result scarcely in the U.S. economic or political interest.

In a pluralistic world economy there will always be tensions from the clash of different systems, but that does not imply that trade between nations need be managed. No foolproof solutions can be found, but a better way to ease tensions is to define practices that are generally recognized as unjustifiable and then to ensure they are eliminated.

It would be especially inappropriate for the United States to legitimate a system of controls now that market forces are shifting trade trends in its favor. Following the sharp change in the dollar-yen exchange rate in 1986–87, American exports have expanded at a 25–30 percent annual rate, and the Japanese trade surplus, on both a global and a bilateral U.S. basis, has declined dramatically. Trade negotiators, understandably, get caught up in sectoral particulars, but it is macroeconomic conditions, not trade in specific industries, that determine overall trade balances.

We should also distinguish between the objectives of the trading system—an open system of international trade—and the negotiating techniques for bringing this system about. Traditionally the United States has relied on the GATT and multilateral negotiations. It should continue to do so. At the same time, the GATT itself acknowledges that broad free-trade areas negotiated bilaterally can encourage the long-term trend toward multilateral free trade. The European Community has proceeded in this direction, and recently the United States has negotiated a major arrangement with Canada. These measures also should continue. Indeed, the European initiative to achieve a high degree of economic integration by 1992 should greatly benefit the United States. First, it should stimulate European growth, which will in turn raise U.S. exports. Second, it should provide the United States and other exporters with a more unified market with common standards. Third, it should undermine nationalistic commitments to protectionism in various European countries and thus promote liberalization. Of course, other countries should be alert to the possibility that the initiative could divert trade away from nonmember countries, but the volume is likely to be small.

Finally, despite all the focus on trade practices, it should be realized that a rapid expansion of the total world market is the most important determinant of U.S. export growth. Developing countries have always been a major outlet for U.S. capital goods exports. A resolution of their debt problems and a resumption of their investment-led growth would therefore be of great benefit to U.S. exporters. Thus it is a mistake for the United States to view the debt crisis solely from the perspective of its banks. It has become evident that some debt relief will be required, and speedy resolution of this issue is in the interest of American industry.

Exchange Rate Policy

In recent years the United States has acceded to the demands of other nations that it cooperate in government efforts to control exchange rates. Pressure is increasing to return to an international monetary system in which exchange rates are fixed by governments. The interest of other countries is understandable because they wish to continue their export surplus with the United States. Although the policy is attractive to American consumers, who have no desire to pay higher prices, it could be dangerous to American workers.

If the United States should adopt a tighter fiscal policy, it would risk higher unemployment. One way to counter that risk would be to reduce the trade deficit, so that jobs would shift from industries that do not engage in trade to industries that do. But for the trade deficit to shrink, U.S. incomes must fall (reducing the demand for imports), or foreign growth must expand (raising the demand for American exports), or the prices of American goods must decline in world markets. The first option is highly undesirable, and the second is beyond American control. The third is the strongest equilibrating force.

Because the U.S. current account deficit is so large, economists are unable to project the precise change in the exchange rate needed to achieve balance on the current account. It will depend on what other countries do to stimulate domestic demand and on the policies they follow on trade. The United States cannot afford to commit itself, at a time of imbalance, to an exchange rate that may be inconsistent with the future achievement of a balance in the current account. Furthermore, without the possibility of a recovery of trade, policies to reduce the budget deficit are likely to translate into higher unemployment.

If the United States does not reduce the budget deficit, the exchange rate may, in fact, rise in the short run. Improved export performance at the current lower level of the dollar, combined with strong domestic spending, may strain the economy's resources and threaten to increase inflation. If the Federal Reserve reacts by tightening credit, U.S. interest rates would rise relative to those of other countries, capital inflows would increase, the exchange rate would go back up, and the improvement in the trade balance would be choked off.

Although the wide fluctuations in the value of the dollar were highly disruptive to the world economy in the 1980s, they should be seen as a symptom of the extreme imbalance in U.S. fiscal-monetary policies, not as a cause of the problems. A return to a system of fixed exchange rates would make deficit countries turn to domestic deflation as the primary means of strengthening their trade performance. Since surplus nations are unwilling to cooperate by accepting higher rates of inflation, the system is biased against growth. A system of fixed exchange rates seems even more impractical in view of the greatly increased mobility of private financial capital, which necessitates that, once confidence is lost, countries adjust their policies very rapidly indeed.

CONCLUDING COMMENTS

In the 1950s, as a dominant and independent economy, the United States could use its international economic influence to achieve political and security objectives. Today the United States is merely the first among equals in an interdependent world economy. Economic developments abroad, once matters of interest only to foreign policy specialists, are now vitally important to economic performance at home. The emergence of large budget deficits and the transformation of the United States into a large net-debtor country have heightened that dependence. Strong foreign growth not only makes the world less susceptible to Soviet influence; it is critical for sustaining U.S. employment as these deficits are reduced.

Although American policies must shift to deal with the changing environment, new policies must be based on a realistic perception of that environment. It is wrong to see foreign growth as damaging to U.S. welfare, erroneous to emphasize improving competitiveness over improving productivity, and inadvisable to abandon the goal of a liberal trading order for a system of managed trade. The future of American living standards overwhelmingly depends, as it always has, on domestic productivity and saving. Given the need to change our policies to achieve these goals, we need an international economy capable of accepting a greatly expanded volume of American exports and a reduction in the U.S. trade deficit. An exchange rate that makes American products competitive in open and rapidly growing foreign markets will be the key.

American foreign policy will have to be more creative in an era in which the United States will be constrained by the need to make painful adjustments in its domestic economic policies. The political battle to restrain spending at home will limit our ability to project influence abroad. Yet our dependence on the international economy has never been greater. The challenge is therefore to join in partnership with our allies to build a liberal international system supportive of our mutual interests. While American power may have diminished, the American interest in U.S. leadership has rarely been greater.

CHAPTER THREE

A Defense Agenda for Fiscal Years 1990–1994

WILLIAM W. KAUFMANN

It has been said that when you take the bull by the horns ... what happens is a toss up. On December 12, 1985, President Reagan signed the Balanced Budget and Emergency Deficit Control Act (P.L. 99-177), sponsored by Senators Gramm, Rudman, and Hollings. In doing so, he seemed to take the deficit bull by the horns. But somehow the bull won out and the deficit went up. Despite this paradoxical outcome, fiscal 1985 proved to be the last year of the great boom in defense funding, a boom that had already begun before President Reagan took office, but to which he had given a mighty impetus. The determination of Congress appeared to be clear. Not only would the deficit be reduced; defense would make a substantial contribution to the reduction. The only issue was, and remains, how deep the cuts should be and where they should be applied.

THE PROBLEM OF DEFENSE SPENDING

Despite this congressional determination, the boom that started with a bang ended with something less than a whimper. During the three fiscal years following 1985, over the most vigorous protests of the president and his secretary of defense, Congress managed to reduce defense budget authority in real terms by about 11.9 percent, which brought it back to where it had been in fiscal 1983 (a very good year for defense). Defense outlays, however, did not actually begin to fall until 1988, and then only by 3.1 percent, which still left them higher than in 1985 (table 3-1).

After yet another long and tedious battle, Congress and the president agreed to set defense budget authority at $290.8 billion and outlays at $285.5 billion for 1989. Thus the decline in budget authority since 1985

Table 3-1. *Defense Department Budget Authority and Outlays, Fiscal Years 1985–89*
Amounts in billions of 1989 dollars

Year	Budget authority		Outlays	
	Amount	Percent change	Amount	Percent change
1985	325.5	...	277.3	...
1986	312.2	−4.1	294.2	6.1
1987	301.6	−3.4	296.4	0.8
1988	292.8	−2.9	287.2	−3.1
1989	290.8	−0.7	285.5	−0.6
1985–89	...	−11.9	...	3.0

Source: Office of the Assistant Secretary of Defense (Comptroller), *National Defense Budget Estimates for FY 1988/ 1989* (April 1988), pp. 88, 97.

will run to about 12 percent in real terms, or $34.7 billion. By contrast, outlays, which are what affect the budget deficit, will rise in real terms by 3.0 percent, or about $8.2 billion.

The principal reason why outlays have proved so relatively intractable to reductions is that the Defense Department carries large balances of prior-year budget authority. And these balances continue to generate outlays at a certain rate (depending on their composition) regardless of what Congress does about current-year budget authority. At present, for example, these balances amount to about $266 billion. Of that total, nearly $225 billion are obligated in the form of contracts for goods and services, and under current law Congress cannot cancel these contracts. As a consequence, previously obligated authority is responsible for about 40 percent of current-year defense spending. The remaining 60 percent comes from budget authority appropriated in the current fiscal year.[1]

If the past is any guide, and if present budgetary plans are implemented, balances of prior-year authority will continue to grow, at least in nominal terms and quite possibly in real terms. Moreover, the defense investment accounts (usually defined as procurement; research, development, test, and evaluation—or RDT&E—and military construction), because they involve a full funding of many programs with long leadtimes—it takes seven years to build a modern aircraft carrier—add most to the balances of prior-year budget authority and mean that outlays will be affected by them over a long period. Between 1982 and 1985, for example, Congress

1. See appendix A, table A–2, for the trend in balances of prior-year budget authority. It should be noted that though Congress may not be able to rescind obligated authority, the administration can still cancel contracts. *Department of Defense Annual Report, Fiscal Year 1989*, p. 127.

appropriated $450.3 billion for investment, most of which has now been spent. Between 1986 and 1989 it appropriated another $496.5 billion for the same accounts, despite reductions that were made in procurement and military construction (but not in RDT&E). The bills for about half of these more recent appropriations will not come due until three or four years in the future. Thus if outlays for defense are to decline significantly during the coming five years, current-year budget authority will have to come under strict control.

CURRENT SOLUTIONS

There are several ways in which defense can be made to contribute substantial amounts to a reduction in the federal deficit, especially since the defense budget is classified as one of the more controllable items in the federal budget. Whether any of these approaches can produce large savings and at the same time ensure the continuation of an adequate defense is another matter. In fact, it is one of the central issues that will face the next president.

Gramm-Rudman-Hollings

One way open to the new president is to allow P.L. 99-177 to take its course. Such a choice, however, is neither pleasing nor productive. Gramm-Rudman-Hollings, even in its modified form, deliberately pre-scribes a bitter medicine. To summarize its contents, if the president and Congress fail in a given year to reach the designated reduction in the federal deficit (let us say they find themselves $20 billion over the target), defense outlays will have to be cut by $10 billion—or half of the $20 billion reduction in the deficit still needed—and all the accounts not fenced off by the president will have to suffer equally. That could easily mean a decline of $30 billion or more in budget authority, depending on where the cuts in outlays were made. Most of them, moreover, would have to come from the pending defense budget, since all but the unobligated balances of prior-year authority would be off limits.

P.L. 99-177 has gone into effect on two occasions: at the beginning of 1986, when it mandated a reduction of $5.8 billion in defense outlays; and briefly at the outset of fiscal 1988, before the president and congressional leaders reached their compromise on federal budget totals and allocations to defense. No one, including the authors of P.L. 99-

177, seems eager to go further and let the law substitute for the more traditional methods of shaping the federal budget.

That attitude is easy to understand. Because the mechanism of the law chops away equally at all unprotected programs regardless of their merits, it virtually ensures that to whatever extent the budget originally reflected a plan for the nation's growth, stability, and security, that plan will suffer a general bleeding, reminiscent of eighteenth-century surgery. Indeed, because of this threat, the propensity grows stronger than usual to obligate prior-year budget authority inefficiently rather than risk losing it, and to engage in excessively optimistic prognoses about the nation's economic growth, thereby making the deficit reduction targets look easier to reach than they are likely to be in reality.

All in all, then, Gramm-Rudman-Hollings seems unlikely to assist much in producing a balanced defense or in reducing the federal deficit. A sword of Damocles it may be, but Congress and the president, having suspended it over the budgetary process, have attached so many strings to it that they have minimized the probability of its ever falling with full force and effect.

The Attack of the Termites

If, by some accident, P.L. 99-177 should come into full play, it would almost certainly produce an even more irrational defense plan than has emerged from the Pentagon during the past eight years. Yet there remains another approach to defense budgeting and reductions that can claim to be its equal. This approach entails a sequence of three basic steps. The first is to look at a given defense budget, not as part of a longer-term set of objectives, plans, and programs, but as a unique entity with no past and no future. The second step is to search for the "fast money" in the budget—that is, the budget authority for items such as pay, spare parts, and fuel that converts almost fully into outlays during the coming fiscal year—and cut the relevant accounts by the amounts necessary to reach the congressional targets for defense. The third step is simply to repeat the first two steps in succeeding years.

Since congressional staff are masters of the art of ferreting out pockets of fast money and padded line items in the defense budget, they can establish an impressive record of savings in that particular way. Unfortunately, however, unless the budget is specifically designed to allow for this kind of exercise, the cuts are almost bound to be at the expense of military and civilian personnel, ammunition, hours of training (with

Table 3-2. *Defense Appropriation Accounts, Fiscal Years 1985–89*
Billions of 1989 dollars

		Operation	Investment				Revolving
Year	Military personnel	and maintenance	Procure-ment[a]	RDT&E[b]	Military construction	Family housing	funds and other
1985	75.3	88.7	110.7	35.8	6.3	3.3	5.3
1986	73.2[c]	85.2	102.4	37.4	5.9	3.1	4.6
1987	78.8	87.8	85.8	38.4	5.5	3.3	1.9
1988	78.5	83.6	83.7	38.0	5.5	3.3	0.1
1989	78.4	85.6	80.0	38.2	5.7	3.3	− 0.5

Source: *Department of Defense Annual Report, Fiscal Year 1989*, p. 297.
a. Although the procurement account declines by 38 percent, most of the reduction occurs in items related to readiness rather than to major weapons systems.
b. Research, development, test, and evaluation.
c. This figure does not reflect the congressional decision to take $4.5 billion from prior-year balances of unobligated authority and apply it to the military personnel account.

their consumption of fuel and wear and tear on equipment), and maintenance. In effect, what happens is that the defense house appears from the outside to be in excellent order while all the parts on the inside that make it function are progressively being eaten away, especially since the major procurement accounts, which consist largely of "slow money," are for the most part spared the erosion in contrast to other procurement (table 3-2). Conceivably we can have our cake and eat it too in the sense of maintaining a strong defense at a reduced cost. But a tactic of concentrating a year at a time on fast-money accounts (some of which are in procurement) is unlikely to achieve that objective.

Reduced Commitments and Arms Control

Arguments have now been made that we should not or need not try to reach the goal of a strong defense. The claim is made in one set of these arguments that the United States, as it has come to play an imperial role in the postwar world (perhaps in a fit of absentmindedness), has undertaken commitments abroad at the expense of its economy at home, and that it will go the way of the Spanish and British empires unless it becomes willing to devote more of its national income to productive investment. To make the necessary changes and get its economic house in order, it must reduce both its overseas commitments and its military capabilities.

In another set of these arguments it is foreseen that a new era in Soviet-American relations will open, that the Intermediate-Range Nuclear Forces (or INF) Treaty will be followed by deep reductions in strategic nuclear and conventional arms, and that many of the regional tensions of the past will subside. In such circumstances, much more modest military capabilities will be needed and a great deal of money can be saved.

As to the first set of arguments, it is probably true that rapidly increased defense spending during much of the Reagan administration, combined with many other factors, has contributed to the current economic problems of the United States. But it may well also be true that increased military spending could have been undertaken—and continued if deemed necessary—without having caused those problems. At 6 or 7 percent of gross national product, defense spending is not a heavy burden on an economy that is more than twice the size of Japan's and 15 percent larger than that of the European Community. Nor is U.S. defense spending correlated in any direct way with the commitments made since World War II. The main factors that drive the size and composition of the American armed forces have to do with the military capabilities of the Soviet Union and its cohorts, the number of theaters in which they might be able and willing to attack more or less simultaneously, the contributions of U.S. allies, the number of theaters in which the United States might choose to establish a defense, and the evolution of technology. At present, depending on how they are defined, the United States has between forty and fifty commitments. But by no stretch of the imagination does it propose to fight in forty or fifty places more or less at the same time. Its force planning—leaving aside its nuclear capabilities, which account for about 20 percent of the defense budget—is based on the assumption that it might have to respond simultaneously to two attacks: one of major proportions (such as an invasion of Western Europe by the Warsaw Treaty Organization, or WTO) and another of lesser size (such as a Soviet effort to seize the oil states of the Persian Gulf or an attack by North Korea on South Korea). Even if a decision were made to reduce U.S. defense commitments by 50 percent, American defense planning would almost certainly take the same form that it now has. Only the allocation of forces might differ.

None of this should be taken to mean that Americans will remain forever committed to the defense of their foreign friends or that several hundred years from now elements of the Seventh U.S. Army will be discovered in the valleys of Switzerland speaking a mixture of English, German, and Latin. Someone other than an American may become SACEUR (supreme allied commander, Europe). Japan and West Germany may find themselves the leaders of the collective security system, such as it is. A strong case of economic nationalism could drive the United

States into a withdrawal of its forces from Europe and Asia and to the adoption of a defense policy oriented to the security of the Western Hemisphere. That such a withdrawal would result in a major reduction in defense spending is, however, doubtful unless the forces withdrawn were also demobilized. Even then, efforts to construct a fortress America—especially one based on defenses against ballistic missiles, bombers, and cruise missiles—could easily result in budgets higher than those proposed by former Secretary of Defense Caspar W. Weinberger.

Nonetheless, the possibility of a real rapprochement with the Soviet Union cannot be dismissed out of hand. Should such a new relationship develop, accompanied by a range of arms control and reduction agreements and lesser involvement in regional disputes, the prospects could prove good for changing the assumptions on which the planning of U.S. nuclear and conventional forces is based. At present, however, the future remains too uncertain to justify major changes in U.S. planning or U.S. forces. It is well to remember, moreover, that compensatory measures have accompanied every important arms control agreement signed thus far. Even the INF Treaty has resulted in a number of suggestions from the Defense Department, including consideration of a new tactical air-to-surface missile, development of a follow-on to the short-range Lance surface-to-surface missile, more nuclear artillery projectiles, and an upgrading of dual-capable aircraft and nuclear gravity bombs. A START treaty leading to a 50 percent reduction in strategic nuclear warheads, instead of cutting strategic costs, could result in greater expenditures on larger numbers of smaller submarines and increased rates of alert for missiles and bombers, together with greater reliability and accuracy in each unit so as to compensate for the loss of numbers. It took a hundred years for the United States and Great Britain to conclude that they no longer were enemies. Whether the United States and the Soviet Union can quicken that pace still remains to be tested.

A NEW FIVE-YEAR PLAN

Meanwhile the question remains: can the United States, faced with all these uncertainties, unilaterally retain an adequate defense posture during the next five-year planning period (fiscal 1990 through 1994) and still reduce defense spending significantly below what the Reagan administration is now proposing? To help answer that question, it becomes necessary to review what has happened to defense since the end of the Vietnam War.

Table 3-3. *Defense Department Budget Authority and Outlays, Fiscal Years 1968–77*
Amounts in billions of 1989 dollars

	Budget authority		Outlays	
Year	Amount	Percent change	Amount	Percent change
1968	289.5	. . .	293.6	. . .
1969	278.2	−3.9	285.1	−2.9
1970	251.0	−9.8	263.0	−7.7
1971	226.5	−9.7	239.1	−9.1
1972	219.3	−3.2	222.7	−6.9
1973	208.7	−4.8	203.8	−14.8
1974	201.2	−3.6	200.0	−1.8
1975	194.6	−3.3	196.5	−1.8
1976	202.7	4.2	189.8	−3.4
1977	212.7	4.9	192.4	1.3

Source: *National Defense Budget Estimates for FY 1988/1989*, pp. 87–88, 96–97.

The Basis for the Defense Boom

When President Reagan entered office in January 1981, he held two strong views about the state of American defenses. First, the armed forces of the United States had suffered a decade of neglect during the 1970s. Second, because of this neglect, a "window of vulnerability" had opened that, if not rapidly closed, would give the Soviet Union an unquestioned superiority in strategic offensive forces and the opportunity to launch a successful first strike against the United States. Others asserted that the risk was not so much of a surprise attack but of threats and pressures to which the United States, knowing of its weaknesses, would be vulnerable. Poor bargaining positions and concessions rather than confrontations would surely follow.

None of these views had much evidence to support it. The armed forces, admittedly, suffered from considerable turmoil during and after the U.S. withdrawal from Vietnam, and defense budget authority fell by more than 49 percent in real terms from its wartime peak in fiscal 1968 to its postwar low in 1975 (table 3-3). Thereafter, however, it began to grow again in real terms at an average rate of nearly 2 percent a year. Moreover (as shown in table 3-4), the defense acquisition system was not exactly idle during the decade. Not only did it fund the production of large numbers of nuclear and conventional capabilities; it also introduced such new systems as the Trident submarine and the C-4

Table 3-4. *Acquisition of Major Weapons Systems,*
Fiscal Years 1974–81
Number of items

Item	1974–77	1978–81
Strategic and tactical nuclear missiles	826	1,192
Trident submarines	5	4
Tanks	3,241	2,524
All other tracked vehicles	3,691	4,420
Surface-launched tactical missiles	173,295	78,199
Air-launched tactical missiles	29,101	19,164
Combat aircraft	1,425	1,841
Airlift aircraft	111	136
Trainer aircraft	227	117
Helicopters	561	612
Major warships	29	16
Other warships	21	28
Auxiliary ships	11	15

Source: William W. Kaufmann, *A Reasonable Defense* (Brookings, 1986), p. 39.

(Trident I) missile, the air-launched cruise missile (ALCM), the M-1 Abrams tank, the M-2 Bradley fighting vehicle system, the AH-64 Apache attack helicopter, the Aegis guided missile cruiser (CG-47), the F/A-18 naval fighter and attack aircraft, the A-10A Thunderbolt II close air support aircraft, and the premier fighters of the Air Force (the F-15 and F-16), all of which provided the backbone of the Reagan modernization program.

Amid this somewhat less than neglectful activity, both the Ford and Carter administrations became concerned about what was considered the growing vulnerability of the intercontinental ballistic missile leg of the strategic nuclear triad (consisting of bombers and submarine-launched ballistic missiles, or SLBMs, as well as ICBMs). The issue was not whether the Soviet Union could deliver a knockout blow against the triad. It could not. Rather, the concern was, first, to prevent an erosion in the U.S. ability to destroy Soviet missile silos on a second strike and, second, to let the Soviet leaders know that if they continued in their efforts to place the U.S. ICBM force in jeopardy, they would have to pay the price both of seeing their own ICBMs threatened and of having to take remedial measures of their own. Accordingly, the United States continued to develop two ballistic missiles with greatly increased accuracies: the MX ICBM with ten warheads and the D-5 (Trident II) SLBM with eight warheads. Although neither launcher had approached de-

Table 3-5. *Growth in Defense Department Budget Authority and Outlays, Fiscal Years 1980–85*
Amounts in billions of 1989 dollars

Year	Budget authority		Outlays	
	Amount	Percent growth	Amount	Percent growth
1980	213.4	. . .	207.1	. . .
1981	241.1	13.0	217.6	5.1
1982	268.9	11.5	232.8	7.0
1983	290.8	8.1	250.5	7.6
1984	303.9	4.5	259.7	3.7
1985	325.5	7.1	277.3	6.8
1980–85	. . .	52.5	. . .	33.9

Source: *National Defense Budget Estimates for FY 1988/1989*, p. 88.

ployment by 1981, it turned out that the then-existing force, even after a surprise attack by the Soviet Union, would probably have had the capability to deliver more than 3,000 nuclear weapons to targets in the Soviet Union. What was more, the same estimates suggested that the Soviet Union was more vulnerable to a first strike than the United States.

Apparently oblivious of these facts, President Reagan launched what was to become the largest and speediest buildup of defense budget authority in American peacetime history. From 1980 to 1985 budget authority as a whole grew by nearly 53 percent in real terms. The main beneficiary of this growth was procurement, which more than doubled in real terms, with RDT&E not far behind, increasing by more than 80 percent. As was to be expected, outlays grew less rapidly; overall they increased by just under 35 percent, although expenditures for procurement rose by more than 63 percent and spending for RDT&E expanded by a healthy 56 percent (tables 3-5 and 3-6).

Several circumstances surrounding this growth deserve notice. Soon after Congress joined the defense bandwagon, it became known that the Central Intelligence Agency (CIA) had revised downward its estimates of the rate at which Soviet defense outlays were rising. According to the new estimates, the rate of increase had fallen in real terms from 4 to 2 percent a year by 1976, and expenditures on procurement were not increasing at all.

Despite what was to become more than a decade of relative Soviet neglect of its military capabilities, the Pentagon continued to stress the growing threat and emphasized that over the previous twenty years the

Table 3-6. *Growth in Defense Department Budget Authority and Outlays for Procurement and Research, Development, Test, and Evaluation, Fiscal Years 1980–85*
Amounts in billions of 1989 dollars

	Budget authority		Outlays	
Year	Amount	Percent growth	Amount	Percent growth
		Procurement		
1980	52.1	...	48.9	...
1981	65.2	25.3	53.4	9.1
1982	82.2	26.1	58.2	9.1
1983	97.9	19.1	67.0	15.0
1984	101.6	3.8	72.7	8.6
1985	110.7	9.0	80.0	10.0
1980–85	...	112.5	...	63.6
		RDT&E		
1980	19.7	...	19.8	...
1981	22.2	12.8	20.8	5.4
1982	25.4	14.4	22.5	8.1
1983	27.9	9.6	25.2	11.6
1984	31.7	13.7	27.2	8.2
1985	35.8	13.1	30.9	13.4
1980–85	...	81.7	...	56.1

Source: *National Defense Budget Estimates for FY 1988/1989*, p. 97.

Soviets had invested nearly twice as much in procurement, RDT&E, and military construction as the United States had.[2] The Pentagon spokesmen failed, however, to note either that the United States and its allies were outspending the WTO or that, since Soviet armed forces were supposed to be twice as large as those of the United States and deployed against what were deemed to be a number of hostile nations and coalitions on their borders, it was hardly surprising that the Soviets' investment budget should be larger—though probably not two times larger—than that of the U.S. Defense Department.

The Objectives of the Defense Boom

The alleged disparity in investment may well have been the driving force behind Secretary of Defense Weinberger's steadily increasing requests for defense budget authority and for the heavy emphasis he gave in them to the investment accounts. Otherwise, as he was later to

2. *Department of Defense Annual Report, Fiscal Year 1988*, p. 18.

acknowledge, the budgetary buildup lacked the combination of central objectives and a well-defined plan for reaching them.[3]

To fill this vacuum, the military services were quick to offer their own plans and programs, none of which was particularly well coordinated with the others. The upshot was not only that they sought an expansion of their forces and their continued modernization with top-of-the-line weapons of the current generation, but also that they hastened the development of a next generation of still more costly capabilities. The Army, despite a personnel ceiling of 781,000, dreamed of a 28-division force, of which 18 would be active duty and equipped with new tanks, new infantry fighting vehicles, new attack helicopters, and even a large fleet of new trucks. The Navy rushed to ensure the construction of a 600-ship navy (the rationale for which appeared later) led by 15 modern aircraft carrier battle groups, 4 reactivated battleships, and at least 100 nuclear attack submarines. The Marine Corps (somewhat mysteriously) limited itself to the amphibious lift for an additional marine brigade and a relatively modest program of modernization. The Air Force was not so constrained as it vied with the Navy for the largest share of the budget. It set out to modernize the bomber and ICBM legs of the strategic nuclear triad with upgraded B-52s, 2 new bombers, a new air-launched cruise missile, the MX ICBM, and eventually the small ICBM known as Midgetman. It also hoped to increase its active and reserve fighter and attack wings from 36½ to 40 and essentially to double the capacity of its intercontinental airlift, to 66 million ton miles a day.[4]

Some Consequences of the Boom

Between 1981 and 1985 Congress appropriated (in 1989 dollars) $1,430.2 billion in budget authority; outlays for the same period (also in 1989 dollars) amounted to $1,237.9 billion, as was seen in table 3-5. Inevitably, improvements in the defense establishment resulted from such a large infusion of funds. Although the services were not able, for the most part, to reach their force goals, they did modernize a significant number of their units with the current generation of weapons. Retention of personnel increased, as did the quality of the people recruited, despite only modest increases in pay. Living conditions improved, as did readiness measured by such criteria as flying hours, steaming days, and days of

3. *Department of Defense Annual Report, Fiscal Year 1987*, pp. 13–25.
4. Ibid., pp. 154, 162–64, 178–79, 182–83, 197, 213–15, 218–19.

battalion training. Stocks of war reserve munitions and matériel rose, but not as rapidly as had originally been hoped.

Several more troubling consequences of the rush to expansion and modernization gradually became evident as well. The Pentagon, though accustomed to the management of large amounts of money and even to periodic increases and decreases in these amounts, was swamped by the magnitude of the growth bestowed on it by the Reagan administration. Scandals and accusations of mismanagement inevitably resulted, followed by the equally ubiquitous efforts to reorganize the acquisition process. Concurrency in the development and production of major weapons systems became increasingly commonplace, and products such as the Army's Sergeant York air defense gun and the Air Force's B-1B bomber became casualties of excessive haste. Even more troublesome, the problem of the foot in the door that had so plagued the Pentagon in the 1950s returned with a vengeance. A large procurement program of current-generation weapons remained to be completed and made continued demands on generous but finite funds. As the services grew more dependent on their National Guard components to round out and augment the active-duty forces, pressure increased to modernize those components as well. Worst of all, more projects for next-generation weapons were expanding in RDT&E (having been allowed in because of low start-up costs) than could be funded at maturity, especially when a program as voracious as the Strategic Defense Initiative (SDI) was planted in their midst. At one point, it was estimated that, to satisfy all these demands, the Pentagon would need at least $750 billion more than it was projecting in its five-year defense program.[5]

THE ISSUE OF CHOICE

Even had defense budgets continued to expand in real terms, it was clear by the mid-1980s that choices among the various activities would eventually have to be made and that something would have to give. It was equally clear that the longer the decisions were delayed, the more

---

5. In fairness to the Weinberger program, the alleged underfunding of $750 billion probably reflected the differences in cost at that time between the Weinberger program and the estimated cost of the "minimum risk" force proposed by the Joint Chiefs of Staff, a force that no one had any intention of buying. See William W. Kaufmann, *A Reasonable Defense* (Brookings, 1986), pp. 100–01. For further information on the defense budget, see Richard Halloran, *To Arm a Nation: Rebuilding America's Endangered Defenses* (Macmillan, 1986), esp. chap. 8.

Table 3-7. *Budget Authority Requests by Defense Secretary Weinberger and Congressional Responses, Fiscal Years 1981–89*
Billions of current dollars unless otherwise specified

Year	Request	Response	Difference	
			Amount	Percent
1981	158.2	178.4	20.2	12.8
1982	222.2[a]	213.8	− 8.4	− 3.9
1983	257.5	239.5	− 18.0	− 7.5
1984	273.4	258.2	− 15.2	− 5.9
1985	305.0	286.8	− 18.2	− 6.6
1986	313.7	281.1	− 32.6	− 11.6
1987	311.6	279.5	− 32.1	− 11.5
1988	303.3	283.2	− 20.1	− 7.1
1989[b]	323.3	290.8	− 32.5	− 11.2
1981–89	2,468.2	2,311.3	− 156.9	− 6.9

Sources: *Department of Defense Annual Report, Fiscal Year 1981*, p. A-9; *Fiscal Year 1983*, p. B-1; *Fiscal Year 1984*, p. 61; *Fiscal Year 1985*, p. 64, *Fiscal Year 1986*, p. 71; *Fiscal Year 1987*, p. 95; *Fiscal Year 1988*, p. 86; *Fiscal Year 1989*, p. 297; and *National Defense Budget Estimates for FY 1988/1989*, p. 94.

a. The original Carter request was for $196.4 billion. Reagan proposed adding $25.8 billion to this amount. See Kaufmann, *A Reasonable Defense*, pp. 24–25.

b. Estimated.

difficult they would become and the more they would cost the taxpayer. Indeed, as Congress began to reduce the defense budget in 1986, the issue no longer was whether cuts would have to be made, but where they could be made without damaging the ability of the United States to retain a powerful nuclear deterrent and sustain a two-theater strategy with its conventional forces.

Yet Weinberger valiantly refused to recognize the inevitable. In 1986 he asked for $313.7 billion in budget authority for the Pentagon, and lost $32.6 billion of it. In 1987, on a slightly more modest note, he requested $311.6 billion and was cut more than $32 billion for his pains. In 1988, though his internal five-year defense program allegedly showed that he would need an average real growth of more than 4 percent a year to fund the program, he proposed a 3 percent real growth for the next five years from a 1988 base of $303.3 billion. Congress ignored the longer-term plan and reduced the 1988 request by more than $20 billion. Finally, for 1989 he proposed a budget of $323.3 billion. But (as table 3-7 shows) the president and congressional leaders ended up by agreeing on a total of $290.8 billion, $32.5 billion below his request.

Despite this succession of setbacks, Weinberger continued to insist on maintaining force structure, pushing the current modernization program (although at a slower pace) and preparing for the early production of such costly new systems as the advanced technology (Stealth) bomber,

Table 3-8. *Budget Authority for Selected New Weapons Systems for the 1990s*
Costs in billions of current dollars

Item	Number	Estimated cost
Advanced technology (Stealth) bomber	132	64.0[a]
MX missile	189	16.3
Rail garrison MX trains	25	9.1
Small ICBM (Midgetman)	645	44.7
Trident II submarine	11	16.9
Trident II (D-5) missile	845	35.5
Strategic Defense Initiative (R&D only)	. . .	50.3[b]
Air defense, antitank system (ADATS)	562	5.7
Light helicopter, experimental (LHX)	2,096	30.0
Advanced tactical fighter (ATF and ATA)	1,270[c]	45.0
F-14D fighter aircraft	527	22.9
Advanced medium-range air-to-air missile (AMRAAM)	24,431	10.5
V-22 Osprey tilt-rotor aircraft	919	29.7
C-17A airlift aircraft	211	35.4
DDG-51 guided missile destroyer	23	20.1
SSN-21 nuclear attack submarine	30	32.0
Total	. . .	468.1

Sources: *Department of Defense Selected Acquisition Reports* (SARs) as of September 30, 1987; "LHX Price Still Growing," *Defense Week*, June 6, 1988, p. 13; Scott D. Dean, "Army Locks onto ADATS, Locks out Liberty in FAADS-LOS-F-H Shoot-off," *Armed Forces Journal International*, January 1988, p. 17; Benjamin F. Schemmer, "USAF's Number-One Conventional Program: Is the Advanced Tactical Fighter a Good or Bad Deal for Industry?" ibid., January 1988, pp. 36–37; and Scott C. Truver, "The Most Controversial Ship in the Navy," ibid., April 1988, p. 56.

a. The advanced technology bomber is a classified program; it is not included in the SARs. The total shown here reflects the author's estimate of the full program cost of 132 aircraft. Other estimates now place the cost of the program at $59.5 billion in 1989 dollars, and rising. George C. Wilson, "Cost of Stealth Bomber Soars to $450 Million Each," *Washington Post*, May 15, 1988. Indeed, according to Richard Halloran, "Bomber Cost Said to Exceed Estimate," *New York Times*, June 9, 1988, the General Accounting Office has now estimated the total program cost at $68.8 billion, or more than $520 million per aircraft.

b. Author's estimate based on Congressional Budget Office, *Modernizing U.S. Strategic Offensive Forces: Costs, Effects, and Alternatives* (November 1987), p. 38.

c. The Air Force advanced tactical fighter (ATF) accounts for 748; the Navy advanced tactical aircraft (ATA) for the rest.

the MX based on railroad trains, the small ICBM, the advanced cruise missile, the D-5 (Trident II) ballistic missile, the V-22 Osprey tilt-rotor aircraft, a new class of guided missile destroyers (DDG-51), the SSN-21 nuclear attack submarine, the advanced tactical fighter, the advanced medium-range air-to-air missile (AMRAAM), the C-17A airlift aircraft, and possibly the first stage of an antiballistic missile defense system based on the Strategic Defense Initiative—at costs running to $468.1 billion (table 3-8). At no point did he appear to have asked how he could reconcile the congressional pressure for reductions in defense spending with his own, understandable, desire for a strong defense. As a result, the irresistible force simply bypassed and ignored the immovable object.

Table 3-9. *Secretary Carlucci's Amended Defense Department Budget Long-Range Forecasts, Fiscal Years 1988–92*

| | Budget authority | | |
| | Billions of | Billions of | Annual |
Year	current dollars	1989 dollars	percent charge
1988	283.2	292.8	−2.9
1989	290.8	290.8	−0.7
1990	307.3	297.0	2.1
1991	324.3	303.7	2.3
1992	342.0	311.3	2.5

Source: *Department of Defense Annual Report, Fiscal Year 1989*, p. 131.

The new secretary of defense, Frank C. Carlucci, after what no doubt were four difficult months (in late 1987 and early 1988), presented Congress with the revised 1989 defense budget and the bare outlines of a five-year defense program. Although he necessarily accepted $290.8 billion as the budget authority to be required for 1989, he proposed that real growth in defense should average about 2 percent a year for the next four years (as shown in table 3-9).

Even if Secretary Carlucci, or his successor, were to achieve this real rate of growth, which seems doubtful, he would still have to reduce the old Weinberger program by more than $229 billion to bring it in line with his own projection. If, as appears more likely, the defense budget will be subjected to continued real reductions on the same order as have occurred since 1985, they could mean still another $246 billion in cuts, or a total of $475 billion from the original Weinberger growth path (see appendix A, table A-3). In either case, the task is not an enviable one. It may indeed prove impossible, considering how much prior-year budget authority is already obligated, unless the secretary is able to provide Congress with a coherent plan and a sensible rationale for reductions of such magnitudes.

So far, Secretary Carlucci has given very few clues about how he will deal with the difficult decisions ahead. In fiscal 1989 he has chosen to spread the pain in a relatively evenhanded way. On the surface, the Army suffers the least of the three services and the Navy the most. However, the Navy had already received some of the funds in 1988 (for carriers and Aegis cruisers) that it was therefore able to take out of its request for 1989. Thus the Air Force has ended up as the hardest hit, in large part because funding for the small ICBM is reduced by more than $2 billion and SDI shrinks by another $1.7 billion from its original target.

What is more interesting is that, these big new programs aside, most of the savings are achieved by what have now become the familiar methods. Carlucci, to his credit, has at least cancelled eight small programs, including ASAT (the antisatellite missile), the Navy's A-6F (an attack aircraft), and the Army's Aquila (a remotely piloted vehicle or drone). He has also stretched out the acquisition of a number of programs such as the MX missile and its rail garrison basing mode, the Bradley fighting vehicle, the AV-8B jump jet, the F-15E fighter and attack aircraft, and several tactical missiles and torpedoes. Active-duty military personnel and full-time civilian employees are to be reduced, respectively, by 36,000 and 33,000 in 1988 and 1989, but the National Guard and Reserve are to be increased by 56,000 during these same years. All three services are required to make modest force reductions on the apparent ground that within existing budget constraints, the slightly smaller capabilities can be better equipped, trained, and sustained. At the same time, however, the secretary has cut the procurement of ammunition, spare parts, and support capabilities by $1.3 billion and protected most of the next-generation weapons, including several (such as the V-22 Osprey and the SSN-21 attack submarine) that are due to receive procurement funding in 1989.[6]

Obviously other choices could have been made, and Congress will undoubtedly make some adjustments to the secretary's recommendations within the overall constraint of $290.8 billion of budget authority for 1989. Nonetheless, granting that this is an interim budget contrived in great haste, the basic question for the next five-year program (1990–94) remains. How are existing capabilities, the completion of current-generation modernization, and the beginning of next-generation acquisitions to be fitted into defense budgets that, at most, will grow by little more than 2 percent a year in real terms, and are more likely to decline, on the average, by as much as 3 percent a year as the battle of the budget deficit continues?

Determinants of Performance

To come to grips with this question, it may be useful to recall one of the Pentagon's clichés (but still a useful one). It says that force performance rests on four pillars: force size and composition, readiness, sustainability,

6. For details, see *Department of Defense Annual Report, Fiscal Year 1989,* various pages; Thomas N. Donlan, "Biting the Bullet: Defense Chief Carlucci Aims for Economy and Quality," *Barron's,* April 4, 1988, pp. 70–71; and Stephen A. Cain, "Defense Budget: Assault on Readiness, The Numbers: Most Training and Logistic Accounts Are Feeling the Pinch," *Military Forum,* May 1988, pp. 22–27.

and modernization. For purposes of emphasis one might add a fifth pillar usually considered a part of readiness and sustainability: intercontinental mobility, since it makes little sense to have powerful forces in the United States if they cannot be deployed in a timely fashion to one or more threatened regions.

Differences of opinion may exist about how ready for combat specific units need to be, and arguments can continue ad infinitum about how long units should be able to sustain themselves in combat, especially when the threat to use nuclear weapons could knock all such calculations into a cocked hat. Similar disputes can and do arise over the size and composition of the nuclear and conventional forces that the United States should support. As a consequence, there is no simple formula to dictate, at various budget levels, the allocation of resources among the principal determinants of force performance.

Despite this range of possibilities, the United States has remained relatively consistent in how it has planned its forces. Today, as for more than two decades, the strategic nuclear forces consist of approximately 2,000 launchers organized in a triad of 1,000 ICBMs, 372 bombers, and 592 submarine-based missiles. Because of technology, not only has the distribution of launchers changed among the three legs of the triad; the number of weapons carried by the force has also risen from over 11,000 to more than 14,000 in the last seven years alone. But as the warhead count has risen, the yields of the individual weapons have on the average gone down.

Although the weapons totals are indeed formidable, it is worth recalling that only parts of the forces are maintained on an alert status and are ready to launch—approximately 68 percent of the total—and that only parts of the 68 percent would reach their targets. Thus it currently takes about three warheads in the forces to ensure the second-strike delivery of one weapon on target. Because of the potential wastage, along with the size of the target list in the Soviet Union (not all of which automatically has to be attacked), there is not much pressure to modify the size and composition of the force short of a major arms reduction treaty or a major technological development. High readiness is accepted as necessary to guard against surprise attacks, but sustainability receives only spasmodic attention, since the idea of a prolonged nuclear war tends to be seen as a contradiction in terms. Modernization, however, is another matter. If cost cutting is to be taken seriously, the number of programs now under way that purport not only to modernize but also to improve the strategic nuclear forces will surely have to be taken into account.

The conventional forces have remained almost as stable as the strategic

Table 3-10. *U.S. Military Personnel in Foreign Areas, End of Selected Fiscal Years, 1980–87*
Thousands of uniformed personnel

Area	1980	1985	1986	1987
Germany	244	247	250	250
Other Europe	65	75	75	73
Europe, afloat	22	36	32	31
South Korea	39	42	43	45
Japan	46	47	48	50
Other Pacific	15	16	17	18
Pacific, afloat	15	20	20	17
Miscellaneous foreign	42	32	38	40
Total	489	515	523	524

Source: *Department of Defense Annual Report, Fiscal Year 1989*, p. 306. Figures are rounded.

nuclear forces. The Army has gone from 16 to 18 divisions, but the number of people in the active-duty component has remained at approximately 781,000 for more than a decade. The Marine Corps, by law, maintains 3 divisions and their associated air wings. The Air Force active-duty fighter and attack wings have risen from 22 to 25, but will fall back to 23 because of the Carlucci cuts. The Navy has added more than 60 ships to its fleet since 1980 and counts 580 of them as deployable battle-force ships, but much of this growth had already been programmed in the 1970s when the goal of a 600-ship fleet first appeared.

Among other things that distinguish the conventional from the strategic nuclear forces is the way in which they are deployed. As of the end of 1987, at least 524,000 American military personnel (or 24 percent of the active-duty force) were stationed overseas. Of this total, 48 percent were in West Germany, and nearly 68 percent in Western Europe as a whole, including the Sixth Fleet in the Mediterranean. Another 130,000 (or about 25 percent of the total) were in the western Pacific, with the main concentrations in Japan (including Okinawa) and South Korea (table 3-10). In addition, more than 18,000 Army and Air Force personnel garrison Alaska, and Hawaii is host to more than 19,000 Army and Air Force people, along with a shifting naval population.

Lord Palmerston once said of the Schleswig-Holstein dispute that only three men even understood its origins. One had died, the second was in an insane asylum, and he himself had forgotten them. The same is not quite true of current U.S. overseas deployments. They are more than simply artifacts of World War II or of some forgotten decision reached at the height of the cold war. Rather, they reflect the roles that U.S. military power plays on the world stage. These roles can be summarized as follows: (1) deterrence of conventional attacks on Western Europe, the Persian Gulf states, and Northeast Asia; (2) the forces deemed necessary, in conjunction with allies, to withstand attacks that could occur with little advance warning, especially in Germany and Korea; (3) the foundation onto which reinforcements can quickly be added; and (4) capabilities at the disposal of the national command authorities to deal with other than the key planning contingencies that are seen as threatening the interests of the United States.

It may be possible to quarrel about the details of these dispositions or about who should pay for them. But it would be difficult to demonstrate in any persuasive way that the United States has acquired excessive insurance (in terms of force structure) against the key planning contingencies on which its force structure is based. The more plausible argument, in fact, is that these dispositions, if anything, reflect certain shortages— in reinforcing units, in intercontinental mobility, and in protection of critical sea-lanes—and an excessive dependence on the threat to use nuclear weapons in regional conflicts. Admittedly, a substantial change for the better in the international environment could occur. Alternatively, a decision could be made to base force planning on only one major contingency (but where?). Conceivably, policymakers could awake to discover that other nations are not only able but also willing to substitute for many of the U.S. dispositions—amid the approval and applause of their erstwhile enemies. But pending such developments, it does not appear practical or desirable, despite what Secretary Carlucci has already proposed, to save large amounts of defense outlays by cutting troop strength, force structure, and overseas deployments. Small adjustments in personnel may be feasible now that the INF Treaty has been ratified and assuming that certain other artificial objectives (such as the 600-ship navy) are abandoned. And certain allies can and should be expected to bear a greater share of the costs of having U.S. forces based on their soil. But if significant savings in defense are to be made during the next five years, the better part of wisdom will be to find them elsewhere. Moreover, if it is true that any significant change in contingencies, troop strength, force structure, and overseas deployments would be counterproductive in the current uncertain environment, then it follows (though not precisely) that levels of readiness, sustainability, and intercontinental mobility become fairly well determined and not subject to large changes. That leaves modernization as the central issue for decision.

Modernization Strategies

Military weapons, equipment, and facilities, like other more or less durable goods, can become more expensive to maintain than replace.

Technological developments can produce more cost-effective capabilities. In the marketplace of military power, the competition can force the rate of change by introducing what appear to be new and superior products at an accelerated pace. Consequently, as is true for used cars, there is no hard-and-fast rule for determining when, how, or at what rate a given inventory of weapons and equipment should be replaced.

Experience, however, provides several general guidelines for the process. First, peacetime service lives for the platforms from which most of the shooting is done are bound to vary. But, on the average, missiles and aircraft seem to last about twenty years, ships and submarines thirty years, and tanks and other tracked vehicles fifteen years. Second, if these platforms are carefully designed, not only can they be readily maintained, but essential components of them can also be upgraded at regular intervals.[7] Third, in the case of very costly platforms, such as aircraft carriers and many other ships, service life extension programs (SLEPs) can add as many as fifteen years to their operational effectiveness. Finally, unless the competition produces a sudden, startling, and significant advance—or your own side does, and it seems worth exploiting—it probably does not make sense to roll over the inventory of military platforms, on the average, more than once every twenty years.

Such a modernization strategy has several implications for the entire acquisition process. It obviously encourages relative speed in the development and production of subsystems (including readily available commercial counterparts) that can be used to upgrade the performance of existing platforms. At the same time, it proposes to allow ample time for the development of the next generation of platforms and puts a premium on building reliability into and testing the platform fully before committing it to production. This strategy can also provide protection against periods of major block obsolescence so long as defense funding proceeds at a reasonable pace and with some degree of predictability rather than in fits and starts. In fact, a process of modular design, periodic upgrades, and generational change (in the chronological as well as the technological sense) should provide greater reliability in performance and less loss of readiness as personnel adapt to technological change in small steps rather than in leaps and bounds.[8]

---

7. Aircraft, for example, may receive as many as five generations of electronic countermeasure sets during the course of their service lives.

8. For a much more comprehensive treatment of acquisition strategies and processes, see Thomas L. McNaugher, *New Weapons and Old Politics: America's Military Procurement Muddle* (Brookings, forthcoming).

It can and should be argued that such a process, unless accompanied by great vigilance and safeguards against surprise, could be exploited by a malevolent and technologically adept competitor. Many indeed would claim that those are precisely the features that characterize the Soviets in their own acquisition process, and that such stately behavior on the part of the United States will simply add to the Soviets' quantitative advantages. Such critics could be right, but the evidence so far does not support them. It is true, for example, that during the past twenty-five years Western observers have seen a series of Soviet tanks that they have labeled the T-62, the T-64, the T-72, and the T-80, whereas they have noted that the United States has stodgily deployed only the M-60 and the M-1. But here as elsewhere changes in nomenclature are being confused with important technological advances. Had the United States chosen to designate the three versions of the M-60 and the two (and possibly three) models of the M-1 as the M-60, the M-65, the M-75, the M-80, and (perhaps) the M-88, no doubt everyone but the Russians would probably have felt more comfortable. Certainly that was the reaction when in the 1960s Secretary of Defense Robert S. McNamara announced the deployment of what was to be the Polaris A-4 missile but had the good sense to call it the Poseidon instead.

In any event, Soviet advances tend to be exaggerated. What seem to characterize the Soviet acquisition process are evolution rather than great leaps forward, the substitution of new and more advanced systems for older ones on less than a one-for-one basis (as in the case of nuclear attack submarines), and a general concern on the part of Soviet leaders that they are not keeping pace with advances in Western military technology. In these circumstances, good intelligence, a refusal to engage in threat inflation, regular upgrades when major overhauls are due, a generational change of basic platforms (where appropriate), and their design to cost rather than to detailed "requirements" (many of which ignore diminishing returns to scale and advantageous trade-offs) seem to be adequate insurance against technological surprise combined with allegedly superior numbers.

THE NEXT FIVE YEARS

During the coming five-year period (1990–94), the modernization problem for the next administration appears to be roughly of the following order. Assuming optimistically that it will obtain slightly more than 2 percent real growth each year, it will accumulate over the five-

Table 3-11. *Estimated Carlucci Five-Year Defense Program,*
Fiscal Years 1990–94
Billions of current dollars

Appropriation account	1990	1991	1992	1993	1994	Total
Military personnel	82.6	86.6	90.2	93.9	97.7	451.0
Operation and maintenance	90.0	94.8	99.1	103.7	108.7	496.3
Procurement	85.3	91.1	98.0	105.6	113.8	493.8
Research, development, test, and evaluation	40.0	42.0	44.0	45.9	48.1	220.0
Military construction	6.0	6.3	6.6	6.9	7.2	33.0
Family housing	3.4	3.6	3.8	3.9	4.1	18.8
Revolving funds and other	0.0	0.0	0.3	0.4	0.0	0.7
Total, budget authority	307.3	324.4	342.0	360.3	379.6	1,713.6
Total, outlays	297.3	311.0	325.9	341.5	357.3	1,633.0

Sources: *Budget of the United States Government, Fiscal Year 1989*, p. 5-6 for fiscal 1990–91, and pp. 6g-8, 6g-16 for 1990–93 total rows; and author's estimates. See table B-2 for the assumptions used.

Table 3-12. *Estimated Congressional Five-Year Defense Program,*
Fiscal Years 1990–94
Billions of current dollars

Appropriation account	1990	1991	1992	1993	1994	Total
Military personnel	81.0	83.6	86.0	88.8	91.6	431.0
Operation and maintenance	85.7	90.1	94.6	99.3	104.4	474.1
Procurement	78.9	73.5	69.2	65.3	61.4	348.3
Research, development, test, and evaluation	40.0	38.9	35.8	32.8	29.8	177.3
Military construction	4.2	4.4	4.5	4.6	4.8	22.5
Family housing	2.6	2.7	2.8	2.9	3.0	14.0
Revolving funds and other	0.0	0.0	0.3	0.4	0.0	0.7
Total, budget authority	292.4	293.2	293.2	294.1	295.0	1,467.9
Total, outlays	282.9	283.7	283.7	284.5	285.4	1,420.2

Source: Author's estimates based on the assumption of a real annual decline of 2.9 percent.

year period a total (in current dollars) of about $714 billion for procurement and RDT&E (table 3-11). Yet it will probably need more than $907 billion to buy out the current generation of weapons, maintain the momentum of the next generation of capabilities now moving through the acquisition pipeline, and sustain major forces in the field (see appendix A, table A-1). If, as seems more likely, defense budgets will continue to decline in real terms for the next five years at the same rate that they have fallen during the last four (but force structure, readiness, sustainability, and intercontinental mobility are protected), only about $526 billion (in current dollars) will become available for procurement and RDT&E (table 3-12). Under these constraints, the problem of choice— at least on the surface—will become even more difficult.

However, a closer look at the real needs of existing capabilities and the application of a systematic acquisition strategy suggest that a continuation of what might be called a congressional five-year defense program—that is, one that declines each year by 2.9 percent in real terms—has its advantages. It can avoid any weakening in U.S. military strength. It need tap U.S. allies for only modest additional support. And it can make a virtue of the necessity for fiscal restraint by continuing the current wave of modernization and deferring the next wave during this period to ensure that its components will not only add significantly to U.S. combat power relative to their cost, but also work reliably in the field.

Strategic Nuclear Forces

The strategic nuclear forces have been undergoing a substantial modernization for more than a decade. The most significant changes have been the introduction of the Trident submarine with 24 launchers and longer-range, more accurate SLBMs and the arming of the bomber force with ALCMs (air-launched cruise missiles), which create complex problems for Soviet air defenses. If the congressional track is followed, both these programs can be continued, and an advanced cruise missile, reportedly with stealth technology incorporated, can ensure a high probability of penetrating even substantially improved Soviet defenses. Furthermore, to the extent desired, a prompt hard-target-kill capability can be maintained by continued acquisition of the D-5 (Trident II) SLBM.

Although the ICBM leg of the strategic triad is thought to be in growing jeopardy, that consideration does not end the usefulness of silo-based missiles. Together with the alert bombers (30 percent of the force), the ICBMs face Soviet planners with the extremely difficult task of coordinating an attack on both forces. Moreover, even if the Soviets could solve the timing problem, they would still have to contend with an SLBM force (including the D-5) that could attack all categories of fixed targets, hard or soft. In the circumstances, and particularly considering the difficulties encountered with the MX ICBM, the B-1B, and the development of a survivable basing mode for ICBMs, it makes sense—whatever the budget level—to defer the time at which new ICBMs and bombers are brought into the strategic forces. A five-year defense program following the congressional track can readily accommodate continued development and serious testing of the small ICBM (Midgetman) and the rail garrison MX, as well as the Stealth bomber. But decisions about their production will have to be deferred until the mid-

1990s. By that time not only will the prospects for strategic arms reduction be clarified, but the roles of land-mobile missiles and the manned penetrating bomber, if it has any, can also be better defined than they are now.

One program that will have to suffer large reductions and undergo restructuring in the congressional program is the SDI. At best, it can be allowed $3 billion a year in real terms during the five-year period of the program. Such a funding constraint will obviously limit the number of expensive tests in space and preclude any thought of beginning the deployment of a first-stage ballistic missile defense by the mid-1990s (a defense currently estimated to cost at least $100 billion and have a 30 percent probability of killing an incoming warhead).[9] But within such a constraint, scientists and engineers should be able to determine what technologies might prove cost-effective in the future and also develop countermeasures to any effort by the Soviet Union to deploy exotic ABM defenses.

Despite this change and the proposed deferrals, the strategic nuclear forces, after a surprise attack, should still be able to deliver more than 3,400 warheads on targets in the Soviet Union. It would be difficult to deny the robustness of such a deterrent to any threat of a first strike.

Tactical Nuclear Forces

The issue of how to distinguish nuclear-armed from conventional cruise missiles will probably continue to pose an obstacle to the conclusion of further arms control agreements. Consequently, both the United States and the Soviet Union will have to review their policies about the deployment of these capabilities, especially their sea-launched versions. During that time it may prove advisable to restrict any further acquisition of SLCMs to the conventional version. Nonetheless, the congressional five-year defense program provides the option to buy another 304 TLAM-N (Tomahawk land-attack missile, nuclear) if further coverage of the Soviet threat to Europe is deemed unnecessary. Based on submarines, TLAM-N could as readily attack fixed targets in Eastern Europe as the Pershing II missiles and GLCMs (ground-launched cruise missiles) that will be destroyed now that the INF Treaty has been ratified.

9. See John H. Cushman, Jr., "Report Sees Countermoves by Soviets on Missile Shield," *New York Times,* June 8, 1988.

Land Forces

The conventional forces of the United States confront four main problems, none of which requires rushing into a next generation of futuristic and much more costly weapons platforms. The Army needs to complete the current modernization of its active-duty forces and to spread that wave of modernization to its Reserve components, on which it has come to depend heavily for both combat and support forces. The congressional program can afford to support this approach to the extent of continuing to buy the AH-64 Apache attack helicopter, the M-1 tank, the Bradley fighting vehicle (or larger numbers of armored personnel carriers), utility helicopters, air defense units, and artillery. At the same time, it must (and should) hold in development and testing such next-generation systems as the new forward-area air defense system (FAADS), the army tactical missile system (ATACMS), and the light helicopter family that have begun playing an increasing role in the Army's budget.

Naval Forces

The Navy during the past seven years has consistently overemphasized its so-called power projection capabilities (that is, its aircraft carrier battle groups and amphibious forces) at the expense of its ability to protect the sea-lanes over which U.S. expeditionary forces, reinforcements, and supplies must for the most part move. Because of this bias, an insistence on buying the most sophisticated and expensive ships available, and a growing shortage of convoy escorts, the Navy had already developed a more voracious appetite for resources than even the Weinberger budgets could satisfy.

As part of curbing that appetite, the congressional five-year defense program would reject the goal of a 622-ship navy and settle for a more modest level of 570 ships. To reach and sustain that level within budgetary constraints, it would defer such programs as the new guided missile destroyer (DDG-51), the SSN-21 attack submarine, and the V-22 tilt-rotor aircraft. It would also adopt a skeptical view toward the "requirement" for 15 carrier battle groups and the amphibious lift for a fourth brigade of marines. However, since Congress has already appropriated funds for 2 new carriers—CVN-74 and CVN-75—the congressional program would phase out 3 older carriers, including the *Enterprise* (which will soon be due for an expensive overhaul) and stop buying any additional amphibious ships. Instead, it would continue to acquire more SSN-688 attack submarines, several more Aegis cruisers, and a new class of guided missile frigates (DDG-X) so as to strengthen the protection of convoys. It would also proceed with the modernization of the support ships in the fleet. In all, 65 new ships would be funded (not including 36 air-cushion landing craft), and 15 older ships—including 2 aircraft carriers and 7 amphibious ships—would undergo conversion and service-life-extension programs.

Tactical Air Forces

Under present geographic and technological conditions, U.S. ground forces are the key to successful offensive and defensive operations in most types of warfare and against most types of enemies. What this means for most purposes is that navies and air forces exist to support and supplement ground forces. But neither the Navy nor the Air Force is content to accept what it sees as a subordinate role in expeditionary warfare. Each persistently seeks to demonstrate that it has a predominant part to play in defeating an enemy, independently of the ground forces. Thus the Navy has invented a maritime strategy that contains more romance than reality as it charges into Murmansk and Vladivostok, while the Air Force attempts to demonstrate that it is the decisive service because of its ability to conduct campaigns made up of strategic bombing against the war production base of the enemy (including bicycle factories in North Vietnam) along with a combination of air superiority and interdiction designed to prevent the movement of reinforcements and supplies of the enemy's ground forces—which will then wither on the vine.

In the case of the Navy, this attitude has led to an excessive preoccupation with carrier battle groups and amphibious operations, the last of which took place under fire in 1950. In some sense, the Air Force has been similarly stricken. It has developed a passionate attachment to the weapons for deep air superiority and interdiction, and a much lesser concern for intercepting the enemy's attack aircraft and providing the Army with close air support. Consequently, even as it modernizes its fighter and attack squadrons with the F-15 and F-16 aircraft, it has begun production of the F-15E as a dual-purpose fighter-bomber, is allegedly experimenting with a stealth fighter, and is pushing for the early production of the advanced tactical fighter (ATF).

Because of these and many other activities, including a heavy emphasis on advanced strategic nuclear systems and precision-guided munitions, the Air Force is living well beyond its expected means. Indeed, it is already being required to give up two fighter and attack wings equipped with older planes in order to accommodate its desire to get on with the next generation of aircraft. However, there is a more prudent alternative, which is incorporated in the congressional program. The two wings dropped by Secretary Carlucci would be retained, but the F-15E would be cancelled and the ATF held in development and extensive testing. In their place, the F-16 would be produced in larger numbers and configured for combat air patrol and close air support, admittedly in default of aircraft more specifically designed for those missions. That does not mean that deep air superiority and interdiction would be abandoned. But because their payoffs tend to occur too late to have a great effect on the outcome of the ground battle, particularly in a critical theater such as central Europe, existing capabilities would be retained rather than augmented, and the funds saved reallocated to aircraft more likely to provide direct and immediate support to NATO ground forces and to attacks on enemy follow-on forces, which could be 80 or more kilometers behind the front.

Mobility

In the realm of mobility, recent experience in Central America demonstrates that several thousand alerted troops can be flown rapidly and efficiently over distances of several thousand miles. But questions arise about the ability of airlift to deal rapidly and efficiently with a hundred times the number of troops over two times or more the number of miles. The questions become more urgent still when the Air Force insists yet again on acquiring an aircraft (the C-17A) that is meant to serve as both an intercontinental and an intratheater lifter and that will cost more than $35 billion for 211 of them (see table 3-8).

No doubt U.S. mobility capabilities should hedge with pre-positioned matériel and airlift, as well as with troops deployed in sensitive theaters, against short intervals between a U.S. decision to move forces and an enemy attack. And the United States is already close to having such a rapid-response capability for use in central Europe. It is not at all clear that we need a great deal more capability simply to be able to move simultaneously and at equal speed into the Persian Gulf or Northeast Asia. Accordingly, the congressional program would defer acquisition of the C-17A. Substituted for it would be 21 more C-5Bs to enhance

Table 3-13. *Allocation of Budget Authority by Major Capability in the Congressional Five-Year Defense Program, Fiscal Years 1990–94*

Billions of current dollars

Capability	Military personnel	Operation and maintenance	Investment					Total
			Procurement	RDT&E	Military construction	Family housing	Other	
Strategic nuclear forces	53.6	94.7	61.9	54.3	5.2	3.0	0.1	272.8
Tactical nuclear forces	6.7	4.7	3.9	1.9	0.0	0.0	0.0	17.2
Land forces	149.1	109.9	61.3	26.0	7.1	2.6	0.1	356.1
Land-based tactical air forces	68.6	72.6	59.7	18.1	1.8	2.1	0.1	223.0
Naval tactical air forces	38.5	39.5	29.5	8.4	0.9	1.1	0.1	118.0
Navy ships	78.6	103.3	66.9	25.2	3.5	2.6	0.1	280.2
Airlift and sealift	14.2	14.0	12.8	9.1	0.0	0.0	0.1	50.2
Intelligence and communications	21.7	35.4	52.3	34.3	4.0	2.6	0.1	150.4
Total	431.0	474.1	348.3	177.3	22.5	14.0	0.7	1,467.9

Source: Author's estimates based on the assumption of a real annual decline of 2.9 percent. See table B-2 for assumptions about allocations.

the reinforcement of Europe, several more maritime pre-positioning ships in the Indian Ocean, and 20 more fast sealift ships, all of which the congressional program can afford.

Summary of Allocations

Total investment in the congressional five-year defense program amounts to $548.1 billion (table 3-13). Of that total, just under $196 billion goes to major procurement, principally to complete the acquisition of the current generation of missiles, aircraft, ships, and tracked vehicles (summarized in table 3-14 and more fully listed in appendix B, table B-5). An additional $152.6 billion is allocated to other procurement, which consists of funds for aircraft modifications and spare parts, support equipment and vehicles, communications and electronics, ammunition, tactical missiles, and miscellaneous equipment (table 3-15). As the table shows, $37.9 billion is provided for ammunition and tactical missiles—enough to continue building war reserve stocks to a level of sixty days of wartime consumption.

Over the five-year period the congressional track cuts RDT&E, as estimated in the Carlucci five-year defense program, by a total of $42.7 billion (see appendix A, table A-3). More than half of that is accounted for by holding the SDI to a five-year amount of $15 billion. While funds for the technology base are kept at a high level, small reductions occur in other accounts as a number of programs are decelerated (table 3-16). Even so, sufficient funds are available to test and evaluate all next-generation programs, including ATB, SICBM, rail garrison MX, SRAM II, FAADS, ATACMS, JSTARS, and the ATF.

The congressional program achieves other reductions of $57.4 billion from various small economies, most of which are offset by additional support payments from Germany and Japan (amounting to $30 billion over five years). Essentially, these offsets cover construction of overseas family housing for military personnel, base improvements, and the salaries of host-nation civilians employed by the U.S. armed forces (table 3-17). The operation and maintenance account (already reduced over the five-year period by $16.5 billion because of the offset payments from Germany and Japan) is reduced by another $7.5 billion not only because of the retirement of three aircraft carriers, but also because of the new and much more costly capabilities forgone. The military personnel account is also reduced by a total of $20.0 billion as the Army's strength is restored to 781,000, but the Navy, Marine Corps, and Air Force are

Table 3-14. *Allocation of Budget Authority to Major Procurement in
the Congressional Five-Year Defense Program, Fiscal Years 1990–94*
Costs in billions of current dollars

Program	Number	Cost
Strategic nuclear forces		
Advanced cruise missile	840	5.1
Trident submarine	5	8.1
Trident II (D-5) missile	168	6.1
KC-135 re-engining	250	4.5
Other[a]	. . .	5.1
Subtotal	. . .	28.9
Tactical nuclear forces		
Tomahawk land-attack missile,		
nuclear (TLAM-N)	308	2.4
Conventional forces		
Tanks	4,035	8.9
Other tracked vehicles	5,626	9.8
Helicopters	1,368	10.4
Combat aircraft	1,937	45.3
Service and support aircraft	866	9.6
Major warships	29	16.7
Other warships and auxiliaries	72	5.9
Airlift aircraft	21	2.0
Sealift ships	22	4.8
Tactical missiles and torpedoes	178,516	21.8
Other[a]	. . .	5.4
Subtotal	. . .	140.6
Intelligence and communications		
(satellite equivalents)	69	23.8
Total	. . .	195.7

Sources: Author's estimates based on *Department of Defense Selected Acquisition Reports* (SARs), as of September 30, 1987; table 3-8; and table B-5.
a. For details, see table B-5.

cut by 53,000 people (table 3-18) to account for the reduction in
programmed aircraft carriers and amphibious lift, and for the phaseout
of the Air Force manned GLCMs (ground-launched cruise missiles), as
required by the INF Treaty.

The main differences between the Carlucci and congressional five-
year defense programs are summarized in table 3-19. The congressional
program permits savings in budget authority of $245.7 billion; reductions
in outlays amount to $212.8 billion in current dollars.

CONCLUSIONS

Because the calculations that have led to these cuts are based on a
five-year perspective and plan, they produce savings in outlays that are

Table 3-15. *Allocation of Budget Authority to Other Procurement in the Congressional Five-Year Defense Program, Fiscal Years 1990–94*
Billions of current dollars

Item	Cost	Program	Cost
Aircraft modifications	18.0	Strategic nuclear forces	22.8
Aircraft spares	21.5	Tactical nuclear forces	1.9
Support equipment and vehicles	33.1	Land forces	34.4
Communications and electronics	25.0	Land-based tactical air forces	30.0
Ammunition	18.8	Navy tactical air forces	13.2
Tactical missiles	19.1	Navy ships	29.7
Miscellaneous equipment	17.1	Airlift and sealift	2.9
		Intelligence and communications	17.7
Total	152.6	Total	152.6

Source: Author's estimates.

Table 3-16. *Allocation of Budget Authority to Research, Development, Test, and Evaluation in the Congressional Five-Year Defense Program, Fiscal Years 1990–94*
Billions of current dollars

Item	Cost
Technology base	24.9
Advanced technology development	9.1
Strategic programs	41.1
Tactical programs	55.4
Intelligence and communications	23.8
Defense-wide mission support	23.0
Total	177.3

Source: Author's estimates.

Table 3-17. *Allocation of Offset Funds from West Germany and Japan in the Congressional Five-Year Defense Program, Fiscal Years 1990–94*
Billions of current dollars

Appropriation account	Amount
Operation and maintenance	16.5
Military construction	8.7
Family housing	4.8
Total	30.0

Source: Author's estimates.

Table 3-18. *Comparison of the Number of Military Personnel*
in the Carlucci and Congressional Five-Year Defense Programs,
Fiscal Year 1989
Thousands of active-duty personnel

	Program		
Service	*Carlucci*	*Congressional*	*Difference*
Army	772	781	9
Navy	593	558	−35
Marine Corps	197	194	−3
Air Force	576	561	−15
Active Guard/Reserve	72	74	2
Total	2,212	2,168	−44

Sources: *Department of Defense Annual Report, Fiscal Year 1989*, p. 305; *Department of Defense Manpower Requirements Report, Fiscal Year 1989* (March 1988), p. II-5; and author's estimates.

Table 3-19. *Comparison of Appropriations in the Carlucci and*
Congressional Five-Year Defense Programs, Fiscal Years 1990–94
Billions of current dollars

	Program		
Appropriation account	*Carlucci*	*Congressional*	*Difference*
Military personnel	451.0	431.0	20.0
Operation and maintenance	496.3	474.1	22.2
Procurement	493.8	348.3	145.5
Research, development, test and evaluation	220.0	177.3	42.7
Military construction	33.0	22.5	10.5
Family housing	18.8	14.0	4.8
Revolving funds and other	0.7	0.7	0.0
Total, budget authority	1,713.6	1,467.9	245.7
Total, outlays	1,633.0	1,420.2	212.8

Sources: Tables 3-11 and 3-12.

relatively modest in fiscal 1990 but grow to what may be considered an excessive size by fiscal 1994. That, however, is the inevitable effect of disciplining the acquisition program, of emphasizing the "slow" rather than the "fast" money accounts, and especially of trying to bring spending from prior-year balances of budget authority under better control.

In addition to these considerations, the only way to maintain a capability compatible with the contingencies that currently shape U.S. force planning is to field modern, ready, and sustainable armed forces, yet accept the near-term fiscal realities by being highly selective about future investments. Admittedly, in light of the rush to fund RDT&E and procurement during the past seven years, and the extraordinary and costly array of programs that has resulted, the option always exists to continue this almost totally uncoordinated activity at the expense of force structure, readiness, and sustainability. And the risk continues that such will be the direction chosen by Congress in default of strong and clear-minded leadership from the Pentagon. Yet precisely because of the changes that have occurred in the Soviet bloc, it seems more than a trifle eccentric to hollow out the defense structure at this early juncture in order, presumably, to obtain greater strength at a time when it may no longer be needed or wanted. The happier course, here as in other matters, would seem to be not too much zeal in support of only one pillar of national security.

Although it is too early to compare the more balanced allocation of resources represented in the congressional five-year defense plan with what may emerge from the strenuous efforts being made by Secretary Carlucci, two final points about greater austerity are perhaps worth making. The first point is that, despite the proposed reductions in funding, U.S. capabilities can actually grow more powerful during the five-year period, not only because of the recommended improvements in the National Guard and Reserve forces, mobility, and sustainability, but also because the defense establishment has by now adjusted its logistics and training to the kind of modernization that is now in progress and would be continued. The services will not suddenly have to make the costly, time-consuming, and disorienting adaptation to yet another generation of systems before they have been fully tested and before units in the field have discovered the full potential of their current weapons and equipment.

The second point is that it should prove relatively easy to adjust the coming five-year defense program to the fiscal realities because of the way budget authority piled up and redundant programs sprouted during the first half of the 1980s. Indeed, such was the rush that enough budget authority accumulated in five years to finance a more prudent, selective, and orderly improvement of U.S. capabilities for another twenty years, even with modestly declining budgets during the next five. But despite this profligacy and the fact that we are paying 70 percent more for U.S. strategic nuclear capabilities than we need to, there is a limit beyond which it would be unwise to count on the defense budget to keep going down.[10]

10. See appendix B, table B-5 for details on the future funding of the strategic nuclear forces.

It has been said on Wall Street that bulls and bears make money, but hogs never do. However one might wish to characterize the recent past, it remains entirely possible that the Defense Department, within the next five years, will manage to dissipate most of the funding that it so easily acquired in the early 1980s. Consequently, without a much improved international environment or greater internal discipline, increases will again become necessary in order to finance the acquisition, operation, and support of yet another and unquestionably more expensive generation of capabilities. One can only hope that before the time comes, and especially during the next five years, the costs of that generation will receive the most detailed scrutiny and that prototype performance will be thoroughly validated in the field before full-scale production begins. If necessity is the mother of invention, perhaps a pinch of modest austerity can become the father of efficiency.

APPENDIX A

It has been said that while money isn't everything, it's way ahead of whatever is in second place. Although the saying may not be precisely accurate in all circumstances, the money the Pentagon is now requesting for the years ahead is a prime concern. The interest is understandable. Clearly, what happens to future defense budgets can have a powerful effect on the federal deficit and on the fiscal and monetary policies of the United States.

This chapter has hypothesized that major savings in defense are possible without doing damage to U.S. security. Further details about the nature of the problem facing the next administration, and how that problem remains amenable to a reasonable, if somewhat painful, solution, are provided here and in appendix B.

By the time the next president takes office, the fiscal 1989 budget will already have been in effect for nearly four months. Although, in principle, the president could still affect the size and composition of that budget by means of rescissions and supplemental requests, his main concerns will have to be with the issues and choices related to the five-year defense program for fiscal 1990–94 and the years beyond.

As the president and his secretary of defense grapple with these issues and choices, they will soon discover that they face a relatively complex situation. The previous administration will have left them with a large number of programs—some already in the procurement stage, and others that are rapidly moving through the process of research, development,

Table A-1. *Estimate of Funded and Unfunded Investment in Defense Programs, Fiscal Years 1990–99*
Millions of current dollars

Item	Estimated cost	Funded	Unfunded
Army			
Aircraft and helicopters	29,646.8	14,080.6	15,566.2
Tactical missiles	42,841.0	15,672.3	27,168.7
Tracked vehicles	38,895.1	18,890.4	20,004.7
Other	30,144.0	500.0	29,644.0
Subtotal	141,526.9	49,143.3	92,383.6
Navy			
Aircraft and helicopters	203,702.0	61,888.1	141,813.9
Shipbuilding and conversion	151,950.9	63,300.0	88,650.9
Missiles and torpedoes	91,082.1	20,518.0	70,564.1
Other	15,120.3	0.0	15,120.3
Marine Corps (ground only)	2,596.9	0.0	2,596.9
Subtotal	464,452.2	145,706.1	318,746.1
Air Force			
Aircraft and strategic missiles	433,459.4	78,600.0	354,859.4
Tactical missiles	23,830.7	1,300.0	22,530.7
Other	69,118.6	0.0	69,118.6
Subtotal	526,408.7	79,900.0	446,508.7
Classified programs	48,900.0	0.0	48,900.0
Total	1,181,287.8	274,749.4	906,538.4

Sources: Author's estimates based on *Department of Defense Selected Acquisition Reports* (SARs) as of September 30, 1987; *Department of Defense Annual Report, Fiscal Year 1988* and *Fiscal Year 1989*; *Armed Forces Journal International*, October 1987, p. 26, November 1987, p. 50, April 1988, p. 20, and May 1988, pp. 56, 84; Congressional Budget Office, "Total Quantities and Costs of Major Weapon Systems Procured, FY 1974–1987," April 4, 1986; CBO, *Effects of Weapons Procurement Stretch-outs on Costs and Schedules* (November 1987), pp. xv, 24; CBO, *Modernizing U.S. Strategic Offensive Forces: Costs, Effects, and Alternatives* (November 1987), p. 38; CBO, *Naval Combat Aircraft: Issues and Options* (November 1987), p. 27; and Annual Report of the Reserve Forces Policy Board, *Reserve Component Programs, Fiscal Year 1987* (February 2, 1988), p. 74.

test, and evaluation—the cost of which could approach $900 billion in less than a decade (table A-1). At the same time, they will have inherited balances of prior-year budget authority (table A-2), most of which will have been obligated in the form of contracts, amounting to more than $271 billion. What is more, this budget authority will continue to convert into expenditures during the next five years regardless of whatever else the new adminstration decides to do about future defense budgets. On top of that, relative austerity in future defense funding will be such that President Reagan's successors will almost certainly find it impossible to raise anything like the $900 billion necessary to complete the programs already on the books. Finally, as they look at the programs constituting the bow wave of the future, they will find a peculiar brew of duplication, complexity, haste, and concurrency in development and production,

Table A-2. *Estimates of Balances of Prior-Year Budget Authority,*
Fiscal Years 1987–89
Millions of current dollars

Budget authority	Start of 1987	End of 1987	End of 1988	End of 1989
Obligated	198,892	214,115	224,794	231,126
Unobligated	59,651	47,621	41,233	40,058
Total	258,543	261,736	266,027	271,184

Source: *Budget of the United States Government, Fiscal Year 1989*, p. 6g-19.

raising at a minimum the probability of renewed waste and at a maximum the possibility of further failures in the tradition of the B-58, Dynasoar, the RB-70, DIVAD, and the B-1B.

Because of the probable mismatch between programs and resources, a mismatch already recognized to some degree by Secretary Carlucci, the next administration will probably have to choose one of four basic options: (1) hollow out current capabilities to protect both current and future investments; (2) reduce force size and composition (including military and civilian personnel) to pay for current and future hardware; (3) maintain current forces and substantially reduce both current and future investments in weapons and equipment; and (4) protect current capabilities and programs, subject the next generation of weapons to rigorous test and evaluation, and preserve the option to begin the procurement of successful prototypes by fiscal 1995. For the reasons given in the main text, the fourth option is seen as the most promising and challenging, but by no means the most likely to be chosen.

To spell out the implications of the fourth option in some detail, three conditions would have to be satisfied. A five-year defense program would have to be provided for fiscal 1990–94, and would have to incorporate the continued buildup planned by the Reagan administration. Specific indication would then have to be given as to what parts of the program would be continued and what parts cancelled or deferred. Other cuts would have to be made to pay for weapons and equipment seen as of high priority but not included in the Reagan five-year defense program.

In principle, such an exercise should be reasonably straightforward. At this juncture, in practice, it is not. As matters now stand, no defense program for fiscal 1990–94 exists. Instead, the only available data are these: the Weinberger internal program totals for fiscal 1988–92, along with some detail about their allocation; the Carlucci program totals for fiscal 1989–93 allocated according to appropriation title by the Office of Management and Budget; the approximate amounts by which Secretary

Table A-3. *Estimates of Budget Authority for the Weinberger, Carlucci, and Congressional Five-Year Defense Programs, Fiscal Years 1990–94*
Billions of current dollars

| | | | | | Differences from | |
| | | | | | | |
Item	Weinberger	Carlucci	Congressional track	Weinberger to Carlucci	Weinberger to congressional track	Carlucci to congressional track
Military personnel	479.9	451.0	431.0	28.9	48.9	20.0
Operation and maintenance	544.0	496.3	474.1	47.7	69.9	22.2
Procurement	584.8	493.8	348.3	91.0	236.5	145.5
Research, development, test, and evaluation	272.1	220.0	177.3	52.1	94.8	42.7
Military construction	38.9	33.0	22.5	5.9	16.4	10.5
Family housing	19.4	18.8	14.0	0.6	5.4	4.8
Revolving funds and other	3.9	0.7	0.7	3.2	3.2	0.0
Total	1,943.0	1,713.6	1,467.9	229.4	475.1	245.7

Sources: Tables 3-11, 3-12, B-1, B-2; Weinberger breakdown based on author's estimates.

Carlucci would reduce the Weinberger program to reach his still ambitious goal of more than 2 percent real growth each year after fiscal 1989; and some data about the out-year implications of the cuts he proposed for fiscal 1989.

The gruel, in short, is pretty thin. Moreover, because of the paucity of data, if the Carlucci five-year defense program is the baseline from which cuts are to be made to reach the levels of the congressional program described in the main text, there is a danger that some of the proposed changes could duplicate recommendations for further cuts that Carlucci presumably will present in January 1989. To avoid double counting, it thus becomes necessary to construct a hypothetical Weinberger program as the baseline from which to make cuts.

Since the Weinberger internal program extends only to fiscal 1992, it has been extrapolated (assuming annual real growth of 5 percent) to fiscal 1994. Another year has also been added to the Carlucci program. These extrapolations, and their allocations by appropriation title, are aggregated and compared with the five-year aggregates of the congressional track in table A-3. Given the assumptions used, total savings of $475.1 billion in budget authority would have to be made to reach the goals of the congressional program. The bulk of these savings would have to come from procurement ($236.5 billion), research, development, test, and evaluation ($94.8 billion), operation and maintenance ($69.9 billion), and military personnel ($48.9 billion). A breakdown of the reductions—and of proposed increases—is shown in appendix B.

APPENDIX B

Because of the problems involved in projecting U.S. defense budgets out to fiscal 1994, as indicated in appendix A, it has proved necessary to make several assumptions about the size and composition of the Weinberger, Carlucci, and congressional five-year defense programs for fiscal 1990–94. Table B-1 shows the three assumed programs on a year-by-year basis in both current and fiscal 1989 dollars. Table B-2 gives the percentages used in allocating the three program totals of $1,943 billion, $1,713.6 billion, and $1,467.9 billion by appropriation account. The Weinberger percentages are based on the budget submissions for fiscal 1985 through 1989. The Carlucci percentages reflect the allocations shown in the *Budget of the United States Government, Fiscal Year 1989.* The congressional percentages relate both to decisions about personnel

Table B-1. *The Weinberger, Carlucci, and Congressional Five-Year Defense Programs, Fiscal Years 1990–94*

| Year | Billions of current dollars | | |
	Weinberger	Carlucci	Congressional track
1990	343.4	307.3	292.4
1991	364.8	324.4	293.2
1992	387.4	342.0	293.2
1993	410.3	360.3	294.1
1994	437.1	379.6	295.0
Total, budget authority	1,943.0	1,713.6	1,467.9
Total, outlays	1,826.4	1,633.0	1,420.2
Average annual growth in budget authority (percent)	8.5	5.5	0.3

| Year | Billions of 1989 dollars | | |
	Weinberger	Carlucci	Congressional track
1990	331.9	297.0	282.6
1991	341.7	303.7	274.6
1992	352.6	311.3	266.9
1993	361.8	317.7	259.3
1994	373.5	324.4	252.1
Total, budget authority	1,761.5	1,554.1	1,335.5
Total, outlays	1,655.8	1,481.0	1,291.9
Average annual growth in budget authority (percent)	5.1	2.2	-2.8

Sources: Tables 3-11, 3-12, B-2; projections in current dollars; constant dollars calculated using Defense Department deflators.

Table B-2. *Percentages Used in Allocating Five-Year Defense Program Totals, Fiscal Years 1990–94*

Appropriation account	Weinberger	Carlucci	Congressional track
Military personnel	24.7	26.3	29.4
Operation and maintenance	28.0	29.0	32.3
Procurement	30.1	28.8	23.7
Research, development, test, and evaluation	14.0	12.8	12.1
Military construction	2.0	1.9	1.5
Family housing	1.0	1.1	1.0
Revolving funds and other	0.2	0.05	0.05
Total	100.0	100.00	100.00

Sources: For Weinberger and congressional track, author's estimates based on *National Defense Budget Estimates for FY 1988/1989*, p. 103; for Carlucci, *Budget of the United States Government, Fiscal Year 1989*, p. 5-6. Figures are rounded.

Table B-3. *Estimated Savings to Be Made in Military Personnel from the Weinberger Five-Year Defense Program, Fiscal Years 1990–94*
Billions of current dollars

| Year | Weinberger program | Differences between Weinberger and congressional track in | | | Congressional track |
		Pay increases[a]	Military personnel[b]	Total saving	
1990	86.5	3.9	1.6	5.5	81.0
1991	91.4	4.7	3.1	7.8	83.6
1992	95.9	5.8	4.1	9.9	86.0
1993	100.6	6.7	5.2	11.8	88.8
1994	105.5	7.7	6.2	13.9	91.6
Total	479.9	28.8	20.2	48.9	431.0

Sources: Tables 3-12, A-3, B-2, and author's estimates.
a. It is assumed that the Weinberger program provides a 4 percent a year pay increase; the congressional track allows increases in pay to cover the cost of inflation.
b. Differences in active-duty military personnel (in thousands) are:

	1989	1990	1991	1992	1993	1994
Weinberger	2,185	2,226	2,259	2,280	2,300	2,319
Congressional track	2,094	2,094	2,094	2,094	2,094	2,094
Difference	91	132	165	186	206	225
Year-to-year change	...	41	33	21	20	19

and programs and to the defense budgets enacted between fiscal 1977 and 1982.

Based on these assumptions, tables B-3, B-4, and B-5 show how the Weinberger totals for military personnel, operation and maintenance, procurement, and research, development, test, and evaluation are reduced to the levels required by the congressional track. Table B-6 breaks down the operation and maintenance account by major function and gives the allocation of the congressional total ($474.1 billion) by percent and billions of dollars. It is worth noting that the total congressional allocation of $14 billion for military family housing allows for the operation and maintenance of 415,000 housing units and the construction or acquisition of more than 100,000 new units. It is assumed that West Germany and Japan would cover the cost of leasing 145,000 units overseas in addition to maintaining on-base housing.

There are bound to be differences of opinion about the desirability of making cuts as large as those described in these tables (especially when Secretary Carlucci is already proposing reductions of more than $200 billion) and about the appropriateness of the specific savings proposed. Because of the START (strategic arms reduction) negotiations and potential constraints on the deployment of SLBMs, it is arguable that fewer than 5 Trident submarines should be funded, that a new and smaller ballistic missile submarine should be designed, and that C-4

Table B-4. *Estimated Savings to Be Made in Operation and Maintenance from the Weinberger Five-Year Defense Program, Fiscal Years 1990–94*
Billions of current dollars

Year	Weinberger program	Indirect hires[a]	Savings			Congressional track
			Operation and maintenance[b]	Total		
1990	94.3	3.1	5.5	8.6		85.7
1991	100.9	3.2	7.6	10.8		90.1
1992	108.1	3.3	10.2	13.5		94.6
1993	116.1	3.4	13.4	16.8		99.3
1994	124.6	3.5	16.7	20.2		104.4
Total	544.0	16.5	53.4	69.9		474.1

Sources: Tables 3-12, A-3, B-2, and author's estimates.
a. A total of 89,000 indirect foreign civilian hires is assumed. They are paid under this calculation by Japan and West Germany.
b. Savings in operation and maintenance result from deferring the introduction of more expensive and sophisticated weapons and equipment. The deferrals are assumed to be as follows: 1990, 77.9 billion; 1991, 107.6 billion; 1992, 144.5 billion; 1993, 189.8 billion; 1994, 236.5 billion.

missiles should be substituted for the more accurate and more expensive D-5. Since sea-launched cruise missiles (SLCMs) are also a source of controversy in the negotiations, a case can be made for ending the acquisition of the TLAM-N. Furthermore, the Defense Department has proposed at various times closing as many as 36 separate bases in the United States; at the same time, the justification for adding 13 new fleet home ports is, at most, minimal. At least $11.6 billion in five-year budget authority could be saved by buying 3 Trident boats instead of 5, substituting the C-4 for the D-5 SLBM, cancelling the TLAM-N program, and a combination of closing old bases and halting construction on new (and unnecessary) naval home ports. These savings could be used either to reduce the federal deficit or to accelerate other programs in the five-year defense program while staying within the constraints set by the congressional track.

Table B-5. *Estimated Savings to Be Made in Procurement and Research, Development, Test, and Evaluation from the Weinberger Five-Year Defense Program, Fiscal Years 1990–94*
Billions of current dollars

Program	Procurement			RDT&E		
	Weinberger	Funded	Savings	Weinberger	Funded	Savings
Strategic nuclear forces						
Advanced technology (Stealth) bombers	37.7	0.0	37.7	16.0	3.0	13.0
Advanced cruise missiles	6.7	5.1	1.6	1.1	0.6	0.5
Rotary launchers	0.4	0.4	0.0	0.0	0.0	0.0
Short-range attack missiles (SRAM) II	1.5	0.0	1.5	0.6	0.6	0.0
KC-135R	7.8	4.5	3.3	0.0	0.0	0.0
OTH-B	1.1	1.1	0.0	0.0	0.0	0.0
MX missiles	11.6	0.0	11.6	1.9	0.5	1.4
Rail garrison MX trains	5.6	0.0	5.6	1.9	0.0	1.9
Small ICBMs (Midgetman)	12.1	0.0	12.1	4.5	2.0	2.5
Minuteman II penetration aids	0.6	0.0	0.6	0.1	0.0	0.1
Minuteman III upgrades	0.3	0.3	0.0	0.0	0.0	0.0
Trident II submarines	8.1	8.1	0.0	0.0	0.0	0.0
Trident II (D-5) missiles	16.7	6.1	10.6	8.9	2.2	6.7
Antisatellite system	2.9	0.0	2.9	1.1	0.6	0.5
TR-1/U-2 surveillance systems	0.4	0.4	0.0	0.0	0.0	0.0
Defense support program	1.9	1.9	0.0	3.4	3.4	0.0
Global positioning satellites	0.2	0.2	0.0	3.3	3.3	0.0
Defense-meteorological support program	0.8	0.8	0.0	1.0	1.0	0.0
Strategic Defense Initiative	0.0	0.0	0.0	50.3	16.0	34.3
Subtotal	116.4	28.9	87.5	94.1	33.2	60.9
Tactical nuclear forces						
TLAM-N	2.4	2.4	0.0	0.0	0.0	0.0

Conventional forces						
Tanks	8.9	8.9	0.0	0.4	0.4	0.0
Other tracked vehicles	15.5	9.8	5.7	0.2	0.1	0.1
Helicopters	23.0	10.4	12.6	5.3	2.3	3.0
Army air defense systems	8.9	0.8	8.1	2.3	2.3	0.0
Air Force combat aircraft	38.8	22.4	16.4	29.1	14.5	14.6
Navy and USMC combat aircraft	51.8	22.9	28.9	33.1	17.1	16.0
Service and support aircraft	20.1	9.6	10.5	0.0	0.0	0.0
Major warships and submarines	53.5	10.3	43.2	18.6	18.6	0.0
Other ships	12.3	5.9	6.4	4.3	4.3	0.0
Ship conversions	5.9	3.7	2.2	0.0	0.0	0.0
Airlift aircraft	9.3	0.0	9.3	8.9	8.9	0.0
Tactical missiles and torpedoes	33.8	21.8	12.0	7.9	7.7	0.2
NATO initiatives	2.8	0.0	2.8	0.0	0.0	0.0
Subtotal	284.6	126.5	158.1	110.1	76.2	33.9
Other programs						
Intelligence and communications	28.8	23.8	5.0	19.0	19.0	0.0
(satellite equivalents)						
Classified	0.0	0.0	0.0	48.9	48.9	0.0
Subtotal	28.8	23.8	5.0	67.9	67.9	0.0
Total	432.2	181.6	250.6	272.1	177.3	94.8
New programs (congressional track)						
16 DDG-X guided missile frigates	...	6.4	−6.4	...	0.0	0.0
21 C-5B aircraft	...	2.0	−2.0	...	0.0	0.0
2 maritime pre-positioning ships	...	0.8	−0.8	...	0.0	0.0
20 fast sealift ships	...	4.0	−4.0	...	0.0	0.0
NATO initiative (barrier)	...	0.9	−0.9	...	0.0	0.0
Total, new programs	...	14.1	−14.1	...	0.0	0.0

Table B-5 (*continued*)

Program	Procurement			RDT&E		
	Weinberger	*Funded*	*Savings*	*Weinberger*	*Funded*	*Savings*
Recapitulation						
Strategic nuclear forces	116.4	28.9	87.5	94.1	33.2	60.9
Tactical nuclear forces	2.4	2.4	0.0	0.0	0.0	0.0
Conventional forces	284.6	126.5	158.1	110.1	76.2	33.9
Other programs	28.8	23.8	5.0	67.9	67.9	0.0
Total	432.2	181.6	250.6	272.1	177.3	94.8
New programs	0.0	14.1	−14.1	0.0	0.0	0.0
Grand total	**432.2**	**195.7**	**236.5**	**272.1**	**177.3**	**94.8**

Sources: Tables 3-15, A-1, and author's estimates.

Table B-6. *Assumptions Used to Allocate Operation and Maintenance Funds in the Congressional Five-Year Defense Program, Fiscal Years 1990–94*

Item	Percent	Billions of current dollars	Item	Percent	Billions of current dollars
Flying hours	10.4	49.3	Reserve forces	7.3	34.6
Ship operations	3.7	17.6	Communications	2.6	12.3
Land operations	4.2	19.9	Transportation	4.9	23.2
Depot-level maintenance	13.0	61.6	Supply operations	4.7	22.3
Modernization	3.4	16.1	Other logistics	7.0	33.2
Real property maintenance	5.2	24.7	Administration	2.8	13.3
Training and education	3.3	15.7	Recruiting, advertising, examining	0.8	3.8
Medical programs	4.6	21.8	Other	6.8	32.2
Base operations	15.3	72.5	**Total**	**100.0**	**474.1**

Source: Author's estimates based on *Department of Defense Appropriation Bill, 1982: Report of the Committee on Appropriations*, H. Rept. 333, 97 Cong. 1 sess. (Government Printing Office, 1981), pp. 51-182.

CHAPTER FOUR

The Prospect of Cooperative Security

JOHN D. STEINBRUNER

In the course of the 1980s, the Soviet political leadership has advanced a strikingly different conception of security from the one it espoused during previous decades. The expression of this "new thinking" has been characteristically blunt and dramatic under Mikhail S. Gorbachev as the Communist party general secretary, but the thoughts themselves are not solely his creation. They have emerged after a series of policy adjustments evidently intended to balance security requirements against the technical and economic capacities of Soviet society, and this underlying, practical gestation lends seriousness to the rhetorical flourish. The implications, at any rate, command attention. If appropriately developed, the new line of Soviet security policy would materially improve the conditions of international security and would reduce the active military requirements of Western defense.

As presented in official and semiofficial pronouncements, the central element of the new conception of Soviet security is the overriding priority given to the objective of preventing war.[1] In and of itself that formulation is not particularly remarkable or particularly new. The prevention of war has long been the Soviets' fundamental declared intent, as it has been for the United States and all other major powers since the advent of nuclear weapons. But it is evident from even the incomplete explanations that have been provided so far that the new declaration is meant to convey a notable shift in perspective—a different diagnosis of the security problem, different doctrinal conclusions drawn from that diagnosis, and ultimately a different security posture. The shift, it is

---

1. The pertinent Soviet statements are reviewed and analyzed in Raymond L. Garthoff, "Soviet Military Doctrine and the Prevention of Nuclear War," in Cynthia Roberts, Jack Snyder, and Warner R. Schilling, eds., *Decoding the Enigma: Methodology for the Study of Soviet Military Policy* (forthcoming).

important to notice, reflects tensions created by modern weapons technology to which the Soviet Union is unusually sensitive.

POLICY TENSIONS

The universally acknowledged purpose of modern military forces equipped with nuclear weapons is to deter a calculated attack by threatening effective retaliation. That has been the primary means by which the Soviet Union and all other states that have nuclear weapons propose to prevent major war. These weapons are so destructive, however, and their means of delivery so rapid that it is hard for any prudent military organization to be confident it can meet the strict demands of retaliation. If either of the principal strategic establishments allowed the opponent to complete a first strike, the effectiveness of subsequent retaliation would be subject to considerable uncertainty. Though a sufficient number of individual weapons would probably survive, the coherence of the organization's arrangements to direct their use might not.[2] That problem is of particular concern to the Soviet Union, where strict and extensive central control over military operations is a matter of the highest priority.

To make the deterrent threat credible, both strategic organizations have prepared for a retaliation rapid enough to complete the basic command functions—authorization and coordination—before an attempted first strike could be fully executed. The distinction between initiation and retaliation thus reduces to a few minutes, and under the pressure of intense crisis it is questionable whether that distinction could be preserved. It is especially questionable given that strategic forces operate on a global scale and that highly proliferated reconnaissance systems generate massive flows of information between the two organizations.

That fact is also of particular concern to the Soviet Union. In conducting military operations just as in managing economic production, maintaining strict central control inevitably slows responsiveness to the flow of information. As judged from normal peacetime practices, the Soviet Union exercises centralized control over a much broader range of operational activities than the United States does, and habitually main-

2. These problems are reviewed from various perspectives in Ashton B. Carter, John D. Steinbruner, and Charles A. Zraket, eds., *Managing Nuclear Operations* (Brookings, 1987), chaps. 3, 16, and 17.

tains most elements of its military establishment in a state less ready to conduct combat operations. The United States, while maintaining strict central control over the authority to use nuclear weapons, habitually disperses the authority to maneuver them and maintains a higher state of readiness. Though there has been virtually no intense crisis experience to provide exact calibration, there are good reasons to believe that the Soviet military forces compare to those of the United States as a marathon runner compares to a sprinter—a distinct disadvantage if the competition in question is a hundred meter dash.

Inherent in this situation is some possibility that a crisis situation not deliberately initiated or effectively controlled by either side could produce an unintended war, even though all parties involved remained powerfully deterred (that is, convinced that war would be unacceptably disastrous). Such a catastrophe would occur if protective alert procedures of the two sides triggered what each understood to be a retaliatory action. The prevention of war therefore requires not only a strong deterrent effect but also effective control of force interactions. Under crisis circumstances there would be sharp tension between these two imperatives; and, again, that tension appears to be disproportionately dangerous for the Soviet military establishment.

Soviet Adjustments

As nuclear weapons were developed and deployed, Soviet security policy adjusted the balance between competing imperatives several times, most notably in a doctrinal shift initiated in the middle of the 1960s.[3]

---

3. The changes in Soviet doctrine and the force structure adjustments associated with those changes have been reviewed and interpreted in Michael MccGwire, *Military Objectives in Soviet Foreign Policy* (Brookings, 1987); Raymond L. Garthoff, "New Thinking in Soviet Military Doctrine," *Washington Quarterly*, vol. 2 (Summer 1988), pp. 131–58; and Garthoff, "Soviet Military Doctrine." The two authors vary in their judgments. But the accounts of both are generally compatible with the interpretation presented here, though neither is exactly the same. Methodological questions can be and have been raised about any interpretive account that uses explicit security logic to connect Soviet doctrinal statements with specific decisions and the results they produce. Rarely if ever are the decisions of a large government entirely determined by the logic used by participants to explain them or by observers to interpret them. Moreover, even logic itself evolves over time and is not perfectly consistent at any given moment. There thus will always be some discrepancy between any logical interpretation and the events it attempts to explain. These discrepancies limit the validity of such an interpretation, as rather aggressively noted in a critique of the MccGwire book by Matthew Partan, "Soviet Military Objectives: Book

Before that time, when Soviet deployments were smaller in number and individually less protected than those of the United States, Soviet military doctrine had declared that the use of nuclear weapons would be an unavoidable consequence of any major war and thereby justified an explicit preemptive strategy. The Soviets had committed themselves to detecting an impending strategic attack before it was actually under way and to initiating their retaliatory operations before the compelling evidence of missiles and bombers in flight would be available. The marathon runner, in other words, would have to jump the gun to have any hope against the sprinter. That commitment entailed an obvious risk of misjudgment, but it offered some protection against a critical vulnerability. If Soviet forces of that period had conceded the initiative and had suffered the full effects of a U.S. attack, their ability to retaliate would have been doubtful.

By the mid-1960s the Soviets had completed a series of basic programming decisions designed to reduce the vulnerability of Soviet strategic forces by increasing their numbers and providing more extensive measures of protection. At that point, when effective strategic parity was in prospect and the North Atlantic Treaty Organization (NATO) was formalizing its flexible response strategy, the Soviets altered their official doctrine to admit the possibility that a major war might be waged, most notably in the European theater, without any use of nuclear weapons. Though somewhat skeptical about the feasibility of such a restrained war, they accepted the prospect as a planning contingency and acknowledged as a corollary that if it occurred they would not initiate the use of nuclear weapons against the United States.[4] Hence, in that instance, they could not execute their previously established doctrine of strategic preemption even though a war in Europe would provide the primary warning evidence on which the decision was to be based.

Review," *International Security,* vol. 12 (Winter 1987–88), pp. 203–14. It would be unwise and impractical to conclude, however, that there is no logic at work or that it cannot be discovered. The Soviet system with its commitment to central planning explicitly formulates its purposes and devotes considerable effort to enforce its formulation. It necessarily reveals in the process a great deal about its intentions. No government, least of all that one, can achieve coherence in its actions without some working logic. Interpreting that logic is a useful, in fact indispensable, means of understanding and predicting Soviet behavior.

4. According to MccGwire's interpretation in *Military Objectives,* this conclusion followed from a simple compelling rule: if the use of nuclear weapons against the Soviet Union itself *could* be prevented, then it *had* to be. By extension, if the United States chose to mobilize and fight in Europe without using nuclear weapons, then the Soviets would

Carrying out the revised logic, the Soviets set a requirement for their conventional forces to engage in rapid, decisive, offensive operations against Western Europe in the initial stages of such a war, in effect transferring the preemptive strategy from nuclear weapons to conventional forces. If they did not win quickly in Europe, they calculated, they would surely lose eventually because of superior American economic and technical potential.

This doctrinal shift was supported by a surge of investment in Soviet conventional forces that ran from the late 1960s through most of the 1970s. The sustained investment substantially improved the ready capability of Soviet conventional forces, but it also triggered within the Western alliance a campaign for greater investment in NATO forces. The United States, as the leader of that campaign, emphasized the application of advanced technology for attacking the infrastructure of Soviet forces far behind the immediate battlefield. Since that capability was designed to stop the planned Soviet advance into Western Europe by stopping the forward movement of reinforcements necessary to exploit a breach in NATO lines, it also would have to be used in the earliest stages of war. The net effect of the mid-1960s doctrinal change, therefore, and of the operational configuration of forces that emerged from it was to inflict on conventional forces the pressures for rapid action and the resulting volatility under crisis conditions that Soviet planners had sought to remove from nuclear forces. Since conventional forces on both sides in the European theater were extensively equipped with nuclear weapons as well and operationally inclined, at least on the Western side, to use them early in the course of any major engagement, the adjustment of the 1960s did not resolve the underlying problem. Indeed it may have worsened the problem by attaching to the nuclear arsenals a conventional fuse that was easier to ignite.

The current shift in Soviet operational doctrine presents a more radical approach. Preemptive options are to be excised from operational doctrine, and the occurrence of global war is to be removed as the central contingency of general security planning. To maximize the chances of avoiding war, as distinct from those of winning it if it does occur, Soviet forces are to be put in a more defensive posture, with nuclear forces sized and configured strictly to retaliate and conventional forces strictly to hold their current positions. Overall security, moreover, is not to rely

---

have to do so as well. With that admitted, the general mobilization of U.S. forces would not provide definitive evidence of imminent nuclear attack, and global nuclear preemption in response to strategic warning would be impractical.

solely, or even primarily, on unilateral military action but rather on international cooperation.[5]

The calculus implicit in these principles accepts some risk about the potential outcome of a hypothetical war in order to increase insurance that it will not be initiated. It assumes that there is no inexorable reason for war between the Warsaw Treaty Organization (WTO) and NATO and that Soviet national security can safely rest on the assumption that major war will be indefinitely avoided. It also assumes that maintaining deterrence is a less urgent security problem than maintaining control of the interaction of forces. These assumptions make stability the central consideration in managing the balance of military forces and shift the element of initiative in security policy entirely into the realm of diplomacy. Initiative on behalf of Soviet state security is to be undertaken in advance of crisis and is to focus on reducing tension between NATO and the WTO and on resolving, or at least containing, regional conflicts outside of central Europe.

American Reactions

There is little prospect that these Soviet doctrinal developments at their current state of abstraction and completeness could be directly convincing to the United States. Most Americans heavily discount any Soviet statements of constructive intent, and for some it is virtually axiomatic that such statements are deliberate efforts to deceive. The United States, moreover, does not vest doctrinal prescriptions with anything like the significance they have for the Soviet planning system and could not readily respond in kind even if there were a general willingness to suspend disbelief. The natural American reaction is to await specific results with polite but skeptical interest and seek to impose on the Soviets the burden of proof, as a judge would do to a plaintiff making an extravagant claim.

The problem with that natural reaction, however, is that the United States itself must necessarily be involved in any systematic implementation of the Soviet doctrinal developments. Though the new line of Soviet policy clearly implies a large reduction and restructuring of military forces, it is unlikely that such changes could or would be done unilaterally. Each of the two establishments has so formalized its requirements in

5. See Garthoff, "New Thinking in Soviet Military Doctrine," pp. 131–58.

reference to the other that the design, the scheduling, and the specific implementation of structural reform has become a mutual affair.

Disengaged skepticism, moreover, does not accord with the degree of American interest. As noted in previous chapters, the looming imperative of a fiscal adjustment in the American economy and the downward pressure on the defense budget that will almost certainly result give the United States a growing stake in mutually organized restraint on military forces. Though it is possible, as discussed, to preserve traditional security commitments under standard threat assumptions despite a declining defense budget, that effort requires much stronger discipline in the internal allocation of resources than the American political system has ever been able to produce. It appears unlikely that such discipline can be achieved unless the related discipline of integrating force posture and arms control arrangements is also pursued.

In addition, for some U.S. allies—most notably West Germany— similar financial pressures on the defense effort are compounded by population dynamics. The age cohort eligible for military service in the Federal Republic will decline by 41 percent from 1987 through 1995, and that stark fact dictates an undeniable interest in force reductions.[6] Our passive skepticism about Soviet doctrinal initiatives and defensive reaction to the diplomacy emerging from them are simply not consistent with maintaining a leadership position either in NATO or in U.S. alliance arrangements globally. If the United States does not muster both the wit and the will to shape the outcome, our international stature will decline.

For all these reasons the combination of opportunity and challenge inherent in the emerging Soviet security conception exerts redirecting pressures on U.S. policy. These pressures may not be sufficient to compel new lines of American thought by sheer force of circumstance, but they certainly do create the condition for new assumptions to take hold and for a new synthesis of American interest to form.

It is reasonable, moreover, to expect some spontaneous responsiveness in the United States to develop eventually as a counterweight to natural skepticism. The basic ingredients of the new Soviet security conception are hardly alien. In fact, much of Gorbachev's new thinking consists of Western ideas being played back.

---

6. U.S. Bureau of the Census, unpublished report prepared for the World Population 1986 Project, table 5.

POTENTIAL OUTCOMES

Both the logic that would be used to implement the emerging Soviet security doctrine and the force structure outcomes that would result have been generally outlined in the course of exchanging arms control proposals. The Soviet agenda was set forth in appeals for conventional force reductions in Europe issued by the WTO in June of 1986 and May of 1987,[7] and in a program for strategic force reductions presented at the summit meeting in Reykjavik, Iceland, in October 1986.[8] Together the two initiatives suggest a comprehensive regulation of the military balance that would render it much more consistent with the new security conception than it now is. The U.S. and allied response to these initiatives has been rather contentious in tone and sluggish in timing but not as fundamentally contrary as the immediate public reactions would suggest. One part of the Reykjavik agenda—the elimination of intermediate-range nuclear weapons—has been formalized in a treaty and is being implemented. That accomplishment has imparted some momentum to the remainder of the program.

Apart from the treaty on intermediate-range missiles, the details of the projected arms control arrangement have not been completely specified; the conventional force initiative is particularly undetermined.

7. See the Budapest Appeal of June 11, 1986, found in "Obrashcheniye gosudarstv-uchastnikov Varshavskogo Dogovora k gosudarstvam-chlenam NATO, vsem yevropeyskim stranam s programmoy sokrashcheniya vooruzhennykh sil i obychnykh vooruzheniy v Yevrope" (Warsaw Pact appeal to the NATO states and all European countries concerning a program for armed forces and conventional arms reductions in Europe), *Pravda*, June 12, 1986, p. 1; and the Berlin Communiqué of May 29, 1987, found in "Communique on Conference of Warsaw Pact States' Political Consultative Committee," *Pravda*, May 30, 1987, pp. 1–2, in Foreign Broadcast Information Service, *Daily Report: Soviet Union*, June 1, 1987, pp. BB10–19.

8. The Reykjavik summit generated a great deal of controversy because of the announced intention to seek the total elimination of all strategic weapons (the Soviet version) or all ballistic missiles (the American version). Radical measures of that sort were consistent with a statement on arms control issued by Gorbachev on January 16, 1986. See "Statement by M. S. Gorbachev, General Secretary of the CPSU Central Committee," *Pravda*, January 16, 1986, p. 1, in FBIS, *Daily Report: Soviet Union*, January 16, 1986, p. AA1. According to the private accounts of participants, however, the initial Soviet position at Reykjavik, stated in a draft agreement, called for a set of more modest and more realistic measures— a 50 percent reduction of strategic nuclear weapons, total elimination of intermediate-range nuclear weapons, adherence to the 1972 Antiballistic Missile (ABM) Treaty, and discussions of additional restrictions on space weapons and on underground nuclear weapons testing. At Reykjavik the idea of more radical cuts in strategic weapons was introduced by the United States.

With some simple logic and a little common sense, however, the potential outcomes can be approximately inferred. The impenetrable intricacies of bargaining maneuvers, political disputes, and bureaucratic staff introduce great uncertainties about the timing of arms control arrangements, but in the end the results are largely determined by underlying national interest powerful enough to be both decisive and apparent.

Strategic Force Reductions

One thing apparent from even the sketchy histories of strategic weapons development yet available is that the number of weapons deployed did not result from any coherent calculated plans, but rather from a sequence of political decisions whose net results did not conform to any of the many participants' earlier intentions. Relating the size of the arsenals to the strategic purposes they are meant to serve has largely been an exercise of rationalization after the fact, and it is not surprising that the exercise has inspired attempts to revise the original decisions. In exchanging proposals for 50 percent reductions in strategic forces, the United States and the Soviet Union are tacitly conceding that their current deployments exceed essential requirements.

An exact measure of these essential deterrent requirements has never been officially proclaimed, in part because it is difficult to form a consensus judgment and in part because it would be awkward to admit candidly that any reasonable definition would fall well below existing deployments. But because of the obvious vulnerability of military organizations and industrial societies to the effects of nuclear weapons, there is little mystery about the limits of what could be considered essential. In both the United States and the Soviet Union, roughly 70 to 75 percent of industrial capacity is contained in 1,500 circular areas over which a single weapon could spread lethal blast and thermal effects.[9] Attacking any substantial part of these targets would devastate both the society and the economy of the victim. Similarly, the infrastructure of either military organization could be eviscerated with that number of weapons, and the targets associated with that theory of attack would substantially overlap with urban-industrial targets. If deterrence works at all, it would presumably work at these levels of threat.

Moreover, as a practical matter, adding yet more weapons to the

9. United States Arms Control and Disarmament Agency, *An Analysis of Civil Defense in Nuclear War* (Washington, D.C.: ACDA, December 1978).

weight of a theoretical attack does not add much to its functional consequence. After absorbing 1,500 to 2,000 delivered weapons, the military and industrial organization of either country would be so severely damaged that additional pounding would largely be a waste of offensive assets. Whether the purpose is simply to punish an aggressor's society or to incapacitate its military establishment, 2,000 is about the limit for the number of nuclear weapons that can be efficiently used.[10]

The presence of more than 10,000 weapons in the deployed arsenals has been justified by the idea that there is safety in numbers. Each side claims that deployment larger than actually required for effective retaliation is necessary to ensure that enough weapons would survive an initial attack. That theory of protection, however, inevitably produces reciprocal fears of preemption, since the excess capacity could also be used to initiate an attack. This problem has been compounded by trends in strategic weapons modernization that have emphasized advances in offensive capability (largely the accuracy of delivery and weapons yield) rather than improvements in measures for protection. In the United States, in particular, two of the principal new weapons programs—the MX intercontinental ballistic missile (ICBM) and the Trident II submarine-launched ballistic missile (SLBM)—are individually no more protected than the weapons they replace, but they are much more capable of threatening the hardened silo installations that have traditionally constituted the bulk of the Soviet strategic force.

An obvious way to stabilize the strategic balance, therefore, and to tailor it to the new security conception is to remove the excess offensive capability on each side, in effect substituting regulation for redundancy as a method of protection. That could be accomplished by reducing deployed forces to a level near the ceiling for efficient retaliation and by limiting weapons modernization to investment in measures for sheltering weapons from direct attack. Under such arrangements neither side could initiate an attack on the opponent's strategic weapons without diminishing coverage of the industrial and military infrastructure targets that are presumed to embody the deterrence effect. Moreover, if the number of warheads is limited relative to the number of missiles and aircraft that carry them, methods of deployment that force any attempted preemptive attack to use two or more warheads for each one destroyed would make this trade-off with the basic deterrent requirement prohibitively severe.

10. The quantitative basis for this judgment is reviewed in Michael M. May, George F. Bing, and John D. Steinbruner, *Strategic Arms Reductions* (Brookings, 1988).

Though it has not yet been clearly articulated in formal negotiations, this distinction between an essential deterrent requirement on the one hand and preemptive attack capability on the other is almost certain to be fundamental to the design of an enduring strategic force reduction agreement. The legitimacy of a deterrent capability must be conceded as the only acceptable justification for those weapons that are allowed. The legitimacy of a preemptive attack capability cannot be responsibly conceded by either side, and the denial of that capability is destined to be the main reason for undertaking strategic force reductions.

In practical terms the distinction denotes different types of targets. Installations associated with the industry and infrastructure of forces necessary to conduct coherent and effective military operations would presumably be included in the essential deterrent requirement against which a retaliatory deterrent threat is accepted. Strategic weapons launchers and their immediate command facilities would presumably be excluded from that requirement, and the capacity to attack such targets would be limited to the greatest extent practical.

The principle of protecting deterrence and denying preemption cannot be translated into a level and configuration of strategic forces with mathematical precision, but the basic design of forces that would approximate that criterion can be derived by applying the standard parameters used to measure the effect of weapons—number, yield, accuracy, reliability—and standard models used to simulate the exchange of forces having these characteristics. Such calculations can hardly predict the realities of an actual war, but they do embody institutionalized expectations in both the United States and the Soviet Union. These expectations inform the calculus of national interest that is the focus of the entire strategy of deterrence.

Figures 4-1 and 4-2 summarize the results of such an assessment. The first shows what the expected effects would be if either the United States or the Soviet Union initiated an attack on the other's strategic forces with inventories of 10,000 weapons on each side—roughly corresponding to the number that would be available under current levels of deployment. The model used assigns weapons to targets in order to achieve the maximum expected effect and then calculates a probable result. The assessment indicates that an attack initiated by the Soviet Union on the United States would use 4,000 weapons to destroy more than 7,000 U.S. warheads but would leave 2,900 U.S. warheads available for retaliation. A corresponding attack initiated by the United States would use roughly 4,400 weapons to destroy about 8,300 Soviet weapons, but 1,700 Soviet weapons would survive to retaliate. The exchange ratios—1:1.8 for the

Figure 4-1. *The Effects of Preemptive Attacks at Current Deployments*
Thousands of warheads

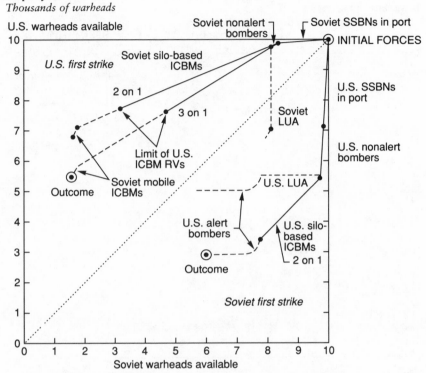

Source: Adapted from Michael M. May, George F. Bing, and John D. Steinbruner, *Strategic Arms Reductions* (Brookings, 1988), p. 18. Solid lines indicate the most efficient use of weapons; dashed extensions denote technically possible but relatively inefficient forms of attack. SSBNs are nuclear ballistic missile submarines; LUA is launch under attack; RVs are reentry vehicles.

Soviets and 1:1.9 for the Americans—favor the attacker as do the residual balances—2.1:1 for the Soviets and 3.3:1 for the Americans. The U.S. force performs somewhat better than the Soviet force.

Figure 4-2 shows the same calculation for forces that have been reduced to 3,000 warheads on each side and configured for maximum protection. The most effective preemptive strike weapons—the U.S. MX and prospective Trident II missiles and the Soviet SS-18—have been removed, and each side is assumed to have deployed 1,000 single warhead ICBMs in a mobile basing mode. If the attacker completely surprised the victim under that configuration of the balance, the first few hundred warheads used would destroy roughly 1,000 submarines, bombers, and ICBM warheads not on alert, but thereafter the attack could not be pursued without the attacker being disarmed and the victim left with

Figure 4-2. *The Effects of Preemptive Attacks with Forces Reduced to 3,000 Warheads and Configured for Maximum Protection*
Thousands of warheads

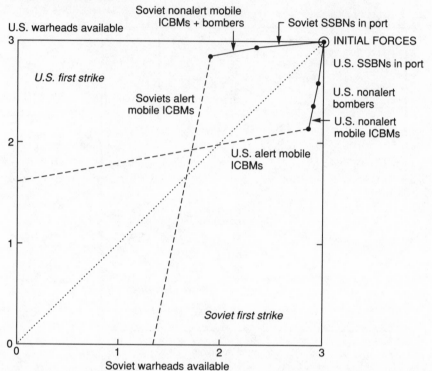

Source: Adapted from May, Bing, and Steinbruner, *Strategic Arms Reductions,* p. 25. Solid lines indicate the most efficient use of weapons; dashed extensions denote technically possible but relatively inefficient forms of attack.

more than 1,000 warheads for retaliation. In contrast to the calculation for 10,000 warheads, the exchange ratios and residual force ratios flip in favor of the defender, as the central principle mentioned earlier would require. Moreover, there is simple equity in the fact that at the reduced level U.S. and Soviet forces appear to perform equally well.

In this assessment, essential retaliatory requirements are adequately covered at both the 10,000 and the 3,000 warhead force levels, reflecting the well-known fact that the deterrent effect is now very strong and showing that it would not be materially diminished by even a drastic force reduction. The main consequence of the illustrated reduction would be to change from positive to negative the incentive to initiate a preemptive strike.

From the perspective of the theory of deterrence, that change appears to be of little practical significance as long as an adequate retaliatory capacity seems ensured. But from the perspective of crisis control that the Soviets are apparently trying to advance, the significance is much greater. As long as a positive incentive exists by these methods of assessment, available weapons will in fact be assigned to attack strategic weapons targets in the prepared plans of both sides, and the operating forces will train to complete these missions as rapidly as possible, since they make little sense unless the timing is preemptive. That feature of prior planning combined with the basic threat to the integrity of the command systems creates much of the impulse for preemption that could be exceedingly dangerous under crisis circumstances.

A reduction and reconfiguration of forces along the lines of the 3,000 warhead example would materially diminish this impulse. That fact is probably a security imperative for both sides strong enough to impose its logic on the eventual outcome.

Conventional Force Limitations

As intended under the principle of preserving legitimate deterrence requirements, a strategic force with 3,000 warheads would give the United States ample capability to threaten a very limited number of targets, whose destruction nonetheless would make an invasion of Western Europe organizationally infeasible.[11] Strictly in terms of military capability, therefore, the illustrated strategic force reductions would not significantly diminish the particular threat U.S. strategic forces would pose to conventional aggression in Europe. But it undoubtedly would diminish political confidence among members of the alliance.

Throughout its history, NATO has believed that its conventional forces could not withstand a fully dedicated WTO assault, and its European members have openly doubted whether U.S. strategic weapons would in the end be used to resist if the United States itself was not under attack. In the late 1950s, after the Suez crisis and the launch of Sputnik had crystallized European doubts about U.S. strategic protection,

---

11. Actual use of any major part of the nuclear weapons now stored in Europe would itself devastate the territory meant to be defended. Insofar, therefore, as the deterrent effect extended to Europe depends on making a credible, militarily advantageous threat, then the implicit level must be held low—on the order of tens of weapons. That number of weapons, if properly timed and located, could probably prevent the movement and supply of forces necessary to mount a successful offensive, particularly if the attack was directed against the early stages of the attempted operation.

NATO forces were supplied with thousands of nuclear weapons, whose presence in the area of potential conflict was accepted as a political guarantee that more remotely located forces could not provide. The greater vulnerability of these NATO forces, which were placed at inevitably well-known locations on the crowded European continent, was discounted in the strategic calculus, but it affected the operational posture that evolved. For more than thirty years NATO forces have ingrained in the training and thinking of their commanders a strong inclination to use their assigned nuclear weapons early in the course of a major battle. That traditional inclination would be strengthened if strategic force reductions were not accompanied by a reduction in the apparent threat of invasion, and the concern would eventually be manifested in a politically charged program for modernizing the tactical nuclear weapons arsenal.

That sequence of events would reinforce the countervailing strategy the Soviet Union adopted during their adjustment in doctrine in the 1960s and would contradict the most recent revision. Over the past decade Soviet tactical air forces have been concentrated in forward positions, with an evident intention to conduct a conventional air interdiction campaign against NATO's nuclear weapons.[12] Since such a campaign would be much more effective if undertaken at the earliest stages of dispersing the NATO weapons from their secure storage areas, a severe burden would be imposed on the judgment of Soviet commanders if NATO ever undertook a protective dispersal of its tactical nuclear weapons in the midst of crisis circumstances. The burden would descend on NATO commanders if they did not disperse. This interaction between the operational postures of the two alliances is one of the more plausible triggers of an unintended war. It would be worsened if a separate strategic force reduction agreement triggers strong efforts to improve the tactical weapons arsenal.

The new conception of security therefore requires not only implementation of the projected change in operational doctrine for Soviet conventional forces but also a corresponding shift in NATO that would subordinate reliance on tactical nuclear weapons to plans for a strictly conventional defense of forward positions. Again, this is a matter of limited significance from the perspective of deterrence, since even with a separate strategic force agreement there would be no rational scope

---

12. An analysis matching the inherent capability of Soviet tactical air forces in Europe with the imputed objective is presented in Joshua M. Epstein, *Measuring Military Power* (Princeton University Press, 1984).

for calculated aggression in Europe. From the perspective of rendering crisis interactions more manageable, however, the changes would be of great importance. There is no circumstance worldwide that could strain the two military establishments as seriously as a mutual alert in central Europe. If that was stabilized, all other potential crisis engagements would be notably eased.

There is little apparent difficulty with the central principle for designing a more stable conventional balance in central Europe. It is now consistent with the policy declarations of both alliances that each should be guaranteed a high-quality defense of its own territory but denied the assets necessary to conduct a successful offensive against the opposing alliance. Moreover, since the defensive mission is generally believed to be easier, particularly if defensive positions are carefully prepared, simple equity produces the desired result. If NATO and WTO conventional forces had equal capability, then neither could attack with confidence and both could be assured of their territorial integrity, with no pressure to initiate operations under crisis circumstances.

The problem comes in the measurement and certification of equity. As summarized in table 4-1, very few of the recognized ingredients that contribute to conventional military power are equal between the two alliances. Nor are their geographic positions, their social conditions, or their economic and technical potential, all of which affect the significance that a given military capability has for overall security. In the absence of anything like the power of nuclear explosions to dominate analytic assessments, no professional consensus has formed on methods for calculating conventional military capacity, and there is no immediate prospect that one will form. The assertion or denial of equity is a matter of judgment about which there are many opinions.

For some, that is effectively the end of the story: the prospect for agreement is destined to be overwhelmed unless there is an accepted basis for designing it. Advocates of this view usually cite the long unproductive negotiations on mutual and balanced force reductions in Europe as historical evidence for their expectation.

But again, that natural reaction seems too negative for the circumstances. It undervalues the power of a new security conception operating within the centrally planned Soviet system. It undervalues the background incentives operating on the more diffuse political system of the United States; notably, the surge in international economic priority and the fiscal pressure on the defense budget. Despite the analytic confusion that besets the topic, a political deal could be struck in which each side improved its security and relieved its longer-term investment burden at

Table 4-1. *Comparison of NATO and WTO Conventional Forces for the Entire European Theater (Atlantic to the Urals)*[a]

Item	NATO	WTO	Ratio of WTO to NATO
Total military manpower			
High estimate	3,000,000	4,000,000	1.3
Low estimate	2,385,000	2,292,000	1.0
Mean	2,696,300	3,573,000	1.3
Main battle tanks			
High estimate	22,200	54,300	2.4
Low estimate	13,500	32,400	2.4
Mean	19,000	47,000	2.5
Armored vehicles			
High estimate	38,400	94,800	2.5
Low estimate	28,900	42,000	1.5
Mean	33,400	68,400	2.0
Antitank missiles			
High estimate	13,300	35,400	2.7
Low estimate	10,100	16,600	1.6
Mean	11,900	23,900	2.0
Artillery, mortars, and MLRS[b]			
High estimate	15,300	46,500	3.0
Low estimate	10,600	23,800	2.2
Mean	12,600	34,700	2.8
Combat aircraft			
High estimate	4,300	7,700	1.8
Low estimate	3,000	5,900	2.0
Mean	3,600	7,000	1.9
Division equivalents			
High estimate	107	192	1.8
Low estimate	88	101	1.1
Mean	96	136	1.4

Sources: British Secretary of State for Defence, *Statement on the Defence Estimates 1988*, vol. 1 (London, 1988); Bundesminister der Verteidigung, *Streitkraftevergleich 1987 NATO–Warschauer Pakt* (Bonn, 1987); John Collins, *US/ Soviet Military Balance: Statistical Trends 1980–1987* (CRS Report 88-425S, April 15, 1988); Anthony Cordesman, *NATO Central Region Forces* (London: Jane's, 1988); Department of Defense, *Soviet Military Power: An Assessment of the Threat, 1988* (GPO, 1988); International Institute for Strategic Studies, *The Military Balance, 1987–1988* (London: IISS, 1987); testimony of Phillip A. Karber, *NATO Defense and the INF Treaty*, Hearings before the Senate Committee on Armed Services, 100 Cong. 2 sess. (GPO, 1988), part 1, p. 230; Benjamin F. Schemmer, "Soviet Technological Parity in Europe Undermines NATO's Flexible Response Strategy," *Armed Forces Journal International*, May 1984, pp. 80–95; interview with Phillip A. Karber, *Armed Forces Journal International*, June 1987, p. 120; and NATO Information Service, *NATO and the Warsaw Pact: Force Comparisons* (Brussels, NIS, 1984).

a. The range of estimates is partly caused by differences in definition between each weapon category. High estimates often include weaponry that could be considered marginal to that category. Low estimates can be caused, in part, by an unusually narrow definition of the weapon category. The mean, and its ratio, is a product of the full range of sources, not simply the high and low estimates. Figures are rounded.

b. Multiple launch rocket systems.

the cost of adjusting long-established planning assumptions and habits of unilateral national decision. As has regularly happened in the course of military history, political actions might well precede a well-formulated rationale.

A potential outcome is not difficult to anticipate in crude outline or even to calculate if appropriately modest claims are made about the calculation. It is acknowledged that the WTO has more tanks, more artillery, and more organized ground combat units than NATO and that these disparities are at the core of NATO's traditional fears of a conventional invasion. It is less explicitly acknowledged, but nonetheless plausibly asserted, that NATO's comparative advantage lies in the quality of its forces—tactical aircraft, in particular, and more generally its ability to apply advanced sensing and information processing technologies to new weapons applications. That sets up incommensurate terms of exchange—current capability of the WTO for future potential of NATO; ground force capability of the WTO for tactical air capability of NATO. Such trades are the despair of analysts, political speech writers, and most officials who must face an imminent election or other political accounting. They are, however, the delight of visionary leaders, since they offer the potential for dramatic redefinition, and that certainly seems to be Gorbachev's attitude.

A deal designed to adjust the conventional balance in Europe in a manner that would be received as dramatic would consist of four main elements. First, there would be a reduction in the fully mobilized size of conventional ground forces, and the reduction would be substantially larger for the WTO than for NATO. The point of that measure is to reduce the disparity in aggregate firepower—from a ratio set at 1.7:1 in the last officially published NATO estimate to one noticeably closer to unity.[13] Second, there would be a relocation of active units away from the inter-German border, and this repositioning would also be dispro-portionately large for Soviet forces in East Germany. The purpose of that measure is to reduce the potential for a rapidly mobilized surprise attack; it could be meaningfully supplemented by expanding regulations

13. *NATO and the Warsaw Pact: Force Comparisons* (Brussels: NATO Information Service, 1984). NATO has not updated this document since 1984. The 1.7:1 ratio applies to armored division equivalents of the two alliances—the most comprehensive general firepower comparison made in the document. (See pp. 7ff and figure 2, p. 8.) The official NATO estimates do not include the forces of France and Spain, even though both are members of the alliance. The reason given is that neither country participates directly in the integrated NATO military command. Many independent accounts do include those forces and therefore estimate the disparity to be less than NATO does.

on the movement and exercising of military units that render each alliance's operations more transparent. There is ample scope for such a redeployment that would not threaten the coherence of the WTO military organization or the predominant Soviet role in it. Third, there would be a reconfiguration and standardization of basic military units in order to constrain their individual offensive capability.

These measures would require the definition and regulation of manning and equipment levels for some fundamental organization unit—most plausibly a regiment. The allowed number and required location of these units would be set on each side and provide the basis for controlling and verifying particular items of equipment strongly associated with offensive missions. Large concentrations of artillery ammunition, for example, would not be allowed in forward positions. Because these stocks are massive and difficult to move, a successful offensive operation requires forward positioning, whereas a defensive strategy logically demands protective dispersal in depth. Similarly, large concentrations of bridging equipment would be prohibited in forward positions, and mine-clearing capabilities even more severely restrained.

Fourth, to balance the disproportionately large reductions and redeployments of WTO ground forces and to alleviate their fears of NATO technical superiority, there would be a corresponding definition, reduction, and redeployment of those tactical air units that are equipped and trained for ground attack missions deep into the opponent's territory. These reductions would also be accompanied by restraints on the rate at which the allowed units could be modernized. Both measures would disproportionately affect NATO's capability, particularly as it has been projected in recent defense plans.

The political deal embodied in these four adjustments primarily affects the United States and the Soviet Union.[14] Each would be formally accepting restraints that would probably be independently imposed anyway as the two countries manage their defense budgets. As the Soviet Union proceeds to modernize its conventional forces at a technical and economic disadvantage compared with the Western alliance, the logic for reducing the base force and the mission aspiration is compelling. By focusing investment on a smaller force and a more realistic objective,

---

14. British and German air forces operate 400 aircraft of roughly comparable quality to those that the United States deploys in Europe to perform deep interdiction missions. They would certainly be counted in the balance, and reduction of these forces would be possible in compliance with the suggested arrangement. The allocation of reductions and of subsequent modernization would be a demanding political task within the alliance.

the Soviets can produce higher-quality security with the assets they have available, whatever the NATO defense program might be. If the reductions can be used to encourage or to formalize technical restraint in NATO, so much the better from the Soviet point of view. Conversely, the emerging pressures on the U.S. defense budget are likely to hold the development of very sophisticated deep interdiction capability well below what has recently been advertised. Budget pressures give the United States its own independent reasons for formalizing the arrangements. The incentives operating in the background on both sides make the deal feasible, even likely, despite the conceptual complexity and analytic difficulty of defining and justifying it.

If the deal is to be executed, however, this political logic must be incorporated in concrete measures. No matter how arbitrarily it is done, the number of units that are to be reduced, redeployed, or reconfigured will ultimately have to be determined, and any explicit connection between the actions of the two sides will set practical terms of exchange. In the absence of a widely accepted calculus, it is much harder to anticipate how the necessary judgments about conventional forces will eventually be made than it is in the case of nuclear weapons. Nonetheless, some rough boundaries can be drawn within which a mutually acceptable outcome can be plausibly expected to fall.

One such boundary concerns the total conventional force assets that each side could potentially assemble in central Europe. Current intelligence estimates indicate that the WTO might be able to mobilize 110 divisions after a 120-day period of preparation. By that time NATO could have 49 divisions in position to resist.[15] Since these divisional units in the two alliances are not of equal size and since their standard level of equipment varies, most methods of comparison begin by aggregating the raw firepower that each of the forces would bring into battle, and the calculated result is usually determined by the ratio of available firepower.[16] Applying the simplest arithmetic to the current WTO-NATO firepower comparison suggests that NATO forces committed to the defense of their forward positions and unwilling to retreat to gain tactical advantage might be damaged to the point of organizational disintegration (50 percent attrition) within five days and completely routed (100 percent

15. William W. Kaufmann, *A Reasonable Defense* (Brookings, 1986), pp. 64, 66.

16. Though it is acknowledged that historical battles have often been decided by factors that are hard to predict—such as the skill of commanders, the spirit of the troops, fortuitous position or timing, and rates of resupply—firepower comparisons are a primary means of stating odds in advance of an actual test. It is presumably on those calculated odds that the deterrent effect depends.

Table 4-2. *Composition of NATO and WTO Tactical Air Forces,*
European Central Front

Item	NATO	WTO
Fighter and attack aircraft	2,800	1,250
Interceptors	800	2,000
Air defense missiles	1,350	2,200

Sources: Congressional Budget Office, *U.S. Ground Forces and the Conventional Balance in Europe* (GPO, 1988); and International Institute for Strategic Studies, *Military Balance, 1987–1988.*

attrition) within fifteen. A net reduction of roughly 45 divisions would have to be extracted from the WTO forces to reverse this result and to make the calculated assessment a stalemate with no loss of NATO territory. With more extensive investment in prepared defensive positions for NATO, the stalemate might be expected to occur if the WTO forces were reduced relative to NATO by 30 to 35 divisions.[17] Net reductions of these magnitudes can be taken as an outer bound for the amount necessary to deny an offensive capability in central Europe. Many would consider the balance acceptable with a lesser adjustment; it is difficult to find a plausible basis for demanding more.

A second boundary of plausible judgment concerns the interaction of tactical air forces. As reflected in table 4-2, the current inventories of NATO and WTO tactical aircraft have a different mix of purposes, with NATO emphasizing both air superiority and ground attack and the WTO forces concentrating on air defense. If both forces committed themselves to an initial battle for air superiority and if NATO aircraft proved to be at least three times as effective as their WTO counterparts, NATO would establish dominant air superiority in three to four days and would emerge with roughly 3,000 fighter and attack aircraft at its disposal. This result would emerge more quickly and with more surviving aircraft available to NATO if the WTO forces diverted their attention from the initial air superiority battle to pursue an interdiction campaign against the NATO nuclear storage sites. If stalemate in the air battle is to be the arranged expectation, then the NATO tactical air capability would have to be reduced by a net of about 1,000 aircraft, and their effectiveness assumed to be no more than twice that of WTO aircraft.

Taken together, these two simple assessments suggest a trade of up

17. This comparison and the one for tactical aircraft presented below was developed by William Kaufmann. The underlying method is partially discussed in Martin Binkin and William W. Kaufmann, *U.S. Army Reserves: Rhetoric, Realities, and Risks* (Brookings, forthcoming). It is more fully presented in an occasional paper by Kaufmann entitled "Quantitative Comparisons of Conventional Forces," Brookings, 1988.

to 14 NATO tactical air wings for up to 30 to 45 WTO ground force divisions in order to bring the central European balance to a state in which both sides are confident of projecting stalemate as the likely outcome of an engagement. That implicit logic can be bolstered directly by considering the performance assumptions for aircraft operating against ground force units that would make those terms of exchange reasonable from the perspective of both alliances. These performance assumptions are an additional means of setting a boundary for plausible judgment.

The primary objective of NATO aircraft in such an engagement would be some 45 Soviet divisions that might be within two days march of the immediate battle line; the central question is whether the aircraft could prevent these divisions from arriving at the point of battle with enough capacity to fight effectively. Since a fully equipped Soviet division contains about 1,250 tracked vehicles (tanks, infantry fighting vehicles and armored personnel carriers, self-propelled artillery, and organic air defenses), the operational requirement for the aircraft is to reduce that inventory by about 50 percent in two days—the same level of attrition at which it was assumed that NATO forces would become ineffective. Extrapolating from peacetime experience, one may reasonably assume that NATO aircraft could fly three sorties a day over two days while maintaining 80 percent of their nominal performance capability and that each of these aircraft could carry eight pods of scatterable munitions, the most effective current form of attack against tracked vehicles. One thousand aircraft meeting these standards could neutralize all 45 Soviet reinforcing divisions in six sorties over two days if they achieved a penetration probability of 95 percent (that is, suffered attrition of only 5 percent per sortie) as well as a kill probability per weapons pod of 95 percent.[18] The same 1,000 aircraft could neutralize 33 divisions—enough to stalemate the battle with prepared NATO defensive positions—while suffering attrition of 10 percent per sortie and achieving a kill probability per weapons pod of only 80 percent. Though it would be difficult to

18. This calculation developed by William Kaufmann projects the maximum potential of tactical aircraft operating against ground units. A standard wing of 72 aircraft with the stated capabilities would be reduced to 56 after flying six sorties with 5 percent attrition per sortie. It would have destroyed a cumulative total of 2,200 tracked vehicle targets, and if those targets were ideally distributed, then approximately 3.5 divisions would have been incapacitated. If assumed attrition is increased to 10 percent per sortie and the kill probability per munitions pod is reduced to 80 percent, then each wing would have been reduced to 46 aircraft after flying six sorties and would have incapacitated a cumulative total of 1,554 tracked vehicles—theoretically removing 2.5 divisions from the battle. Under the former performance assumptions 14 wings could stop all 45 divisions; under the latter assumptions, slightly over 34 divisions would be removed.

Table 4-3. *Cumulative U.S. Defense Budget Savings Resulting from Reductions of Strategic Offensive Forces and Fighter-Attack Aircraft*
Billions of constant fiscal 1989 dollars

	Years after implementation				
Item	1	5	10	15	20
Strategic offensive forces[a]	9.7[b]	48.5	97.0	145.5	194.0
Tactical aircraft[c]	4.5[d]	24.1	52.0	84.4	121.9
Total	14.2	72.6	149.0	229.9	315.9

Source: Adapted from the budget estimates by William W. Kaufmann presented in chapter 3.

a. The strategic forces assumed are those presented in figure 4-2 and consist of 47 bombers with 470 air-launched cruise missiles, 1,000 small ICBMs, and 192 Trident I SLBMs.

b. Cost savings are estimated from the lower "congressional track" budget presented in chapter 3. The strategic forces assumed here would cost $19.2 billion a year. The savings of $9.3 billion is the difference between that number and the $28.9 billion a year strategic forces budget projected in chapter 3.

c. It is assumed for the purposes of this table that U.S. F-15s would constitute half of the total 1,008 tactical aircraft reduction. The other half would come from Toranados currently deployed by the Federal Republic of Germany, the United Kingdom, and Italy. Savings are estimated for the 504 U.S. aircraft only.

d. The calculation assumes that the tactical aircraft being removed would otherwise have been replaced by more advanced aircraft at an amortized annual rate. The specific figure is derived by assuming (1) that the current capital base of the aircraft is $45 million each, (2) that annual investment costs (spare parts and eventual replacement) are 10 percent of this capital base, (3) that annual operating costs are an additional 10 percent of the capital base, and (4) that the capital base itself must be increased by 3 percent a year to amortize the cost of technical improvements incorporated into replacement aircraft. The savings estimates aggregate 2, 3, and 4 but exclude the capital base itself, which has already been spent.

argue that this idealized performance assessment is empirically likely, it does fall within the theoretical potential of the aircraft, and thus defines an outer boundary of plausible judgment.

IMPLICATIONS

The theoretical objective of sharply reduced, protectively configured strategic forces and the more loosely defined vision of a stabilized conventional balance in central Europe offer substantial scope to implement the doctrinal and diplomatic initiatives that have recently been emerging from the Soviet Union. They also offer a major opportunity for the United States to improve security while relieving its long-term financial burdens. As summarized in table 4-3, the force reductions outlined would diminish the U. S. defense budget by about $15 billion a year in fiscal 1989 dollars. At 5 percent of the current budget, that amount would nearly double the rate of reduction projected in chapter 3 as an extension of recent congressional actions, and at least 90 percent would be realized as an addition to the savings from more efficient reallocation that were presented in that chapter.[19] Over the normal life

19. The defense budget reductions suggested in chapter 3 would postpone the

cycle of the weapons systems in question—approximately twenty years—these additional savings would total more than $300 billion, the equivalent of an entire year's budget.

Though it remains uncertain whether these potential force reductions will actually be achieved in whole or in part, the prospect alone is sufficient to alter the political conditions of international security and thereby to pose security interests for the United States that extend well beyond the standard conceptions of deterrence and containment formulated during the cold war. In this, as with fiscal deficits, trade balances, and defense budget allocations, evolving circumstances have created strong reasons for adjustments in policy, but they will probably not generate the immediate sense of crisis the United States has habitually relied on to make demanding political decisions.

In principle, there are compelling reasons for the United States to initiate a policy adjustment comparable in spirit to the Soviet doctrinal developments but more specific in content and broader in scope. Even full implementation of the strategic force reductions and conventional force limitations outlined would not establish a complete regime of cooperative security. Any diplomatically feasible reduction of strategic forces, for example, would necessarily continue restrictions on strategic defenses,[20] but not necessarily extend these restrictions to protect surveillance and communication assets in space. Yet that latter protection is essential for preserving the coherence of the respective command systems—the most important single problem in controlling crisis interactions. Similarly, reasonable limits must eventually be set on this

---

introduction of a technically improved replacement aircraft, but the annual costs for an improved model are included in the cost estimates from which table 4-2 is derived. At the extreme this postponement might last the entire twenty-year period, in which case the estimated savings would be only 90 percent of those presented in table 4-2.

20. This necessity has been obscured and even directly contradicted in the political and technical rhetoric that has accompanied the Strategic Defense Initiative (SDI) in the United States, but it has been implicitly acknowledged in specific decisions. The core fact is that any deployment of strategic defenses must be precisely regulated—that is, subjected to mutual agreement—if it is not itself to become an incentive for initiating offensive operations under crisis circumstances. The reason is that a given offensive force will do much better in penetrating a given defensive system if it initiates with optimum coordination than if it retaliates after suffering initial damage—an effect that becomes increasingly important as offensive forces are reduced and, perversely, as the effectiveness of defensive forces is increased, right up to the (impractical) point where those forces are literally perfect. Despite rhetorical commitment to an SDI program unilaterally pursued, the U.S. negotiating position after the December 1987 summit meeting in Washington has accepted that strategic force reductions will have to depend on an agreement regarding strategic defenses.

protected surveillance and communication capability, in order to distinguish the legitimate, essential functions of operational control and verification on the one hand from the unacceptably intrusive observation required for preemptive targeting on the other. In general, as the technical determinants of military power shift from developments in nuclear explosives and rocket propulsion to developments in sensing and information processing, the most critical issues of regulation also shift. The problem of reliably preventing war is not just one of correcting force imbalances inherited from the past, but even more of avoiding those that have yet to develop.

In practice, however, the United States is poorly prepared to undertake such an initiative. Through the political process the issues of security have been fragmented into those readily expressed either in budget decisions or in specific treaty positions. Political debate has been largely focused on immediate marginal increases or decreases in the defense budget, on individual weapons projects, on compliance with disputed treaty arrangements, and most recently on a vision of a perfect defense, inspired far more by domestic politics than by strategic or technical reality. The problems of operational interaction that appear to be motivating the Soviet doctrinal initiatives and that are at any rate emerging as leading security problems have been at best only dimly grasped in U.S. political discussion; the policy process within the government sharply separates this subject from the more familiar topics of the defense budget and arms control. Even the projected budget savings would be experienced as accounting abstractions that do not readily impress American public opinion, and political decisionmakers are moved by things that do.

There is no simple remedy to this disparity between the requirements of security policy and the inherent limitations on its formulation imposed by the nature of the American political system. The tension between substance and process is clearly a major drama in the evolution of democracy. One can readily identify, nonetheless, a necessary and constructive first step. The United States is unlikely either to initiate its own changes in policy or react appropriately to Soviet diplomacy until there is a better developed, more widespread conceptualization of the need to do so. Nothing can substitute for a more extensive, more penetrating public discussion.

CHAPTER FIVE

Rationalizing Technology Investments

KENNETH FLAMM
THOMAS L. MCNAUGHER

The application of advanced technology is critical simultaneously to the security, the economic prosperity, and the international stature of the United States. Though that judgment is difficult to prove with standard statistics, virtually no one would doubt it in summarizing the experience of the past four decades or in anticipating the next four.

It is certainly apparent in studies of the prime symbol and leading instance of technical change, the electronic computer. The cost of information processing capacity has declined for decades at a stunning rate, averaging more than 20 percent a year, perhaps 25 percent in real terms. This is roughly an order of magnitude greater than the most rapid price decreases registered in the peak decades of the first great industrial revolution at the dawn of the nineteenth century. Shipments of computer hardware alone are now rapidly approaching 2 percent of U.S. gross national product, and a reasonable calculation suggests that one year's technological advance in computer engineering brings with it a benefit of 0.3 to 0.8 percent of GNP.[1] In an era when annual growth rates in national income are 2 to 3 percent, this constitutes an extraordinarily important contribution to improving the standard of living. Moreover, since the trend of technological advance will continue unabated for at least another decade and because information is an essential element of

---

1. See Kenneth Flamm, *Targeting the Computer: Government Support and International Competition* (Brookings, 1987), pp. 32–35. An approximation to this number may be arrived at by noting that a 25 percent reduction in the cost of computer shipments, which are approaching 2 percent of GNP, is 0.5 percent of GNP. Calculations that take into account the sensitivity of computer demand to price, and use a range of plausible values for the price elasticity of demand and the annual rate of technology-driven improvement in price performance, yield the ranges mentioned in the text.

most economic activity, the basic structure and operating patterns of modern economies should be far more profoundly affected than we have yet been able to appreciate—and similarly for military forces.

Public policies to support the development of advanced technology in the United States have historically been primarily preoccupied with national security applications.[2] As the United States invested in its military establishment in the years following World War II, commercial industries were stimulated, largely as an unforeseen outcome.[3] Since that time, as military technologies have matured, the demands of security investment have diverged from those of commercial application, while the broad economic implications of the new technology have become as important to its society as achieving purely military objectives.

Today we live in a different world. Industrial societies that were still recovering from the damage of World War II when the U.S. acquired its general technical advantage have learned to adopt our accomplishments. U.S. businessmen now increasingly complain that American innovations in basic science and technology are being commercialized abroad with little of the profit flowing back into the pockets of Americans whose tax dollars financed much of the initial investment. These industrial rivals, moreover, have come to undertake their own technical investments in amounts comparable to the United States', and since they direct a higher proportion of it to commercial purposes, their investments now exceed our own in that area.[4] Meanwhile, defense research and development seems less effective than it once was in generating commercial benefits and is itself more in need of the discipline and innovative impulses that well-developed markets provide.

Changing circumstances call for changing policies. A new world of

2. One of the major historical exceptions was the U.S. government's support for agricultural research, begun in the nineteenth century. The limited ability of small farmers to undertake such investments, and the difficulties of capturing and commercializing the results in an era when farmers were a potent political force, foreshadow some of the dynamic that is driving government to take a more supportive role in industrial R&D today.

3. Though the scale and significance may be unprecedented, military investment was also crucial in advancing American industrial technology in the last century. Public investment in state-of-the-art armories and munitions factories spurred the growth of the metalworking and machine tool industry. The American system of large-scale manufacture was honed on the military market: Samuel Colt's pioneering use of interchangeable parts in mass-produced revolvers was an experiment paid for by military procurement. See, for example, David A. Hounshell, *From the American System to Mass Production, 1800–1932: The Development of Manufacturering Technology in the United States* (Johns Hopkins University Press, 1984), chap. 1.

4. National Science Board, *Science and Engineering Indicators, 1987* (Government Printing Office, 1987), p. 3.

peers and competitors means that, more than ever before, public investments in technologies expected to benefit either the U.S. industrial base or the defense effort must be effective and efficient. And the increasing maturity of much U.S. military technology, and tightening budgets, mean military R&D can no longer be expected to build the commercial technology base. Where military investment is in frontier technologies, expanding the outer envelope of technological advance, defense investments can help create technologies that will ultimately benefit industry. But the existence of nimble and able foreign competitors means that speed and effectiveness are essential in reaping commercial returns, and the defense establishment is simply not organized for rapid and efficient application. The core defense technologies—ships, aircraft, and tracked vehicles—are more mature, increasingly specialized, and inherently remote from commercial markets. The expense of each item and the limited scale of production mean that the relationship between the evolution of design and the ultimate product must be very different. For both economic and security reasons the United States must reconsider the way it organizes investments in technical innovation.

While the details are still uncertain and disputed, the guiding principles of necessary reforms seem clear enough. Public support for developing the commercial technology base ought to be defined and justified on its own terms. It should not depend on a concocted claim that it is needed to maintain national security, an appeal designed to tap the deep pockets of the defense establishment. Conversely, military requirements for technology ought to be defended in military terms, and not draped with claims of commercial spillovers when the logic of military necessity seems weak. Programs to support either objective—commercial or military—should be designed with efficiency and effectiveness in mind. An effective military research and development effort means scraping away the bureaucratic incrustations that have grown over defense R&D contracting in recent years and providing for the operational experience required to master increasingly complex technical applications. Improving the effectiveness of investment in commercial R&D means creating an agenda responsive to the technological needs of industry. It also means experimenting with new forms of organization designed to increase cooperation within industry and between industry and academic research institutions.

THE HERITAGE

World War II marked a fundamental change in the importance of R&D in American economic life and in public support for technological innovation. The war involved an unprecedented mobilization of American scientists and engineers in a vast military R&D project.[5] Federal expenditures on R&D rose from $97 million in fiscal year 1940 to $1.38 billion in 1944 and $1.6 billion in 1945. After the war, support continued; in 1947 the military spent $500 million (out of $625 million in federal research funds) on R&D, 80 percent of which was contracted to industrial and university laboratories.[6] Before World War II the government had paid for 15 to 20 percent of U.S. research; after the war it funded more than half of a vastly expanded national effort.[7] After falling sharply in the 1970s, federal funding today pays for more R&D than does funding from the private sector.[8]

It was in this postwar environment that the computer industry took off, and this industry's success has become a symbol of the nation's entry into the era of high technology. But the nation's initial experience with commercial spillover from rapidly changing military technologies began after World War I, with airplanes and, especially, their engines. Although federal support for the aircraft industry was proportionally smaller and less direct than it would be for the computer industry, it was crucial to the industry's survival.

Aircraft and Engines

The story of innovation in the aircraft industry and the crucial role played by defense spending has been told in detail by others.[9] Here it is

5. For example, in 1935 less than 4 percent of Bell Laboratories personnel worked on military projects. In 1943 roughly 75 percent of the Bell staff and 80 percent of the Bell Labs budget went to defense activities. Bell Telephone Laboratories, *A History of Engineering and Science in the Bell System*, vol. 2: *National Service in War and Peace (1905–1975)* (Murray Hill, N.J.: Bell Telephone Laboratories, 1978), pp. 11, 356.

6. Roughly half the 1944 expenditure, $730 million, was accounted for by the Manhattan Project. National Science Foundation, *Federal Funds for Science, II. The Federal Research and Development Budget, Fiscal Years 1952 and 1953* (GPO, 1953), pp. 11–13.

7. Flamm, *Targeting the Computer*, p. 6.

8. National Science Foundation, *National Patterns of Science and Technology Resources, 1987*, NSF 88-305 (GPO, 1988), table B-5.

9. See Irving Brinton Holley, Jr., *Buying Aircraft: Matériel Procurement for the Army Air Forces* (Office of the Chief of Military History, Department of the Army, 1964); David C. Mowery and Nathan Rosenberg, "The Commercial Aircraft Industry," in Richard R. Nelson, ed., *Government and Technical Progress: A Cross-Industry Analysis* (Pergamon, 1982), pp. 101–61; Robert Schlaifer and S. D. Heron, *Development of Aircraft Engines*

necessary only to draw a few conclusions. First, federal support was essential to the development of an industry in what has always been an exceptionally volatile and risky business, with its unpredictable demand and the steadily rising costs of developing new models.[10] But the greatest source of risk has been technological advance in a host of aircraft subelements, which has produced rapid obsolescence in existing models, great market uncertainty, and a constant need to face the risks of technological research.[11]

In his comprehensive history of early aircraft engine development, Robert Schlaifer argued that it was "not only inevitable but desirable that the government should guide the general course of development, since the record shows that private industry cannot be relied upon even to advocate, let alone finance, the development of every type of needed materiel."[12] Thus federal—largely military—support for R&D was instrumental in advancing the state of the art in aviation.

Military funding went well beyond support for scientific advance, subsidizing the industry at all levels. Income from military production contracts served to buffer aircraft firms from ebbs and flows in the commercial side of their business. In the 1930s every major aircraft manufacturer, including Douglas, whose DC-3 dominated the commercial market, did at least half, and often much more, of its business (measured as a percentage of sales) with the military.[13] Profit from military

---

and Fuels (Harvard University Graduate School of Business Administration, 1950); and R. Miller and David Sawers, *The Technical Development of Modern Aviation* (London: Routledge and Kegan Paul, 1968).

10. Today a manufacturer that decides to build a new model "is literally betting the company, because the size of the investment may exceed the company's entire net worth." John Newhouse, *The Sporty Game* (Knopf, 1982), p. 3.

11. Before World War II the most startling advances lay in improving the thrust and trimming the weight of aircraft engines, although improvements in airframe design had only slightly less disruptive effects on the industry's advance. An ingenious combination of these advances gave Douglas dominance in the industry after it introduced the DC-3 in the mid-1930s. The development of jet engines just before World War II introduced a new phase in aircraft design, complemented somewhat later by the introduction of electronics components. The costs and complexity of new models rose accordingly.

12. "Nowhere in the world," he continued, "did a single established engine builder undertake the development of turbojets until either persuaded to do so by government, as in Germany, or confronted with a demonstrably successful turbojet developed with extensive government aid as in England and in the United States." Schlaifer and Heron, *Development of Aircraft Engines,* pp. 27–28, 29.

13. During the 1930s, for example, when the Douglas DC-3 dominated commercial aircraft markets, "the greater unit value of military aircraft enabled other producers to avoid financial disaster." Mowery and Rosenberg, "Commercial Aircraft Industry," p. 108.

aircraft production contracts tended to serve as a hidden subsidy for R&D.[14]

For engines, in which technological change was most pronounced, the military services were "the main market . . . particularly for new types and models."[15] This held true in the jet as well as the piston age. Demonstrated just before World War II, jet engines saw considerable development during the war, all for the military market. After the war, work on strategic bombers contributed substantially to the development of turboprop as well as turbojet engines. And the early high-bypass-ratio engines crucial to commercial aviation in the 1960s were first developed and built for the military.[16]

The military's drive for high-quality products tended to pull the commercial side of the industry along in its wake. Although the military purchased commercial or near-commercial aircraft like the DC-3 and the KC-135 (which, with some modification, became Boeing's very successful 707), the aircraft industry benefited more broadly as a "borrower" of technologies successfully applied in military aircraft.[17] It is in this sense that funding for purely military R&D paid dividends to commercial aviation. That firms were engaged in developing both military and commercial aircraft was obviously crucial, since industrialists were in a position to make rapid and informed judgments about when best to move a new technology into commercial ventures.

The way federal support was provided also made a difference. Schlaifer, for example, distinguished between federal funding of R&D and federal performance of R&D. "A private firm must maintain a proper balance in directing the general program of development," but "a government establishment tends to become a collection of specialists, each promoting his specialty whatever the effect on more necessary objectives." Thus, army engine projects failed "to sacrifice individual features of merit in

14. See Holley, *Buying Aircraft*, p. 24.
15. Schlaifer and Heron, *Development of Aircraft Engines*, p. 7.
16. Significantly, by this time aviation and engine firms had acquired their own R&D facilities. Thus the industry contributed 32 percent of the financing for development of the turbofan engine, with the military contributing 55 percent and the Federal Aeronautics Administration and the National Aeronautics and Space Administration 13 percent. Mowery and Rosenberg, "Commercial Aircraft Industry," p. 131.
17. Mowery and Rosenberg use the word *borrower* in three contexts. First, "significant innovations in commercial aircraft design . . . were originally developed by manufacturers of airframes and engines for military applications." Second, "important benefits are reaped by airframe and engine manufacturers who are able to share development, or less often, production tooling costs between military and civilian designs that are less closely related." Third, aircraft "have benefited to an unusual extent from technological developments in other industries." Ibid., p. 102.

order to hasten the success of the engine as a whole."[18] As principal customer, the government had the power to control "even the work done by private firms in all its details, but development [of engines] was fully successful only when the services gave the firms all possible freedom in deciding on details of design and development."[19]

The most successful vehicle for funding aeronautical research was not a military organization per se but rather the National Advisory Committee on Aeronautics (NACA), created in 1915 and funded separately from military service budgets, just as its successor, the National Aeronautics and Space Administration (NASA) has been funded separately from the Defense Department. Although NACA's formal mission was to attend to problems facing military and air mail aircraft, its work covered "problems of aerodynamics and aeronautics common to both military and commercial aircraft."[20] NACA's elaborate test and research facilities, principally at Langley Field, Virginia, and Moffett Field, California, provided test data to the industry as well as the military. Equally important, these research centers served "as training schools for the vitally necessary aeronautical engineers of industry."[21] NACA's greatest contribution was made before World War II; by the 1950s, commercial aircraft firms had developed their own R&D facilities.

Significantly, NACA's strong suit was not only or even mostly basic research. Indeed, much of the basic research and inventing in aeronautics was done outside the United States, notably in Germany, immediately before and during World War II. Rather, NACA excelled in taking basic scientific ideas to a point at which "they could easily be applied by manufacturers."[22]

The Computer

The great technological strides made during the war convinced the military officers, scientists, and engineers involved that continuing support

18. Schlaifer and Heron, *Development of Aircraft Engines,* pp. 23, 24.

19. Ibid., p. 8. "Government intervention in technical details," he continued, "always led to very considerable delay, and often to a poorer product in the end."

20. Mowery and Rosenberg, "Commercial Aircraft Industry," p. 128.

21. Holley, *Buying Aircraft,* p. 23.

22. See "Statement Submitted by Dr. David R. H. Sawers, Princeton University, in *Economic Concentration,* Hearings before the Subcommittee on Antitrust and Monopoly, Senate Committee on the Judiciary, 89 Cong., 1 sess. (GPO, 1965), app. 7, pt. 3, p. 1505. Sawers goes on to argue that by 1945 "German designers had built or were testing nearly all the ideas" that were to be incorporated in American aircraft in the next twenty years. This research was mostly financed by the German government.

for research (albeit at more reasonable peacetime levels of expenditure) could pay great strategic, economic, and social dividends. The computer industry became a principal recipient of this support, and rapid progress in computing technology was directly linked to government-sponsored research projects.

Between 1945 and 1955 the U.S. government became the dominant (almost exclusive) force in computer development; all major computer technology projects in the United States were supported by government or military users or both. Between 1955 and 1965 the emergence and rapid growth of a commercial, business-oriented market for computers drastically reduced the government share of the overall marketplace. Government users still dominated in high-performance, large-scale scientific computers, however, and advanced technology projects paid for by the federal authorities accounted for much of the continued rapid technological advance.

From 1965 to 1975, as the commercial market matured, the emerging economics of competition in this technology-intensive industry dominated developments in the commercial marketplace. A shakeout occurred, and a few firms firmly entrenched in specific market niches survived. Entry into the competition in hardware was largely confined to firms specializing in new low-end applications (often based on minicomputers), and high-end, very large scale computers (supercomputers). The government played little direct role in the entry of the cheaper, low-end hardware producers, but a very direct and significant one in the supercomputer marketplace. The government's overall support of advances in technology generally declined, however, consistent with a broader pattern of reduced support for research caused by the financial burden of the Vietnam War. Federal support for computer R&D now focused on advanced, precommercial concepts and more exotic technologies, and on support for basic research.

From 1975 to the present, falling hardware costs have led to the emergence of the computer as an inexpensive, mass-produced good. Competition in the commercial marketplace has dominated the continued restructuring of the industry at home and abroad.

In the early years of the computer industry, the government's role in spurring technological development was so pervasive that its critical role in industrial and technological development is virtually self-evident.[23] But the tremendous growth in the commercial markets since the 1960s

---

23. A skeptical reader may wish to consult Kenneth Flamm, *Targeting the Computer*; and Flamm, *Creating the Computer: Government, Industry, and High Technology* (Brookings, 1988).

makes current government funding for R&D and procurement of computers now seem of minor proportions.

However, for experimental computer technology too visionary or too costly to be a sound private investment of scarce research dollars, federal support has continued to be crucial. As limits to advances in computer performance using tried-and-tested solutions became evident, the American government again took the lead in supporting research that explored parallel processing, exotic semiconductor materials, and optical and cryogenic components. A new generation of advanced computer products—sophisticated networks, systems based on concepts of artificial intelligence, high-performance graphics, reduced instruction set computer architectures—drawing on government-funded R&D of the 1970s and early 1980s has just begun to come to market. And a heavy new round of investment in advanced computer technology promises further returns.

Superconductors

The discovery in 1986 of new materials that transmit an electrical current without resistance at relatively high temperatures may prove to be the same sort of radical technological breakthrough in the 1990s that the computer proved to be in the 1950s. The transmission of power without loss through heat promises to revolutionize electrical generation and storage. Superconducting digital switches promise levels of circuit density and speed in electronic systems such as computers that would be impossible with conventional elements. Without the need to dissipate heat, magnets of unprecedented power and minimal weight and volume seem attainable. New types of sensors for all types of electromagnetic radiation seem possible by using such devices as Josephson junctions that could previously only function in temperatures maintained by liquid helium. The ability of the new materials to work at much higher temperatures with considerably smaller refrigeration costs, and the possibility that room-temperature operations might one day be feasible, have stirred much commercial interest.

The new materials build on a knowledge base formed by a long-term investment in the theory and application of condensed-matter physics. The phenomenon of superconductivity was discovered in the Netherlands at the beginning of this century.[24] European researchers—primarily in

---

24. This section draws heavily on Kenneth Flamm, "Government's Role in Computers

the Netherlands, Germany, Britain, and the Soviet Union—made significant advances in exploring the phenomenon in the 1930s. However, the materials used were low-temperature superconductors, requiring refrigeration using liquid helium at 4.2 degrees Kelvin (− 490 Farenheit) to exhibit their peculiar characteristics. Before World War II perhaps ten laboratories in the world (two in the Soviet Union) had mastered the exotic technologies required to liquify helium.

Even earlier, superconducting materials had been used in constructing ultrasensitive magnetometers. Germany and the United States invested significant resources in developing infrared detectors in the 1940s, but World War II ended before a production system saw action. Sensors for microwave radiation were also investigated in the 1940s. During the war reliable cryogenic refrigerators were developed and put into volume production. Liquid oxygen, which requires refrigeration to 90 degrees Kelvin, was routinely used in high-altitude fighters by the Allies.

Just after the war ended, about the same time as the new Office of Naval Research turned its attention to computers, cryogenics and superconductors were also placed on its research agenda. Within the first few years of its existence, the ONR had established and funded a major research program in low-temperature physics that was a significant influence in training scientific personnel. Most American workers in the field can trace their roots—or the antecedents of their professors or graduate research programs—to the ONR program.

By 1950 the first practical result of the ONR support—a vastly improved helium liquefier—transformed low-temperature physics into a much less difficult and demanding pursuit. This apparatus, the Collins cryostat, was the backbone of a highly productive low-temperature physics research program begun at the Bell Telephone Laboratories in 1953. In 1954 a team at Bell used this cryostat to push critical temperature for a superconducting niobium-tin alloy to a new high, 18 degrees Kelvin.

Progress in the theory of these new materials was also made during the 1950s, funded in part by Defense Department research contracts. John Bardeen, Leon N. Cooper, and John R. Schrieffer later received the Nobel prize for work supported in part by such a contract. A rash of studies followed in the late 1950s and early 1960s, many funded by the Defense Department, showing superconductivity in a variety of new

---

and Superconductors," prepared for the U.S. Congress, Office of Technology Assessment, under contract H36470, March 1988. See also U.S. Congress, Office of Technology Assessment, *Commercializing High-Temperature Superconductivity* (GPO, 1988).

materials. Perhaps the most remarkable aspect of this increased under-standing is the way in which the locus of technical advance moved from its prewar center in Europe to the United States. This had much to do with the migration of many European physicists to America and the research investments of the government (through the Defense Department in general and the ONR in particular) and the Bell Labs.[25]

Though public investment in superconductivity research had slowed before the discovery of high-temperature superconductors, the military services continued to fund significant efforts until diminishing returns appeared to set in. The major Defense funders were ONR; its sister organizations, the Air Force Office of Scientific Research and the Army Research Office; and the Defense Advanced Research Projects Agency (DARPA). On the civilian side the National Science Foundation (NSF) has been an important source of support since the 1970s, and the discovery in 1987 by Paul Chu at the University of Houston of a material that was superconducting at 95 degrees Kelvin was financed by a NSF research grant. DARPA's involvement with the basic research on mate-rials, in fact, is an excellent example of some of the problems that have made military support for long-term research less forthcoming in recent decades.

DARPA AND THE INTERDISCIPLINARY LABORATORIES. The Advanced Research Projects Agency (DARPA; the "D" for Defense was added in 1972) launched a major initiative into materials research, including superconductors, soon after its formation in 1959.[26] From 1960 to 1962 interdisciplinary laboratories were begun at twelve major American research universities. Funded at $15 million to $20 million annually, the laboratories were intended to strengthen American materials science at the universities. Though solid-state physics and metallurgy were among the interests supported by the laboratories, and superconductivity re-search was part of the program, the laboratories are best known for building American technical capacities in ceramics, composites, semi-conductor materials, laser components, and basic theory. By the mid-1960s their budget had doubled to nearly $30 million annually, and they increased the supply of faculty and post-doctoral researchers at the

25. Paul K. Hoch, "Migration and the Generation of New Scientific Ideas," *Minerva,* vol. 25 (Autumn 1987), pp. 215–17, 225–36.
26. The information in this paragraph and the next is drawn from Richard J. Barber Associates, *The Advanced Research Projects Agency, 1958–1974* (Alexandria, Va.: Defense Technical Information Center, 1975), pp. V-45–V-48, table VI-1.

universities by more than 50 percent, almost doubling the number of graduate students and research assistants.

In the mid-1960s the laboratories originated the concept of coupling with industry to transfer university expertise in basic research to help industry solve problems with defense-related materials. But the Defense Department believed the program was not oriented toward specific defense needs, and the funding pressures of the Vietnam War caused funding to be cut to $4 million in fiscal 1968, though it was to rise again to $15 million in 1969–70. The issue was clearly that too much unfocused research was being done and not enough development. At that point Congress passed the Mansfield amendment mandating that the Defense Department support only research directly related to defense needs. DOD used the amendment as the excuse to begin the process of reducing its investment in the centers.[27]

In fiscal 1972 the program was passed to the NSF, and the centers were renamed the Materials Research Laboratories. In 1973 and 1974 four new MRLs were started, and a fifth began in 1982. From 1977 to 1986, however, eight were terminated, leaving nine still in operation today. The link to current research is that the latest high-temperature superconductors are ceramics, and the processing techniques for these materials will undoubtedly draw heavily on the knowledge base built in these centers.

With the interdisciplinary laboratories gone, DARPA's Materials Office turned increasingly to more applied science. New materials for use in military applications were investigated, and some support was given to the Navy's Annapolis research laboratory, where a superconducting motor and generator propulsion system were being developed. While propulsion systems using high-temperature superconductors will undoubtedly build on the experience gained in this program, DARPA concluded in the mid-1970s that the field had reached a dead end and moved out of superconductivity research.

APPLICATIONS. In the late 1950s and early 1960s government agencies began to seek applications for low-temperature superconductors. The National Security Agency funded a program to develop superconducting switch elements, but devices that depended on relatively slow phase

---

27. The Mansfield amendment was clearly used to shut off projects in competition for scarce budgetary resources during the Vietnam War. An internal Defense study found that only 4 percent of DOD projects failed its definition of the Mansfield test (and none was in DARPA). Ibid., pp. VIII-20–VIII-21, VIII-59.

changes in superconducting materials were too slow to compete with the rapidly evolving semiconductor electronics, another discipline that greatly benefited from defense research investments. In 1962 a different and much faster mechanism usable in a superconducting switch was set out by Brian D. Josephson in a Nobel prize–winning paper. The NSA mounted a major effort to build prototype computer components using the Josephson effect at IBM in the mid-1970s, an effort that grew to about $20 million a year by 1981, with the agency paying a quarter of the cost. Continued advances in increasing speed and reducing power dissipation in semiconductor technology again doomed the effort, which was saddled with the additional difficulties of working at liquid helium temperatures, and the project was terminated in 1983.[28] But if a new project using the high-temperature materials is begun—which seems likely—it will build on research on the structure of devices and the manufacturing techniques learned in these earlier efforts.

In the 1960s the predecessors of the Energy Department began to develop magnets with extremely strong fields by using low-temperature superconducting materials. These turned out to be the first practical application of superconductivity, and were used in particle accelerators and detectors. Difficult manufacturing problems were solved and materials improved through collaboration between the energy research laboratories and private manufacturers. Today the major commercial application of superconductivity—medical magnetic resonance imaging—uses materials first developed for these earlier magnets. (The other, and much smaller, commercial application is Josephson-effect devices, which draw on technology for superconducting electronics developed at IBM and other organizations as part of the research effort of the 1970s.)

Thus in a pattern typical of the early development of computers and aircraft, the few early commercial applications of superconductivity drew directly on the first applications sponsored by the government. Unlike computers and aircraft, however, superconductors have not yet become a significant large-scale commercial industry.

THE LOGIC OF GOVERNMENT POLICY

Public support for investment in technological innovation stems from two very different motives. One of these—historically the major justifi-

---

28. Flamm, "Government's Role in Computers and Superconductors," pp. 50–51.

cation in the United States and the driving force behind investments in computers and aircraft—has been to develop superior technology for use in weapons. The second motive, the basis for the current intense interest in high-temperature superconductors, is that investment in technology can bring economic benefits to society exceeding the private return to those undertaking the investment. In these cases some sort of government subsidy or incentive may be called for as a matter of public policy.

The economic argument for public support of R&D was not articulated until the late 1950s, and such support has only recently gained wide acceptance in this country as a legitimate function of government. The rationale recognizes two main issues. Private firms may be unable to appropriate (that is, capture for their exclusive use) the benefits of certain types of investments in technology, particularly basic research. And imperfections in capital markets make very risky and costly projects less likely to be undertaken than might be beneficial from society's perspective. Projects that entail radical innovations (as opposed to incremental advances) suffer on both counts, because much of the uncertainty in defining new existing demands can be resolved only by actually developing and marketing a highly innovative good at great cost. Prospecting for profitable innovations on the technological frontier yields information about the nature of demand that is as easily grabbed by claim jumpers as by the risk-taker. Private firms have a considerable incentive to avoid hazarding their own capital in removing these uncertainties. Over time, government support has assumed its greatest role in the most basic research and the most radically innovative projects.

Government has generally played its most important part at the birth and in the infancy of new technology. In superconductors, aircraft, and computers, government programs (and the Bell Labatories, which might in the days before divestiture have best been thought of as a quasi-public source of research support) paid for virtually all the initial work— research, development, and perhaps most significantly the initial market sales. But as commercial products emerged in computers, for example, and commercial markets developed, the volume of commercial sales came to dwarf the government market.

Commercial sales are dominated by an R&D effort that is mainly focused on development, typically five times greater than spending on research performed in the computer industry, for example. Thus, even though government pays for perhaps 40 percent of computer-related research in the United States, and maybe 65 to 75 percent of basic research, its share of total computer R&D is only about 20 percent.[29]

It may be appropriate, then, to think of a life cycle in federal support for the development of a new technology. In the earliest days, when there are few trained people and little knowledge, and commercial products are merely a glimmer on some visionary's mental horizon, the government funds most of the research and buys the product. Private individuals would have to bear too much of the cost and risk and get too little of the return (because of imitation or hiring away trained people by others, for example) to make those first, very expensive investments.

But the resulting products can often be adapted at low cost into commercial products, and a new market carved out. After a self-sustaining commercial market has proved itself, private interests are perfectly willing to invest in development, where results take the form of incremental improvements and informal know-how that is more difficult for a competitor to steal. The return is more easily captured for the benefit of the investor risking his resources. In short, in the early, precommercial days of a new technology, government's role is often broad and pervasive. As the technology matures, private interests take over the job of refining the product and directing it toward the commercial niches that they know best.

Computers and aircraft are relatively mature technologies in the later stages of this life cycle. Superconductors are in the early stages. The closest thing to a commercial market for them is in medical instrumentation, and even here the products are still only a few small steps away from their roots in research magnets and sensors. Thus it is natural to expect government-sponsored research to be far more critical and pervasive in the near-term growth of commercial applications.

Our reading of the historical record also provides a corollary. The further from an established product or market a particular technology lies, the more likely an R&D investment will have inappropriable economic consequences or a scale and risk that might rationally motivate government involvement. Econometric studies also show that more basic research has greater social returns. The more mature the technology, the more tailored it is to a well-defined market, and the narrower and closer to product development the effort becomes, the less likely it is that the R&D performed is going to yield far-reaching technological benefits to

29. Flamm, *Targeting the Computer,* pp. 101–05.

the nation. Because significant economic benefits spilling beyond the organization undertaking the project are less likely, the economic rationale for public support is weaker, and (in the cases we know) the role of government in moving the technology forward becomes less critical. Since the broad outlines of the last four decades of American high technology are consistent with this cycle, it is all the more remarkable that one of the key architects of postwar U.S. science policy articulated much of the argument back in the 1940s, when the first great debates over American technology policy occurred.

Dr. Vannevar Bush served as czar over much of the unprecedented wartime R&D effort in the United States. In his capacity as head of the Office of Scientific Research and Development, Bush drew on an extensive background as a practicing engineer and scientist, professor and dean of engineering at the Massachusetts Institute of Technology, consultant to industry and government, and a key participant in the flowering of modern industrial research within corporate America in the 1930s. Though he was a firm believer in the value of markets in directing resources, Bush was an equally stubborn believer that private efforts alone could not produce the research base required by the new industrial technology. When basic research competed for scarce research dollars in a corporation, Bush argued, it would inevitably be cut back in favor of product and process development.[30] Bush's law paralleled the argument outlined above (which was not to be articulated in its modern economic form until 1959) that a private company could less easily capture the benefits of basic research effort than it could the benefits of product development.[31]

To protect basic research from open competition with development efforts, Bush proposed creating a national research foundation to insulate

30. "Applied research and development differs in several important respects from pure science. Since the objective can often be definitely mapped out beforehand, the work lends itself to organized effort. If successful, the results of applied research are of a definitely practical or commercial value. The very heavy expenses of such work are, therefore, undertaken by private organizations only in the hope of ultimately recovering the funds invested. . . . The distinction between applied and pure research is not a hard and fast one, and industrial scientists may tackle specific problems from broad fundamental viewpoints. But it is important to emphasize that there is a perverse law governing research: under the pressure for immediate results, and unless deliberate policies are set up to guard against this, *applied research invariably drives out pure.*" See Vannevar Bush, *Science: The Endless Frontier,* A Report to the President on a Program for Postwar Scientific Research (GPO, 1945), p. 77.

31. See Richard R. Nelson, "The Simple Economics of Basic Scientific Research," *Journal of Political Economy,* vol. 67 (June 1959), pp. 297–306.

investments in basic research from the pressures of profitability.[32] Today's National Science Foundation, with its elaborate systems of peer review oriented toward pure intellectual merit and away from economic or commercial return, is the modern legacy of Bush's vision.

Although Bush did not make the point, his law may apply to much technology spending in the public sector as well. In such "mission" agencies as Defense or Energy or NASA, stringent budgets have typically meant cutting back on longer-term, more speculative research in favor of delivering the functioning systems that commanders, or department heads, or mission specialists are clamoring for. The projects most distant from clear or immediate missions are sacrificed—and this too means development is favored over research.

Even within the NSF, the growing awareness and importance of economic "competitiveness" in the 1980s have skewed the budget increasingly toward applications and engineering. The relative share of its traditional grants to individuals for basic research projects has steadily declined in recent years.[33]

If the private sector can be counted on to fund more applied research and development, then, and the public sector has designed institutions such as the NSF and the National Institutes of Health to insulate basic research from the pressures of funding competition, is there yet another significant need that goes undefined? We believe so.[34]

Between the very basic and the very applied lies an ill-defined but critical no man's land in which basic science is first translated into practical new concepts for products and processes. Although the eventual link to commercial returns may be more visible than it was at the basic research stage, the same concerns apply: inexpensive imitation by competitors and the scale and risks required in proving new ideas can lead to the same sort of underinvestment that motivates society to supplement private support for more basic research.

In the American system of R&D, in which basic research is performed mainly in universities and applications and development mainly in private corporations, this middle ground between idea and product is also where linkages between distinct participants, particularly academia and the private sector, are required. Mechanisms for translating the basic research

32. See Bush, *Science*, p. 17.

33. National Science Foundation, *Report on Funding Trends and Balance of Activities: National Science Foundation, 1951–1988*, NSF 88-3 (GPO, 1987), p. 8.

34. Arguments of the sort that follow have been made in Flamm, *Targeting the Computer*, pp. 180–84, and Martin Neil Bailey and Alok K. Chakrabarti, *Innovation and the Productivity Crisis* (Brookings, 1988), pp. 113–18.

of universities into new products developed by our corporations are clearly at the root of current concerns over our ability to translate what is widely perceived to be the world's best system of support for basic science into competitive and timely commercial innovations.[35]

This middle-ground research, where relatively costly investments in developing and proving practical new concepts are made, constitutes the current challenge to public policy. It is here that huge investments were required to convert the theory of computing machines developed in the 1930s into the first working behemoths of the 1950s. This middle ground was where the government poured resources into translating the deepening understanding of aerodynamics, structures, and materials into functioning prototypes of superior flying machines in the decades after the 1920s. This is the middle ground where engineers and scientists currently worry that foreign competitors are poised to pluck basic research on high-temperature superconductors and rush to market with new products.

Yet these are relatively recent preoccupations. Why does a system that seemed to work so well in the 1950s and 1960s now need restructuring? What has changed that makes our traditional reliance on the technologies developed for military systems less effective in pushing the civilian industrial technology base forward?

CHANGING CIRCUMSTANCES OF MILITARY AND COMMERCIAL R&D

Two changes make the institutions we developed during and after the Second World War less reliable today. One is external: the development of significant technical capacity and challenge by foreign competitors. The other is internal: an increasing divergence in the objectives of military and commercial technology and the decreasing commercial and military returns of investments in defense technology.

International Competition

New technology has raised the American standard of living in three distinctive ways. First, because it has helped our national stock of

35. For example, see Council on Competitiveness, *Picking Up the Pace: The Commercial Challenge to American Innovation* (Washington, D.C., 1988).

resources—people, land, minerals, and capital—produce more and better products than before, it has directly improved our economic welfare.

Second, in an international economy, if Americans "own" a new technology, they can charge foreigners through direct sales of the rights to its use, or indirectly by setting up factories overseas to build products embodying the new technology, or by exporting the products directly and building into the price a premium reflecting the superiority of the good. Such "technological rents," may be a significant component of U.S. national income beyond gains experienced by Americans consuming American goods.[36] Many economists studying the huge increase in American direct foreign investment in the 1950s and 1960s, for example, believe that superior American technology gave U.S. firms the edge required to overcome their natural handicaps in foreign markets and make attractive profits. The handsome returns on these investments contributed to the high U.S. standard of living.

Third, new technology may improve U.S. living standards by lowering the price and improving the performance of imports. Even if foreign suppliers earn a technological rent on their sales to the United States, as long as some of the improvement is passed on to consumers, Americans still gain.

The first and third routes to improved standards of living do not necessarily cost Americans anything. Individuals, firms, and countries invest in creating new technology because they believe that if their investments are successful, they will for a time be able to earn technological rents that will justify research and development investments and a continuing investment in innovation. Typically, however, technological innovation has a way of diffusing. Eventually, when the technology is freely available, one can no longer charge for its use or charge a premium for a product that uses it. The window for collecting technological rent has effectively closed.

So if the United States is willing to wait for the technological developments of other nations to diffuse, or is willing to settle for whatever part of the benefits of innovation is not subtracted by technological rents in imports from abroad, Americans can effectively gain something for nothing. Certainly many foreign competitors have benefited

---

36. Technological rents can also be collected by American firms in sales of high-technology goods to American consumers, but from the perspective of the nation as a whole this is merely a transfer of income from one group of Americans to another.

from eating the crumbs at the U.S. technology table as they caught up relatively cheaply.

But is waiting a sensible U.S. strategy in a new epoch of intense international competition? For one thing, it means losing out on significant economic returns that can only be gained by investing in technology. Without investment, there is no ownership and control during the window for technological rents. America would be giving up rents that could have been earned, and this country certainly has the human and technical resources that give it a comparative advantage in such investment. Furthermore, America would be losing the potential improvement in productivity that the technology would bring to the use of national resources. Finally, if everyone tried to act as a free rider, global investments in technology would fall, and all would be worse off.

An important part of America's leadership in the global economy in the past four decades has been its willingness to invest in such international "public goods" as technological innovation (especially basic research), even when it realized that significant returns would be captured by others. Once, this mattered less because U.S. firms captured the lion's share of the returns on the least appropriable investments. Today it matters more because others are in a better position to capitalize on U.S. research investments. Of course, America might be content just to continue to invest in the basic science, even if U.S. firms do none of the commercialization and earn no private returns. It is still an investment yielding positive social benefits, since imported cars and computers make lives better. But again, this would mean sacrificing potential technological rents and tolerating lower productivity as Americans waited for the technology they helped build to drift to these shores. This strategy may be better than receiving no technological innovation, but Americans would be far from enjoying the standard of living they could have. And, though impossible to prove, some involvement in creating new technologies is needed to effectively master their use.

Concern for national security means that the United States will be involved in high technology whether or not it chooses to capitalize on potential economic benefits of that technology. Given that reality, not to take steps to maximize those benefits seems foolish.

The picture is further complicated by the fixed, sunk-cost nature of expenditures on research and development. The costs of developing a new product are not much affected by the scale on which the product is later produced. So volume of sales and size of market can greatly affect the average cost of producing a technology-intensive product: the largest producer may well have the lowest costs.

The economies of scale inherent in the use of technology have made high-technology industries unswervingly international in focus: a significant foreign market can greatly increase the rate of return on relatively fixed R&D investments. In one sample about one-third of the return to private investments in industrial technology was earned in foreign markets.[37] In computers, perhaps 40 to 50 percent of sales and profits are earned from sales abroad.

Thus in the 1970s, when foreign competitors began to achieve technological parity with American firms in such key areas as semiconductors, ceramics, metal alloys, machine tools, and robotics, and sometimes pulled ahead, the situation was particularly galling. For the first time since the end of the war, American firms faced foreign competitors seeking the same technological rents in international markets and sometimes managing to be the first to capture private returns on new technologies. Often the new products and processes capitalized on basic science originating in the United States.

In a less competitive world it did not really matter whether U.S. investments in R&D were made at minimum cost to achieve maximum results. Effective overseas rivals were few, and returns, where and when they materialized, were invariably captured by American firms. Today, however, speed and timing are everything. Lean and hungry foreign competitors have proved their ability to develop and market technologically innovative products. If institutions are not designed to ensure that American R&D investments are effective, efficient, and quickly translatable into technological rents earned by American firms, those returns will be siphoned off into foreign pockets and diminish the ability to sustain the technological base on which American industry depends.

Furthermore, the increasingly pervasive role of high technology in the American economy raises worrisome new concerns. An argument for "strategic" investments in technology to preserve a viable American industry in critical areas threatened by foreign competitors has been given force by the current plight of the American semiconductor industry.

In a world of perfect competition, of course, economic arguments for supporting a strategic industry make little sense. If foreign competitors can produce more cheaply, why shouldn't America take advantage of its comparative edge, purchase the product from them, and shift its resources to industries in which it does have an advantage?

---

37. Specifically, 29 percent in the chemical industry and 34 percent in other industries. See Edwin Mansfield and others, *Technology Transfer, Productivity, and Economic Policy* (Norton, 1982), pp. 50–52.

High-technology industries, however, are clearly not places to look for perfect competition. If a foreign producer has a monopoly on an advanced technical process or product, industries that use it and that might otherwise be competitive may find themselves at a disadvantage. The foreign producer will generally maximize profit by entering the user industry and thus has the incentive to squeeze out American firms there.[38] Monopoly control also gives him the means.

Until recently, this seemed like a very academic and abstract argument. But the operation of the Semiconductor Trade Agreement, signed by the United States and Japan in 1986, has given it force. One Japanese response to the pact was to form a de facto production cartel for dynamic random access memories (DRAMs), a cartel whose effectiveness was made possible because Japanese producers controlled an overwhelming percentage of DRAM sales in the open market. Restrictions on production and investment helped drive up the price of a key commodity used by a highly important and competitive U.S. computer industry and cost the American economy billions of dollars. It also enabled Japanese producers of semiconductors, who themselves manufacture computers, to make rapid inroads into the American market with lower prices.[39] What seemed a textbook curiosity has become the focus of an industry crisis.

The point is that high-technology products have become so pervasive and essential an element of the U.S. economy that access to them at reasonable and stable prices is every bit as important as access to, say, oil. Maintaining national technical capacity in such areas may be a form of anticartel insurance, a guard against predation by foreign monopolists every bit as sensible as the development of alternative energy sources.

These issues were of little concern in the United States during the first two postwar decades. They have since become vitally important as technical competitors have risen to absorb rents generated by new technologies, even to control access to the new technologies themselves. The need for efficiency in technology investment is obvious. The question is whether that efficiency can be provided by the nation's traditional, defense-oriented approach to technology investment.

---

38. This was first shown by John M. Vernon and Daniel A. Graham, "Profitability of Monopolization by Vertical Integration," *Journal of Political Economy,* vol. 79 (July–August 1971), pp. 924–25.

39. One study estimated that the Japanese market share in U.S. personal computer stores jumped by 50 percent between the first quarters of 1987 and 1988. See Steven Burke, "U.S. PC Firms Suffer as Japan Reigns Supreme in Memory-Chip Market," *PC Week,* June 7, 1988, p. 166.

The Military Procurement Muddle

Unfortunately, as the world economy has become more competitive and less tolerant of inefficiency, military R&D has lost many of the characteristics that once helped generate commercial returns. It has lost them largely because it never consciously sought to establish them in the first place. Much of what was good about U.S. military R&D during and just after World War II, especially the way it generated commercial returns, was the product of crisis. During World War II itself, R&D was handled as the nation generally handled war, by mobilizing the scientific community, funding the effort at an extremely high level, and relaxing political accountability to "get the job done." During the 1950s military R&D retained much of this wartime urgency, especially after the bomber gap scare of 1956 and the Soviet launching of Sputnik late in 1957. Thus this decade too was characterized by fiscal and political largesse. In any case, large-scale military R&D *in peacetime* was novel; although the military services had some institutions in place to handle it, Congress and the newly created Defense Department did not. Novelty and urgency together thus left the military R&D effort relatively free from intrusive political oversight.

As this novelty and urgency have passed, politicians have sought to bring military procurement, and with it military R&D, under greater control. The drive has been legitimate and understandable: legitimate because military procurement uses public money to create a public good called national defense, and understandable because weapons acquisition in the 1950s was marked by rampant interservice rivalry and a lack of coherent strategic direction. But the disciplining effort has imposed on military R&D a set of political incentives and an encrusted organizational structure that are relatively insensitive to the increasingly complicated technological undertaking that forms the core of the acquisition process. This has had unfortunate consequences for the quality of U.S. military R&D generally and more specifically for its usefulness in generating commercial returns.

SHORT-TERM PERSPECTIVES. Congress is charged with "providing for the common defense," and as the common defense came increasingly to depend on R&D and procurement, Congress moved to control them. In 1955 only the defense subcommittees of the House and Senate Appropriations Committees routinely reviewed military R&D budgets. In 1959 the Armed Services Committees acquired responsibilities for authorizing the procurement of some kinds of weapons, but given the small size of its staff, no one expected the Senate Armed Services Committee to oversee R&D.[40] In 1962 the committees acquired precisely this authority, and by the end of the decade subcommittees were examining every corner of the R&D budget.[41] Today program managers for the military's R&D projects spend substantial time testifying on Capitol Hill, briefing the staffs of individual members of Congress, or responding to congressional inquiries.

Although the growing intrusion of American political processes into the oversight of military R&D followed legitimately from the enormous and sustained increase in this component of the federal budget since the early 1950s, Congress has also been pulled in more deeply by the consistently unsatisfactory way the Defense Department establishes program budgets.[42] Deeply institutionalized incentives encourage both industry and military program managers to be optimistic in the early stages of development.[43] Thus long-range budget planning documents, the five-year defense plans, consistently underestimate future program costs, producing the so-called bow wave of escalating procurement costs. Escalating costs force military planners into an often frenetic annual effort to revise their five-year plans, which essentially become annual planning documents. The need for annual reallocation of insufficient funding would itself require legislative action. But from the congressional point of view the Defense Department seems always to mismanage its

40. Raymond H. Dawson, "Congressional Innovation and Intervention in Defense Policy: Legislative Authorization of Weapons Systems," *American Political Science Review,* vol. 56 (March 1962), p. 53.

41. See Andrew Mayer, *The Authorization Process: A Brief History of Authorizing Legislation, with Particular Reference to Its Use by the Armed Services Committees* (Congressional Research Service, 1976), pp. 23–25.

42. Although historically the Armed Services Committees had attended principally to military construction and basing, by the end of the 1950s members had recognized that politically important allocations had moved elsewhere in the defense budget, and the committees shifted focus accordingly. The procurement budget was of course considerably larger than the R&D budget, but most of the important weapons choices were made during the development stage of a new project. Hence the concern for procurement inevitably led to concern for R&D. Prodding the committees was competition among congressional committees and individual members of Congress. Control over defense funds is power; congressional gaming for control has ultimately helped produce a more complicated budget system.

43. See, for example, Merton J. Peck and Frederic M. Scherer, *The Weapons Acquisition Process: An Economic Analysis* (Harvard University Graduate School of Business Administration, 1962), pp. 412–24. For a more recent statement, see Blue Ribbon Commission on Defense Management, *A Quest for Excellence: Final Report to the President* (GPO, 1986), pp. 45–46.

budget, not to mention individual programs whose costs seem forever on the rise. Thus the department needs help, and members of Congress are usually happy to provide it.

What they provide as well, unfortunately, is a short-term perspective that makes sense politically but is anathema to the needs of creative R&D. Congress was relatively generous with military R&D in the 1950s, funding multiple projects and alternative technical approaches to especially risky ventures. Not all duplication was planned in an orderly fashion; some of it was the result of fierce and largely uncontrolled interservice rivalry. Still, congressional generosity created an environment in which developers could explore uncertainties and cope productively with the surprises that so often mark good R&D. And duplication, even some spawned by interservice rivalry, often provided developers and policymakers alike with useful hedges against failure in risky weapons programs.

By the end of the decade, however, most members of Congress had begun to see multiple projects as wasteful duplication, befitting their tendency to justify every dollar spent for its short-term benefit. Thence began a shift away from funding multiple approaches to technical problems in developing weapons and toward the use of analysis to select a single "best" approach. In the early 1960s Robert S. McNamara carried the efficiency drive farthest by seeking not only to eliminate most vestiges of interservice rivalry but also to enforce cooperation where requirements seemed compatible.[44] Within projects, meanwhile, the duplicative work on components and subsystems that had been commonplace in the 1950s was replaced by extended study leading to firm choices imbedded in the elaborate detail of "total package" contracts. To be sure, extended study often proved to be an inadequate guide to the technical challenges posed by sophisticated systems and components.[45] Yet reforms like the Packard Initiatives, inaugurated in 1969 to foster more prototyping of alternative technologies, often fell victim to the

44. Such, for example, was the rationale for the F-111 project, which was intended to fill the Air Force's need for a new fighter bomber and the Navy's need for a new fleet interceptor. Robert F. Coulam, *Illusions of Choice: The F-111 and the Problem of Weapons Acquisition Reform* (Princeton University Press, 1977), esp. chap. 4 and pp. 128–29.

45. The Air Force spent $1 billion, for example, to develop the F-111's Mark II radar, only to prove that original performance specifications could not be met. At much greater cost the aircraft itself was proved to fall short of the full range of expectations written into the original contract. Coulam, *Illusions of Choice*, pp. 128–30; and Allen D. Lee, *A Strategy to Improve the Early Production Phase in Air Force Acquisition Programs*, P-6941-RGI (Santa Monica: Rand Corporation, 1983), pp. 99–101.

search to eliminate wasteful duplication. "The shift from prototype test to analysis as a basis for major management decisions," a Rand Corporation report noted in 1981, "has been almost total."[46]

Obviously, there is nothing wrong with thinking hard at the start of a new project; certainly some of the inefficiencies of the 1950s acquisition process could have been curbed with such extra thought. But it is not clear that all technological uncertainties can be resolved by analysis; indeed, the distinguishing characteristic of R&D is precisely the tendency for problems and breakthroughs to appear by surprise. What is clear is that the rich and varied menu of technologies that reached reasonably advanced development in the 1950s has since been narrowed considerably. Fewer technologies are now being brought to the preproduct stage that proved so important in producing commercial returns in the aircraft and computer industries, and proportionately more investment is going into development.

SOCIALIZATION OF DESIGN. Another perverse consequence of the effort to discipline weapons acquisition has been the absorption of decision-making for technical matters into an increasingly complicated Pentagon bureaucracy. The antipathy to wasteful duplication and interservice rivalry helped produce the Defense Reorganization Act of 1958, which among other things enlarged and strengthened an additional layer of defense organizations housed in the Office of the Secretary of Defense (OSD). The effort has continued. The Defense Acquisition Improvement Act of 1986, for example, created an undersecretary of defense for acquisition, whom members of Congress often refer to as the acquisition czar. Yet the reorganization neither eliminated nor redefined the duties of the deputy secretary of defense, who formerly handled acquisition and retains the charter to do so. And in bringing the Office of the Joint Chiefs of Staff and the nation's regional commanders more fully into decisionmaking, the reorganization gave still more agencies an official say in directing military R&D.

Nor has Congress reorganized itself *out* of the acquisition process. The growth of staffs has only added to the pervasiveness of congressional

---

46. G. K. Smith and others, *The Use of Prototypes in Weapon System Development*, R-2345-AF (Rand Corporation, 1981), p. 2. Symptomatic of the shift toward analysis has been the marked growth in the length of the "concept formulation" phase of most system development projects. G. K. Smith and E. T. Friedmann, *An Analysis on Weapon System Acquisition Intervals, Past and Present*, R-2605-DR&E/AF (Rand Corporation, 1980), pp. v–vi, 38–39.

oversight. And the interaction between the Pentagon bureaucracy and congressional staffs has created the potential for lobbying by Defense Department agencies as well as defense firms, making it difficult indeed for the acquisition czar or the secretary of defense to fully centralize control over weapons acquisition.

Military program managers who must report frequently to Congress, their own service staffs, and various agencies in OSD at least annually are in no position to leave the defense firms working for them much freedom to make design choices. Rather, they face what the Packard Commission referred to as a "sea of advocates" in the Defense Department, all anxious to see their ideas reflected in ongoing R&D projects. Requirements for new systems, once relatively brief and oriented toward performance, are now long and detailed lists achieved by extensive interagency negotiation. Once written, they are difficult to violate. Thus program managers have a pronounced tendency to sacrifice cost and schedule to meet original performance requirements.[47]

The management of military R&D has, then, become increasingly politicized. At the very least this means that military R&D is likely to move more slowly today than its commercial counterpart. More important, design choices lie in the hands of an elaborate government bureaucracy, which makes R&D management too inflexible. Industrialists are less in charge now, and thus are less likely to be able to move new technologies rapidly into commercial production.

THE MATURATION OF DEFENSE TECHNOLOGIES. Most of the technologies under development in the 1950s—jet engines, supersonic airframes, rockets, computers, and electronics components generally—involved relatively new and unexplored technologies. Developmental risks were quite high, but so was the promise of improved performance and decreasing costs. In the metaphor often used to describe technological evolution, these technologies generally lay on the rapidly rising slope of the S curve.

This is precisely the phase in the technological life cycle when government support is both necessary and most productive, and the military's freewheeling approach to technology development was more or less appropriate to this phase in the cycle. Given in addition the deep involvement of industry's engineers and designers in the work carried

47. For evidence on this point see Edmund Dews and others, *Acquisition Policy Effectiveness: Department of Defense Experience in the 1970s*, R-2516-DR&E (Rand Corporation, 1979), pp. 25–27.

out during this period, it is not surprising that there was a substantial spillover from the defense effort into commercial high-technology enterprise.

The technologies under development in the 1950s remain at the core of the nation's force posture to this day. For the most part, however, they are now mature technologies, well up toward the "flat" of the S curve. As development has become increasingly a matter of refining and perfecting basic technologies, military and commercial designs have diverged; the Air Force's F-100 jet engine, with its high fuel consumption and capacity to rush quickly from idle to full throttle in response to the needs of air combat, has little in common with commercial jet engines, which are designed for low fuel consumption and very steady throttle play. Advances in engine components may of course still spill over into commercial developments. In comparison to the 1950s experience, however, a larger share of defense R&D funding for jet engines and other mature military technologies is now of little use to commercial firms.

RAIDING BASIC RESEARCH. Managerial inflexibility and short-term perspectives are more evident in development than in basic research. Research is a separate enterprise, often carried out by different organizations that face incentives and strictures different from those operating on managers of development projects. Thus defense research spending might arguably still produce commercial spin-offs despite problems in the way the Defense Department handles system and component development.

But what this argument ignores is that commercial returns from defense spending were never wholly or even mostly the result of spending on basic research; indeed, an important force behind the commercialization of defense technologies was defense investment in new applications and the provision of an early market. Equally important, this argument ignores the extent to which the instability built into procurement budgeting makes the defense budget an unreliable source of funding for research. Because procurement costs continue to rise and because Congress is no more anxious than the services to cancel weapons projects, project schedules are usually stretched to lower their annual cost while other parts of the defense budget are raided to fund them. Although the most visible target for such raids has been the "operations and support" line of the defense budget, funding for basic and applied research is equally vulnerable.

That funding for research has tended to rise and fall disproportionately in relation to the Pentagon's overall R&D budget (see figure 5-1) suggests that raiding is more likely when budgets are shrinking.[48] But even this may not reflect the entire reality. In particular, money appropriated for research may in fact be used to fund project-related development. The same pressure would also appear to operate in the industry, where the character of so-called independent R&D spending has changed over time: "The main criterion for reimbursement used to be the innovativeness of the work; today the controlling question is apt to be whether industry's R&D is sufficiently related to an ongoing weapons program."[49]

The diminished commercial returns to defense R&D may reflect a recent trend toward spending relatively less on research, even in times of rising budgets. In figure 5-1, for example, funding for research did not rise proportionately with the pronounced increase in R&D funding initiated by the Reagan administration. The contrast with 1958–66 is especially stark. Among other things, the contrast reflects different management styles in the Defense Department. Robert S. McNamara wielded considerable control over the budget and insisted on substantial funding of basic research; Casper W. Weinberger left the services free to manage their own budgets, and they chose to emphasize projects rather than research.

At bottom, the bow wave is symptomatic of fundamental instability in the way the Defense Department budgets for weapons acquisition, R&D in particular. Project costs are habitually underestimated at their start, later forcing the services to scramble for money from whatever spending category can be raided. The most obvious source of project funding is readiness; another is research. If the nation needs a stable effort to develop its technology base, the defense budget is not the place to lodge the effort.

---

48. For a discussion, see U.S. Congress, Office of Technology Assessment, *The Defense Technology Base, Introduction and Overview: A Special Report*, OTA-ISC-374 (GPO, 1988), p. 5. Although raiding pressures are understandably at their worst when defense budgets are shrinking, recent work by the Congressional Budget Office shows that even during the height of the Reagan-era defense spending surge the Defense Department was unable to fund many of its programs adequately. This suggests that the bow wave is large indeed and that pressures to raid technology base funds for project support are likely to operate even when defense budgets are increasing. U.S. Congress, Congressional Budget Office, *Effects of Weapons Procurement Stretch-Outs on Costs and Schedules* (CBO, 1987), pp. 9–16.

49. Commission on Integrated Long-Term Strategy, *Discriminate Deterrence* (GPO, 1988), p. 46.

Figure 5-1. *Defense Department R&D Obligations, 1956–87*
1982 dollars

Index, 1972 = 100

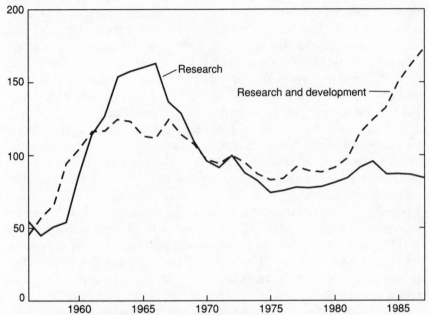

Sources: National Science Foundation, *Federal Funds for Research and Development: Detailed Historical Tables,
Fiscal Years 1955–1986* (NSF, n.d.), pp. 3–18, 21–36, and *National Patterns of Science and Technology Resources,
1987*, NSF 88-305 (GPO, 1988), pp. 53–55. GNP deflators are from *Economic Report of the President, February 1988*,
p. 25.

NEW STRATEGIES FOR INVESTMENT

If defense R&D spending is now less apt to produce useful commercial
returns, one way to revive commercial competitiveness would be to go
back to the freewheeling, throw-money-at-it response of the 1950s.
Political circumstances are not likely to permit such a reversion, however.
Bureaucratization and political oversight have been growing, while
reforms that run against these trends have failed. Even if reversion were
politically possible, however, it would be neither technically nor finan-
cially desirable. Military technologies and the force posture they support
have reached a maturity that calls for a new managerial approach tailored
to the needs of national defense. This leaves commercial R&D where it
belongs—on its own, deserving public support that entails managerial
strategies tailored to commercial needs.

A New Approach to Military R&D

The stakes involved in further developing a mature technology can be both higher and lower than they are for a new technology. They can be higher because developers can spend a great deal of money for marginal improvements in performance, and because mistakes can be costly. Holding out for another thousand pounds of thrust from a jet engine can push unit costs up far more than the improved performance is worth.[50] The stakes can be lower because no revolutionary breakthrough is likely to catapult one's adversary far ahead of one's own capabilities. Indeed, at some point it makes no sense to seek to maintain a technological advantage in mature technologies. What does make sense is to stabilize development while seeking advantage in a newer technology.

If progress is slower and more predictable in mature technologies, development need not be rushed. And if both mistakes and innovations are likely to be costly, development should not be rushed. These arguments become even more powerful when design complexity is considered. Modern systems present technical integration problems many times more difficult than the relatively simple weapons of the 1950s. Designers need freedom and flexibility near the end of the design cycle, when pieces of the system must be fitted together, as well as at its beginning. Artificially compressing the design process for complex weapon systems leads to costly retrofits or performance problems.

A final reason to adopt more judicious development is that integrating a new weapon into an existing force configuration disrupts operational routines as both line users and support organizations struggle to adapt to new technologies and capabilities. Conversely, the established complexity of the force will affect the new weapon as users encounter design problems and suggest useful changes. These interactions have become more wide-ranging and unpredictable as U.S. forces have grown more complex. Developers and military users alike thus confront an increasingly complicated force integration problem that demands time, patience, and care.

In developing new weapon systems, the military services still adopt a

50. Analysts at the Rand Corporation concluded from their study of technological change in tactical aircraft, for example, that it "has become increasingly difficult to sustain the rates of technological improvement that we have grown accustomed to in the past." William L. Stanley and Michael D. Miller, *Measuring Technological Change in Jet Fighter Aircraft*, R-2249-AF (Rand Corporation, 1979), pp. 44, 47.

crisis approach more appropriate to the 1950s. They rush systems into production and deployment on the basis of scant test data, almost guaranteeing that some development work will have to be retrofitted into production systems. This practice also ensures force disruptions and increases the cost of responding to design changes. The resulting costs are at least partly recognized, but they are accepted as the only way to remain technologically ahead of the Soviet Union. Indeed, there is widespread pressure to shorten rather than to lengthen the time required to develop new systems: "We forfeit our five-year technological lead by the time it takes us to get our technology from the laboratory into the field."[51]

In such cases the political system, in concert with the military services, moves precisely in the opposite direction from that required. In a sense, Congress and the military are operating on two premises—that shiny new hardware in the field equals effective military force and that moving quickly to full production is the best way to capture economies of scale. But new hardware will produce effective combat power only after design flaws have been addressed and forces learn to use it. And whatever savings accrue in the move to full production must be balanced against the costs of retrofitting design changes to systems in the field. The nation's security would benefit from slowing down the cycle of weapons replacement, allowing time for operational testing and design evaluation to sort out possible force integration problems before full production begins.

This recommendation sounds counterintuitive for a nation anxious to exploit its advantage in military technology. It is also out of keeping with the practice of commercial high-technology firms, which rush new products to the market in order to exploit an early technological lead, and thereafter improve the product as technological evolution and the market dictate. But the recommendation applies principally to weapon systems. The Soviets take as long to develop these as the United States, suggesting that slowing the process will not substantially threaten the U.S. lead. In any case, major system components have now matured, and the nation's technological lead rests on subsystems using new, fast-moving technologies. It is these, rather than the system as a whole, that should be modernized quickly to retain the nation's technological lead.

Yet even here commercial practice remains a poor model for the military. The military "market" is a large force resting on a complex logistics structure; modernizing even at the subsystem level is thus an

_____

51. Blue Ribbon Commission, *Quest for Excellence,* p. 47.

immensely more costly and complicated process for the Defense Department than it is for most businesses. Additionally, the military's market test is not everyday use but war. If war is not very likely, it makes little sense to buy a new, high-technology component in quantity, since technological change will quickly make the component obsolete. Conversely, if war is likely, the organizational perturbation that often comes with wholesale modernization may actually undermine force effectiveness. In many cases it makes more sense to test new devices in a small portion of the force until they have matured somewhat, are better understood, and are changing less rapidly than to engage repeatedly and at great cost in modernizing the entire force.

Impediments to this kind of reform spring less from some enemy threat than from political and financial pressures in the U.S. acquisition process. From the earliest phases of the cold war, the rush to production has been a useful way to generate political support for a system and thus ensure its production. This suits industry as well as the military services because industry's profits have traditionally come from production more than R&D. Indeed, given the congenital optimism that marks the early stages of weapons development, defense firms usually have to fight to make profits on R&D, often accepting less than what they regard as adequate. Thus to remove some of this pressure to rush new weapons into production, the U.S. system must more fully separate design from production and provide an adequate reward for each.

Slowing the system design process will produce the desired results, however, only if designers have the flexibility to respond to problems. Thus in addition to separating design more fully from production, the design process itself must be relieved of the bureaucratic encrustation that has overtaken program management. There is no easy way to do this; much of the bureaucracy has resulted from the natural workings of the American political process. One approach, however, would be to use competition more extensively in developing near-production-ready weapons that can be operationally tested and modified in a competitive environment. This would satisfy political demands for accountability—competition is normally the only politically acceptable alternative for congressional oversight—while providing the political system with choices from among reasonably complete weapons. The divisive politics of weapons procurement would be focused on production choices rather than on the design process.

Of course, producing competing systems of this level of maturity smacks of wasteful duplication; indeed, it runs counter to the short-term perspective that dominates the nation's political process. But if the nation is to face the problems of the next decade squarely, even politicians will have to recognize the high price paid for the current approach to military R&D. Quality weapons—quality R&D—cannot be had on the cheap; that would be false economy. To pay more up front is to put R&D funds where they will do the most good.

Significantly, lengthening the design process could also create more reasonable choices among candidates for production. As William Kaufmann's chapter shows, this may be the only way the nation can meet its security commitments in what promises to be an era of stable or declining budgets. Reforming the way America buys weapons is thus linked directly with broader reforms in the way the nation's force posture is shaped.

A Strategy for the Industrial Technology Base

If military R&D on mature technologies is less productive commercially, and if more international competition requires more efficiency and speed in commercially relevant development, how ought the nation respond? The desirable elements of a new policy are highly debatable— there is, after all, no single provably correct answer, derivable from either theory or history, as to the best organization of public support for the technology base of the economy. America should probably look at this as an area for enlightened experiment, should take what seem to be useful ideas, develop them in different ways on a small scale, and find the ones that seem to work best in the context of its economic and political institutions. We can then steer a pragmatic course, building on successes and discarding failures. While definitive guidelines for policy cannot be provided, there are some useful directions for navigating the high-technology economy of the next century.

A LEGITIMATE INTEREST OF GOVERNMENT. America must first recognize that supporting, facilitating, and organizing investments in precommercial technology—both basic science and middle-ground research—is an important function of government. The debate ought to be how best to organize this investment to build the most advanced industrial economy in the world. If building a commercial technology base is crucial, we ought not be burdened by the need to devise elaborate ruses and stratagems so that other missions of government can be teased and stretched to provide the funds.

THE INEVITABILITY OF CHOICE. Public policies intended to correct for the underinvestment in research caused by problems of appropriability, or risk and scale, ought to address the specifics of these problems. That is, public resources should be directed where appropriability problems are greatest and the risks large and indivisible. This means basic and middle-ground research, and radically innovative, or large, risky projects.

Market signals should be integral to these choices, but at the same time, since market signals miss opportunities that society nonetheless considers economically desirable, they must be supplemented by decisions that implicitly choose where to invest resources.

Some general level of subsidy, such as tax credits, to support R&D across the board may be useful (since empirical studies generally show that social returns to research exceed private returns), but subsidies cannot distinguish between projects with slight problems of appropriability and those with severe problems. In extreme cases, when no benefits can be captured for the exclusive use of a private investor, no partial subsidy can transform them into attractive, money-making propositions. And a general subsidy that makes a highly inappropriable project worthwhile does so at the cost of making much more appropriable R&D projects excessively attractive. Thus, while some type of general R&D tax credit would seem useful, it should be supplemented by policies targeting research and radical, high-risk projects whose returns are much more difficult than average to capture.

NEW INSTITUTIONS. Funneling support for precommercial middle-ground research through existing institutions is subject to Bush's law. Administered through so-called mission federal agencies, such support inevitably competes with more applied, mission-related projects, and presumably suffers in battles over scarce R&D dollars within the agencies. One might argue for adding these objectives to the National Science Foundation's mandate, but imposing criteria of long-term economic and commercial relevance on choices would conflict with the NSF's historical mandate to divorce basic research funding from commercial tests of any sort.

What is needed is a separate institution, with its own new and important mission: to protect support for economically significant middle-ground R&D projects from the ravages of Bush's law. If the budget for these sorts of projects is to be altered, let it be by explicit congressional or executive mandate, not by budget wars within agencies with only a peripheral interest in the health of the commercial technology base.

Bush himself may have summed it up best when he described "two basic principles for successful government participation in scientific research. First, the research organization must have direct access to

Congress for its funds; second, the work of the research organization must not be subject to control or direction from any operating organization whose responsibilities are not exclusively those of research."[52] We would add to Bush's formula only the suggestion that identical principles be applied to federal support for commercially relevant, middle-ground research and the thought that differences in objectives and orientation make a distinct organization responsible for funding the middle ground as necessary as one responsible for basic research.

INDUSTRIAL RELEVANCE ON THE AGENDA. Industrialists are certainly in closer contact with the market than bureaucrats and may have valuable insights into what technologies are potentially of greatest commercial importance. Industry must therefore be allowed a significant voice in setting the agenda for supporting research intended to strengthen the commercial technology base. Rather than allowing the Pentagon or any other government agency to devise plans and issue directives, a separate government institution should serve as a contact point, facilitator, collector of information and scanner on the world horizon, to which industry would come with proposals. Such an organization might even distribute reports and proposals to industry for comment and possible expressions of private-sector interest.

The projects selected should always be designed to benefit the technology base of an *industry*, however, not an individual firm or group of firms. And the projects should not be a sophisticated form of pork barrel. Public resources should be invested only if industry is willing at least to match the funding. Sharing costs and risks creates incentives for allocating resources efficiently. Funds should flow only into projects industry believes are productive, ones in which it is willing to sink its own resources, but where benefits are difficult to capture privately and individual efforts unlikely to succeed.

DIVERSITY IN DECISIONMAKING. Federal agencies sponsoring R&D have rarely seen eye-to-eye on what was and was not worth funding. Development of the original mammoth computers—ENIAC, Whirlwind, ILLIAC—was often fiercely opposed by one set of potential funders, staunchly supported by another. Money was perhaps wasted on some dead ends, but other projects paid off many times over. The point is that no one is omniscient, and diversity—parallel approaches—is worth

---

52. Testimony of Vannevar Bush, "Research and Development," Hearings, House Committee on Military Affairs, 79 Cong. 1 sess. (GPO, 1945), pp. 4–5.

maintaining. The United States would be much poorer technologically if some single funding authority had been granted an exclusive franchise to decide research priorities. It would be a mistake, therefore, to create some superagency to reign as undisputed czar over the government's nonmilitary technology investments. Each agency has its own mission and ought to be encouraged to invest in technological innovation when it provides a solution to a particular problem. What is needed is a federal entity focused specifically on the commercial technology base, an ombudsman for industry and an advocate for policy. A strong nimble organization to speak up for commercially relevant technology, to facilitate proposals by industry, and to work to couple academia and commerce would provide a new dimension to public debate.

ADVANTAGES OF COUPLING AND COOPERATION. One lesson that emerges from the history of both computers and superconductors is the advantage of collaboration in research among universities, federal laboratories, and industry. Coupling between the universities and industry played a major if sometimes inadvertent role in developing the first computers. The university computer projects strongly influenced the technical designs of products that emerged in the 1950s, though the mechanism for transfering technology was often people who left academic projects and joined industrial laboratories. In the 1950s and 1960s such large military projects as the SAGE bomber defense system, Project MAC (computer timesharing), or the ILLIAC IV supercomputer often teamed university-based researchers and industry. This coupling provided a continuing conduit between the basic research undertaken in universities and the industrial laboratories working on concrete applications, and it directed the basic researchers to interesting problems with direct relevance to useful applications.

These projects were also characterized by considerable cooperation and sharing of knowledge among the industrial contractors that teamed up on them. SAGE, for example, brought together IBM, Burroughs Corporation, RCA, General Electric, the System Development Corporation (SDC), the Bell Labs, and MIT. Project MAC included General Electric (and later, Honeywell Corporation), MIT, and the Bell Labs. ILLIAC IV involved Burroughs, Fairchild Industries, Texas Instruments, and the University of Illinois. Part of the successes achieved included diffusion of the common knowledge and experience accumulated on the job to a wide cross section of the industry.

Private firms may also duplicate precompetitive applied research as they develop commercial products. Such duplicated effort cannot be easily translated into a competitive advantage and will reduce the overall return on the industry's investments in R&D. Reducing duplication and underinvestment in more basic resarch can be a powerful motive for experimenting with cooperative research ventures.[53]

It is worth remarking that the Japanese have made cooperative research programs, jointly pooling private and public funding, the focus of public support for R&D. By sharing knowledge and eliminating unnecessary duplication, they have economized on resources invested in more basic, precompetitive areas of research and appear to have derived significant industrial payoffs from relatively modest sums of public funding. Sharing also encourages private firms to combine resources on research for which risks and potential returns are great but the possibility that any single firm will capture the bulk of the return appears modest. Their approach has been very much one of flexibility and pragmatism, experimentation and pursuit of avenues that have proved productive. Their continued use of this model suggests that all parties consider it a solid and useful investment.

WORKING FOR AN OPEN INTERNATIONAL SYSTEM. As long as the economic future of the United States continues to be linked to high technology, it must support an open global economy. U.S. high-technology industries have always sought the widest possible market to earn the best possible return on relatively fixed R&D investments. If the United States responds to apparent provocations of others by erecting protectionist barriers around its markets, it will undermine the principle of an open system. In the long run protection will strangle the returns, slow investments, and stunt growth. Clearly, America should instead seek to strengthen the principle of open markets, to knock down barriers, not reinforce them.

It is unproductive to suggest that foreign governments should be prevented from subsidizing R&D intended to benefit their countries' firms commercially, since essentially all governments—loudly and openly or quietly and covertly—do so. One might, however, suggest that all would benefit (through reducing duplication, for example) by making reciprocal participation in such national R&D programs a matter of bilateral negotiation.

---

53. See Michael L. Katz, "An Analysis of Cooperative Research and Development," *Rand Journal of Economics,* vol. 17 (Winter 1986), pp. 527–43; and Michael Spence, "Cost Reduction, Competition, and Industry Performance," *Econometrica,* vol. 52 (January 1984), pp. 101–21.

On the other hand, the relatively heavy U.S. investment in basic research has the character of an international public good in today's world of rapid, inexpensive, and essentially uncontrollable scientific communication. When such basic science was mainly commercialized by American firms, this investment was no burden. But in a world of technological peers who are just as likely to commercialize products that draw on advances in technology, it is appropriate to internationalize some of this expenditure as well, to ask that others spend to replenish the common pool in rough proportion to their withdrawals. Foreign countries may have to increase contributions to U.S. basic research programs and to do more research themselves. To some extent, this is already occurring—in Japan, for example—and should be further encouraged.

To conclude, the United States in the 1980s faces the maturation of its military technology and international economic competition with technological peers. On the military side, measured and careful investment driven by mission and requirement is the appropriate response to shrinking budgets and diminishing returns to investments in technology. On the economic side, the United States should ask other nations to support a commensurately larger share of the burden of investing in the least appropriable basic research, and should move to help firms earn returns on technology investments. This in turn means it must recognize the government's role in maintaining the industrial technology base. New policies must be designed to help American firms commercialize products that draw on American advances in science and technology. Effectiveness and efficiency must become hallmarks of the R&D investments intended to benefit the economy of tomorrow.

The world has changed, but America has not. Can we face our ·challenges from a position of strength, in full command of our extraordinary resources, or will we ignore them until forced into full retreat, in crisis, with our strength diminished? These problems are now evident to many in our society, and a new consensus can emerge. The time to restructure is now.

CHAPTER SIX

Socialist Reforms
and the World Economy

HARRY HARDING
ED A. HEWETT

Socialism began this century as an idea of little practical significance, a European-based body of thought attractive to intellectuals and others alienated by the impersonal, sometimes brutal, and often unfair practices of capitalist societies. It was a capitalist world in 1900, and socialists were on the fringe, advocating what seemed then to be a farfetched notion that society could perhaps be organized under a fairer, more humane, and even more efficient system than capitalism.

As the century draws to a close, almost one-third of the world's population lives in self-proclaimed socialist societies, which produce a little less than one-fourth of world GNP.[1] Russia, which started the century as a monarchy with a weak military system based on a peasant economy, now presides over the Union of Soviet Socialist Republics, a universally acknowledged superpower whose only military rival is the United States. Socialism in China, encompassing more than one-fifth of the world's population, is now entering its fifth decade with a vitality that has captured the world's attention.

Besides transforming the lives of the third of the world's population directly affected, socialist regimes have also dramatically changed the fortunes of the remaining two-thirds. The U.S.-Soviet military confrontation has dominated the second half of this century. Since World War II most of America's wars and military confrontations have been conducted against socialist adversaries: the Korean War, the several Taiwan Straits crises, the Bay of Pigs episode and the Cuban missile crisis, the war in Vietnam, and the interventions in Grenada and Central

---

1. Central Intelligence Agency, Directorate of Intelligence, *Handbook of Economic Statistics, 1986: A Reference Aid,* CPAS 86-10002 (Government Printing Office, 1986), pp. 22, 34–35, 55.

America. The military establishment of each superpower is configured and deployed to deal with the other. Soviet and American policies toward Latin America, Asia, Africa, and the Middle East are designed largely with an eye to superpower competition.

But though the geopolitical effect of socialist regimes on the rest of the world has been impressive, their economic and ideological importance has been less notable. The repressive regimes characteristic of real-world (as opposed to theoretical) socialism have gradually eliminated any moral force they might once have exerted on other nations. The socialization of the means of production and the rigid enforcement of egalitarian principles have so stifled incentives in the socialist economies that their systems have tended toward extreme inefficiencies. These in turn have reinforced the inclination to minimize economic contacts with the rest of the world. As a result, socialism enjoys little moral authority except in some less developed countries; very few would argue that it should serve as an economic model; and it has proved to be of modest importance in world commerce. These systems as a whole constitute a fairly self-contained, high-cost, generally low-technology island in a dynamic world economy.

For socialist countries this situation has proved untenable. The Stalinist model, adopted in or imposed on all socialist countries, has been adept enough at achieving industrialization but is hopelessly ill suited for managing an industrialized economy. The political system, designed to control and collectivize uneducated peasants, is crumbling at different rates in individual socialist countries in the face of growing pressure from increasingly sophisticated populations. Innovations in the world economy based on new technologies in information, biotechnology, materials, and other areas have begun to widen the gap between socialism and developed capitalism in ways that are increasingly obvious to all, including the people living under socialism.

For many socialist countries, therefore, the developments of the last decade have produced a serious systemic crisis. In Poland a combination of economic stagnation, political repression, and foreign control has created chronic political turbulence that has shaken the regime to its foundations. Post-Mao China experienced a popular "crisis of confidence," particularly in urban areas, that was rooted in twenty years of frozen living standards and ten years of political chaos and exacerbated by a growing awareness among educated Chinese of the superior economic and political performance of the rest of East Asia. By 1980 Chinese leaders themselves were worriedly comparing the collapse of the legitimacy of their regime to the explosive situation in Poland. In the Soviet Union the crisis has been somewhat less dramatic, but no less real. The Soviet people, too, were frustrated by the bureaucratic and economic ossification of the Brezhnev era; and their leaders have become acutely conscious that their dream of strategic parity with the United States cannot be realized if Soviet economic efficiency and technological levels fall ever farther behind world standards.

In response to these pressures, virtually all the socialist countries have begun the painful process of economic and political reforms that could eventually change the very nature of their societies and of their relations with the rest of the world. The most prominent and potentially important reform efforts currently under way are those of China and the USSR. Events in Eastern Europe—which went through a round of generally unsuccessful reform efforts in the 1960s—are less interesting, but that should soon change.

Reforms in China and the USSR, if they are pursued vigorously, will have major implications for the global economic and political system. China's early successes with economic reforms and an opening to the West—though partial and modest—provide a glimmer of what might occur. If China and the USSR were simultaneously to implement radical economic reforms, Eastern Europe would quickly follow. The result would be important new investment opportunities in rapidly growing economies, growth in exports to the East, and eventually a reverse flow of manufactured goods from socialist countries in far greater quantities than ever seen in the postwar period.

Reform could also significantly affect international geopolitical and ideological trends. A common commitment to economic liberalization and political restructuring would remove the ideological foundations of the Sino-Soviet dispute and greatly reduce friction between the two countries. Successful economic revitalization and political reform throughout the socialist world might well enhance the attractiveness of communist ideology in the third world, reversing the long decline in the ideological appeal of socialism.

Above all, economic reform may have significant implications for the foreign policies of the large socialist states. For China, the concentration on economic modernization and reform has led Peking to seek a peaceful and stable international environment, to build economic relations with a broad range of trading partners, to reduce tensions with most of its neighbors, and to adopt a more flexible and pragmatic approach to many international issues. The Soviet Union, too, has seemed eager to reduce its international burdens so as to maximize the resources it can devote to *perestroika*, agreeing to the abolition of intermediate- and short-range nuclear missiles, withdrawing its troops from Afghanistan, working for a negotiated settlement in Cambodia, and trying to improve its relations with Peking.

Over the longer run, the effect of economic reform on world geopolitics remains uncertain. It could well be that the foreign policy associated with the early stages of reform—an interest in stability, reduced tensions, and wider economic relationships—will become institutionalized in both China and the Soviet Union. But it is also possible that the increased economic and technological resources produced by reform will be devoted to national assertiveness, with each country renewing its drive for major power status. It is also conceivable that reform could stimulate a stronger Sino-Soviet relationship, in ways detrimental to American interests.

The existence of such possibilities is not in itself new; the compelling economic logic supporting radical reforms has been evident to all socialist countries for a long time. The issue now is whether the very strong commitments to reform in China and the USSR signal truly profound changes in these two societies. Are the two great socialist countries, finally, on the verge of radical reforms? If so, what are the potential implications for the world economy? And what does that mean for U.S. foreign policy? How should the West relate to these ongoing changes? Should we do something to help them along? Will they have a marked effect on the evolving role of the United States in the world economy?

Typically a discussion of issues such as these would proceed by first describing actual developments in reform efforts, then analyzing their potential impact on Soviet or Chinese links with the outside world. In this case, however, it seems more promising to proceed somewhat differently, first examining what reforms are necessary to fully transform relations between socialist countries and the world economy, and then comparing these "necessary" reforms with what has actually occurred and what might plausibly happen in the future. The result is a gauge of how far the reforms must go, as well as some notion of how measures already introduced will affect socialism's economic relationship with the rest of the world.

Because this is a brief essay, it must be fairly general. The details of reforms in China and the USSR have been discussed amply elsewhere.[2]

2. See Harry Harding, *China's Second Revolution: Reform after Mao* (Brookings, 1987); Ed A. Hewett, *Reforming the Soviet Economy: Equality versus Efficiency* (Brookings, 1988); Jerry F. Hough, *Opening Up the Soviet Economy* (Brookings, 1988), and *Russia and the West: Gorbachev and the Politics of Reform* (Simon and Schuster, 1988); and Karen Dawisha, *Eastern Europe, Gorbachev and Reform: The Great Challenge* (Cambridge University Press, 1988).

The purpose here is to elucidate the fundamental issues, develop an analytical framework, and use that framework to peer into the future. We focus primarily on the USSR and China because of their dominant positions in the socialist world and the enormous potential of changes under way in both countries. We discuss other socialist countries, such as those of Eastern Europe, primarily as sources of information on potential difficulties awaiting Soviet and Chinese reformers.

CAUSES AND CONSEQUENCES OF SOCIALISM'S ISOLATION

By their own choice the socialist countries have until recently remained fairly isolated from the world economy. In 1985, for example, these countries together accounted for almost one-quarter of the world's GNP, but only 12 percent of world exports.[3] Their share of financial flows was surely even more modest than their share of trade, though the data are difficult to construct.[4]

Not only has the role of the socialist countries in world trade and financial flows been modest but also the structure of their foreign economic relations has been simple. The socialist countries have for the most part engaged in straightforward exchanges of raw materials for manufactured goods and food, of some manufactured goods for others, and so on. Prior to reform, these countries rejected direct foreign investment from the West, engaged in limited scientific or technological exchanges with capitalist countries, and remained apart from the principal institutions, such as the World Bank and the International Monetary Fund (IMF), that shape the international economic system. The internationalization of the production process (with different components manufactured in different countries), of financial institutions, and of corporations has been, with few exceptions, a practice limited to the

3. CIA, *Handbook of Economic Statistics, 1986*, pp. 22, 25.
4. One, admittedly imperfect, way to measure socialist countries' participation in international financial transactions is to estimate the share of international assets held by socialist banks. For the Soviet Union and Eastern Europe, which account for slightly under 11 percent of world trade, their holdings of international assets amounted to four-tenths of 1 percent of all international assets in 1983. Ralph C. Bryant, *International Financial Intermediation* (Brookings, 1987), p. 34. There is no similar number for China, and it would be difficult to construct because of the rather complex role of Hong Kong. But clearly the socialist countries play an insignificant role in international financial markets.

capitalist world. And naturally the benefits of that process in increased efficiency, product quality, and consumer choice have also been limited to the capitalist countries.[5]

This relative isolation from the world economy is primarily the choice of the socialist countries themselves and is rooted in some of the central assumptions of communist doctrine.[6] First, to a certain extent a commitment to public ownership of the means of production is inherently autarkic—that is, tends to promote national economic self-sufficiency and independence. Even if loosely applied, this principle excludes majority foreign ownership of joint ventures. If strictly applied, the principle of public ownership precludes any direct foreign investment at all. The outcome is to limit the international financial flows of socialist countries primarily to balance-of-payments borrowing or project finance tied solely to a commitment for deliveries of the resulting products.

Second, the logic of central planning reinforces the tendency toward autarky. In their effort to control all productive activity, central planners isolate the domestic economy from the vicissitudes of the "unplanned" world economy through a foreign trade monopoly and through total control over the use of foreign exchange. Thus the internationalization of products or production processes is the exception, not the rule, in such a system.

A third set of assumptions that promotes autarky in socialist systems is associated with the Stalinist development strategy based on a "big push" toward heavy industry. Several features of this strategy lead to chronically excessive demands for imports. The tendency of central planners in socialist systems to run their economies at close to full employment and full capacity produces constant bottlenecks that can be satisfied only by imported products. In particular, the emphasis on high rates of investment produces a chronic hunger for imported technology, and the exclusive priority assigned to heavy industry creates a constant demand for imported consumer goods. The central planners are well aware that such demands, if satisfied, would place intolerable strains on limited foreign exchange earnings and reserves. As a result,

5. It is true that these constraints have not prevented the socialist countries' international trade from growing faster than their GNP, which indicates an increasing role for international trade in their systems. But the growth has been in raw materials or simple manufactured goods in exchange for food and more sophisticated manufactured goods, a very traditional pattern with clear limitations as an engine of technological progress.

6. The U.S.-led embargo of those countries in the postwar period provided an additional rationale for those who advocated autarkic policies, but it was not the main reason for them.

they maintain strict central controls over all links between the domestic and world economies.

Finally, the legacy of Lenin's theory of imperialism also limits the willingness of socialist leaders to engage in a wide set of international economic relationships. In essence, the theory assumes that the international economic institutions associated with mature capitalism are inherently exploitative, designed to favor the interests of powerful industrialists in the larger developed countries at the expense of the interests not only of their own workers but also of smaller and less developed countries abroad. More recent versions of the theory propose also that socialist systems are vulnerable to various forms of cultural and ideological penetration from the West—what the Chinese have recently called "spiritual pollution"—that could weaken public commitment to Marxism, socialism, and Communist party rule.

In line with this thinking, both China and the Soviet Union traditionally assumed that socialist countries should separate themselves as far as possible from the international capitalist system. Chinese and Soviet leaders viewed the world as divided into two competing economic blocs, one socialist and one capitalist, which would have little interaction. When socialist countries engaged in foreign economic relations, their partners tended to be other socialist nations, not capitalist ones.

The tendency toward autarky in the socialist countries is evident in their decision to maintain inconvertible currencies—currencies that cannot be freely exchanged for the currencies of other countries. All socialist countries now have inconvertible currencies, largely for two mutually reinforcing reasons. First, because of years of absolute protection, they make products that are usually uncompetitive on world markets. This deficiency severely limits these countries' export possibilities and, in turn, the attractiveness of their currencies as a form of payment for anyone exporting to them. Conversely, the inefficiencies and poor-quality products characteristic of domestic industry in socialist countries create a huge potential demand for imported goods. To be sure, Soviet oil, Chinese textiles, and Eastern European pharmaceuticals are all readily sold on world markets and earn foreign exchange. But those export earnings are not sufficient to support fully convertible currencies.

Central planning also contributes to currency inconvertibility. The essence of central planning is the predominance of direct central control over resource allocation, at the expense of markets. Planners in Soviet-style systems exercise particularly close control over the allocation of the factors of production, including foreign exchange as well as land, labor, financial capital, capital goods, and technology. Planners jealously guard their right to determine what will be produced and who will receive it; money follows rather than determines their decisions. Thus foreign nationals, even if they have Soviet rubles and know of Soviet products they wish to purchase, find that central planners, not rubles, determine access to those products. Planners' absolute control over the disposition of national output, and the limited share of this output that is competitive on world markets, combine to create strong barriers to the convertibility of socialist currencies.

This self-imposed isolation from the world economy, symbolized by inconvertible currencies, has clear advantages for socialist countries. Insofar as they affect the socialist countries at all, shocks in the world economy—for example, the rapid escalation of oil prices in the 1970s and early 1980s—are absorbed first by the state and then distributed to the population over time. For the USSR, a major petroleum producer, the oil shocks meant higher imports of food and machinery equipment without new debt; for Eastern Europe, net energy importers, they meant reductions in domestic spending primarily through investment declines. In both cases the effects on employment, the income distribution, and the price level were muted and spread out over time, which, from a social point of view, is a positive consequence of the insulation from rapid changes in the world economy.

But the costs of autarky are huge. Stalinist central planning is, in its international dimension, the most extreme form of protectionism; the planning, price, and financial systems form mutually reinforcing barriers between the domestic economy and the rest of the world economy. Enterprises exist in a hothouse, free of competition from imports. The constant pressure for high growth, along with the equivalent of an easy money policy, means that enterprises can almost always sell their output, irrespective of its quality. The fully predictable result in all socialist countries is a tendency toward limited consumer choice, high production costs, low quality, low productivity, and a general inability to compete internationally. Insulated from the increasingly internationalized competitive process that drives technological change, these countries fall further and further behind.

A MODEL OF SOCIALIST INTEGRATION
WITH THE WORLD ECONOMY

If China or the Soviet Union—or any socialist country—decided to reject its autarkic policies of the past and fully integrate itself into the world economy, it would have to change dramatically the ways in which its productive enterprises related to the rest of the world, and ultimately the degree to which its currency was freely convertible into those of other countries. These moves would imply, in turn, equally far-reaching changes in its intellectual assumptions about both its domestic economy and the nature of the international economic order.

To achieve a successful opening to the world economy, enterprises in socialist countries will need to meet three conditions. First, they must have the incentive to compete in world markets and the autonomy to do so effectively. That requires a high degree of independence from both central planners and intermediate party and state bureaucracies. Second, they need adequate information about world markets so that they can compete in those markets. That, in turn, means enterprises that wish to export can deal with potential customers directly, rather than through the cumbersome intermediacy of state foreign trade corporations. Third, enterprises will require the material means to develop products that are competitive on world markets. In essence, that means access to efficient factor markets through which enterprises can acquire financial capital, raw materials, personnel, technology, and so forth.

These three conditions—competition in world markets, market information, and material means—are interconnected. Information about world markets comes through competing with the world's producers, either in your own market if they are allowed to sell there, or in other markets as you seek to take away their business. Such competition presupposes that domestic producers have the right to travel outside the country; it also presupposes that when a producer has a good idea, he can find enough capital, foreign exchange, and materials to put together a product with a chance of competing in world markets.

The interconnections among the three conditions are such that measures addressing any two will be ineffective. For example, most reforms in socialist economies have somehow made special funds available to encourage exports and provided special access to materials (condition 3); and they have allowed producers to learn more about foreign competitors, through travel, the acquisition of technical information, and so on (condition 2). But the incentive to export has usually been a rather modest quota of their foreign exchange earnings. Excess demand continues on the domestic market. Since each producer experiences minimal, if any, competition from other domestic firms or from imports, it can sell its output without great effort. In this context, exports—which require great effort and which even then may result in failure—are an unappealing option. Clearly the first condition is the most important one: the incentive to export must be strong, and the costs of not exporting must be high.

But it is also true that incentives alone will be ineffective. Central planners may give enterprises incentives to export, and enterprise managers may genuinely desire to increase the sale of their products overseas. But without accurate information about the international marketplace and the needs of potential clients, firms will be unlikely to produce goods of the design, quality, and price that will be attractive on foreign markets. And without effective factor markets, they will find it difficult to obtain the additional labor, financial capital, equipment, and raw material necessary to increase their production.

Just as currency inconvertibility symbolizes the degree to which socialist countries are insulated from the world economy, so too would currency convertibility symbolize their openness to the world economy. The free convertibility of a currency means that anyone who holds it can, without restriction, either use it to buy available goods in the country issuing the currency or exchange it for the currency of another country. The liquidity of a convertible currency means that people will willingly accept it in payment for goods, knowing that they can either use it immediately to acquire other goods (in this or another currency) or hold on to it, being confident that later they can purchase goods with it. The freely convertible currency can be held by, and sold or purchased by, anyone—whether they are residents of the country issuing the currency or citizens of other countries.

As a practical matter, convertibility of a country's currency requires that the country produce a range of goods and services competitive on world markets and that anyone holding the currency be allowed to purchase those goods.[7] In that situation, those who hold the country's currency will feel confident they can either buy the goods of that country or sell the currency to someone else who wishes to do so. If, on the other hand, the country's exportables are generally uncompetitive on world markets, or the goods that are competitive are not sold to foreigners, people are reluctant to accept the currency. There is little or nothing they wish to buy with it that they can buy, and they find it hard to sell the currency since others share that view.

7. Theoretically, there is an exchange rate at which any country will have a comparative advantage in producing and selling some range of products. But as a practical matter, most governments in countries with a large share of manufacturing that is uncompetitive on world markets are not willing to allow the exchange rate to fall enough to change that situation.

From this analysis we can draw two important conclusions about the possibility of currency convertibility under socialist central planning, and more generally about the potential for a more active role for socialist countries in the world economy. First, the free convertibility of a country's currency and traditional socialist central planning are incompatible. Traditional central planning is a conscious rejection of the role of money in resource allocation; free convertibility of a currency assumes the primacy of money in domestic resource allocation, and it internationalizes that primacy. Free currency convertibility is, therefore, impossible unless radical reforms are implemented that shift the bulk of decisionmaking on resource allocation from planners to markets. And even then, currency inconvertibility will remain as long as domestic industries are protected from the competitive pressures that would force them to develop viable exports for world markets.

Second, and most important, the measures socialist leaders must take to achieve convertibility in their currencies are precisely the same as those needed to attain the goals of their economic reforms. Domestic industries in socialist countries will decrease costs, raise quality, and develop exports salable in the West only if they are freed to make their own decisions and can operate in markets, under competitive pressures, in a general policy framework set by the state. To create these competitive pressures, the state would have to, more or less simultaneously, eliminate obligatory planning, move to a flexible price system linked to the world economy through a meaningful exchange rate, encourage free entry in industries to foster competition, and use banks and other financial instruments to move capital from where it accumulates to where it can be put to best use. Such radical economic reforms not only will bring about improvements in economic performance but will also move a socialist country closer to convertibility.

Currency convertibility is not something socialist planners can "declare," nor is it something that will come early in a reform process. Rather, it is a measure of the success of economic reforms and of the efforts to engage in more profitable interchange with the world economy. Currency convertibility will be a consequence, not a cause, of socialist countries' integration into the world economy.

Notice that neither of these conclusions suggests the need for socialist countries to abandon all the principles on which socialism rests. The primacy of markets and a convertible currency do not preclude an important role for the state in economic affairs. For instance, state-owned companies, if they operate with the right set of incentives, can operate in markets; and a socialist government can reduce disparities in the distribution of income and wealth in a society without destroying incentives to economize.

But the definition of what is *socialist* will have to change as these societies search for integration with the world economy. To begin with, they will have to abandon some of the basic assumptions of the Soviet model of economic development, particularly the single-minded focus on the central management of the details of resource allocation. They will also have to modify significantly, if not discard, the traditional Leninist assumptions about international political economy. Rather than see the world as divided between two competing blocs, economic as well as political, the socialist countries must recognize the existence of a single world market into which countries are integrated to varying degrees.

CURRENT REFORMS IN THE SOVIET UNION AND CHINA

Efforts to reform socialist economies date back more than a third of a century, and virtually every socialist country, with the possible exceptions of Albania and North Korea, has tried at least once to reform its system. In general, the initial impetus for these reforms is political, stemming from the party's fear that poor economic performance threatens the party's ability to control society. That, in turn, leads to various measures designed to improve efficiency and accelerate economic growth, thereby expanding the quantity and improving the quality of goods available to the society.

Increasingly these reforms are beginning to assume a more internationalist tone. In the 1970s the socialist countries began to enter international economic organizations—the General Agreement on Tariffs and Trade (GATT), the IMF, the World Bank, and others—in a process that required compromises on both sides. The result now—unthinkable several decades ago—is that economic policymakers in Hungary, or Poland, or China must negotiate with the international economic community about their own macroeconomic and microeconomic policies. Most socialist countries are seeking to attract foreign investors by providing opportunities for direct foreign investment, ranging from minority positions in joint ventures to 100 percent foreign-owned enterprises. Participation in international financial markets has grown significantly in recent years, both in magnitude and complexity. The economics profession in many socialist countries is showing an increased curiosity and objectivity about how the most advanced capitalist economies function and how the international economy operates.

All these changes suggest that the elites in socialist countries are beginning to perceive the strong connections between their goal to increase efficiency and the need to integrate their economies into the world economic system. The logic of specialization and trade as engines of technological advance, understood for some time by economists in socialist countries, is increasingly appreciated at leadership levels. Many leaders in socialist countries now worry openly about investor confidence in their system, the possibility of making their currencies convertible, or the role of socialism in the world economy.

Of most importance here is the increasing sophistication of the two great socialist countries, China and the USSR, in their thinking about their role in the world economy. China led the way with a quick and bold opening to the West in the late 1970s. It has now joined almost all the principal international economic organizations, including the World Bank, the IMF, and the Asian Development Bank, and has applied for membership in the GATT. Its share of exports in national output, which was 5.6 percent when reform began in 1978, reached 16.1 percent in 1987.[8] Peking borrowed at least $25 billion between 1979 and 1987 from almost every conceivable source: from commercial banks, from foreign governments, from international financial organizations, and on world bond markets.[9] By offering investment incentives, creating special economic zones and open cities along the Chinese coast, and liberalizing the legal restrictions on foreign ventures, Peking has opened the entire eastern coast of the country to direct foreign investment and has absorbed more than $10 billion from foreign entrepreneurs between 1979 and 1987.[10] As China moves to assimilate Hong Kong, it will gain even more experience, setting the tone for the rest of the socialist world.

The USSR has traditionally been far more conservative in its approach to the international economy. But under Gorbachev, Soviet leaders' thinking about, and policy toward, the Soviet role in the world economy

8. For 1978–86 figures, see Harding, *China's Second Revolution*, p. 139; for the 1987 figure, see Guojia Tongjiju (State Statistical Bureau), *Zhongguo tongji zhaiyao, 1988* (A statistical survey of China, 1988) (Peking: Chinese Statistical Publishing House, 1988), pp. 6, 85.

9. For 1979–86 figures, see Harding, *China's Second Revolution*, p. 154; for the 1987 figure, see Xinhua News Agency, February 23, 1988, in Foreign Broadcast Information Service, *Daily Report: China*, February 23, 1988, p. 12.

10. For 1979–86 figures, see Harding, *China's Second Revolution*, p. 154; for the 1987 figure, see Xinhua News Agency, February 23, 1988.

has grown in sophistication. The USSR is now actively pursuing the possibility of joining international economic organizations (the GATT, and possibly the IMF and World Bank), regimes governing trade in specific commodities (for example, the Multifiber Arrangement), and regional economic organizations (for example, the Pacific Economic Cooperation Conference and the Asian Development Bank). The Soviets have floated their first bond issue in Switzerland, have availed themselves of note issuance facilities, and are now involved in debt swaps with Western banks. Joint ventures are now legal in the USSR; there is talk of special economic zones; and Soviet leaders are anticipating the convertibility of the ruble, first within the communist-bloc Council for Mutual Economic Assistance and then in trade with the West.

Still, socialist leaders have a long distance to travel in moving from autarky to a truly internationally oriented view of their economies. Although many socialist countries have taken a more inventive approach to their foreign economic relations—through such devices as joint ventures and special economic zones—their general orientation is still to promote exports, not to subject domestic industry to foreign competition. There is still a tendency to consider foreign economic relations simply as an export promotion problem in which the basic goal is to increase the efficient production of competitive exports in order to finance the importation of a bill of goods determined by central authorities. Protection of domestic industry remains, perpetuating the isolation of the domestic from the world economy; all that has changed is central pressure to improve export performance.

That, for example, is clearly the logic of the current Soviet reforms. Essentially all enterprises in the manufacturing sector now have, or will soon have, the right to direct export and import. When they export on their own account, they retain part of their foreign currency receipts, which they can use for imports. But the bulk of hard currency available for imports comes from proceeds of energy sales—in some years loans—and those are still centrally controlled and allocated, apparently with a strong protectionist bias. Thus imports will become competitive only when enterprises, using their own funds, import goods that Soviet producers also offer. So far those funds are limited. More important, a clear import licensing policy for these "free" imports has not been established.

Soviet joint ventures—legalized in January 1987—could potentially be a source of competition for Soviet domestic industry. But so far the policy has moved slowly. As of June 1988 only about fifty joint ventures had been arranged, few of which are large. More critical, the Soviet partners for the joint ventures will usually be under the ministries that produce the product lines in question, and those authorities are unlikely to create competitors to their own enterprises. When the joint ventures begin operation, they will probably soon find themselves deeply entangled in the bureaucratic thicket of what is still essentially a traditional centrally planned economy. The only potential for a real procompetitive bias in Soviet joint ventures will come if the government truly encourages cooperatives, soon to be operating under broad legal powers, to pursue the legal rights given them to form joint ventures.

China has been somewhat bolder than the USSR or Eastern Europe in its effort to expand contacts with the international economy. But though China's approach is much more liberal than the USSR's, Peking shares Moscow's emphasis on promoting exports and limiting access to the domestic market. Thus the bulk of China's foreign trade reforms are intended to make it easier, and more profitable, for the country's enterprises to export. As in the USSR, factories that produce for the international market, together with the administrative bodies that supervise them, are allowed to retain a certain proportion of the foreign exchange earnings obtained from export. An increasing number of enterprises are allowed direct contact with potential customers abroad, and foreign trade corporations are increasingly serving as the agents of export enterprises, rather than simply as the procurement arm of the central government. In contrast, imports are restricted by a wide range of taxes, tariffs, and quotas; and Chinese industry is permitted, even encouraged, to draw up lists of goods that should be denied import licenses on the grounds that they can be manufactured at home.

China's regulations on direct foreign investment also illustrate the country's biases in favor of exports and against imports. The provisions give preferential treatment to those ventures that will produce for the export market and those that will produce goods which can substitute for imports, or at least those that will bring advanced technology to China. Conversely, projects that are intended simply to produce for the domestic Chinese market are discouraged, primarily by giving foreign investors only limited opportunities to convert profits earned in Chinese currency into foreign exchange for repatriation.

The main difference between China and the USSR in this regard is that China's reforms seem to be moving in the direction of a regulated market economy in ways that will encourage foreign investment. The relaxation of mandatory planning has made it increasingly possible for foreign ventures to obtain needed inputs—whether labor, capital, or raw materials—in burgeoning domestic markets without applying to central or provincial planners. Moreover, though the Chinese still insist that the creation of a fully convertible currency is unfeasible under present circumstances, they are beginning to experiment with limited foreign exchange markets, in which foreign ventures (and, increasingly, domestic Chinese enterprises) with a foreign exchange surplus can sell their hard currency, at a premium, to those willing to buy it.

On balance, however, the reforms in both China and the Soviet Union still focus largely on export promotion and import restrictions. Much of the motivation is financial, particularly the desire to avoid excessive indebtedness by limiting trade imbalances. But political factors are also at work. In some sense also socialist countries have used protectionism to shore up support for the party's management of the economy. Protection from the capricious whims of the world economy, encouragement of technological self-sufficiency, and most important, the guarantee of full employment, all have been realized in part through the institutionalized protectionism of central planning. Understandably, as the leaders of socialist countries are compelled to face up to the costs of their relative isolation, their first instinct is to try to encourage exports, while protecting domestic industry from what could be devastating competition from imports and foreign-owned enterprises.

Conversely, reformers in socialist countries normally have little understanding of, and no sympathy for, the benefits of reduced protectionism. As yet they give little credence to the notion that foreign trade, along with expanded competition among producers at home, forces domestic producers to lower costs and raise quality. In an open economy domestic producers constantly struggle among themselves and with foreign producers to preserve markets, with the exchange rate acting as a safety valve to equilibrate the balance of payments. The result is constant pressure on all competitors to meet customer needs at minimal cost, which in turn leads to the efficiency and gains in quality characteristic of capitalist markets but absent from most socialist systems.

In socialist countries the protectionist component of the ideology, and a constant preoccupation with the balance of payments, are so strong that the case for opening the economy to import competition is rarely made, and if it is, is never accepted by the government. Economic reforms usually come about because of difficulties in economic performance, including balance-of-payments problems, and leaders are in no mood to contemplate proposals for increased imports that—whatever the long-term consequences—would have the initial effects of closing some domestic enterprises and increasing the trade deficit. Rather, the guiding principle is, "We should import only what we cannot ourselves produce, and we should try to produce everything."

Since the government has so carefully walled off the home market for domestic producers' exclusive use, enterprises not surprisingly show little enthusiasm for their new-found rights to export directly to foreign markets. The notion that Western enterprises export, not because it is fun, but because they have run out of options in domestic markets, has not yet penetrated into the thinking of the much more protectionist-oriented reformers in socialist countries.

COULD THE FUTURE BE DIFFERENT?

Clearly the policy climate regarding the role of the international economy in China has changed, and it is beginning to change in the USSR. China is already showing an ability to compete on world textile and clothing markets, and other labor-intensive products, such as consumer electronics, are also being developed. Although direct foreign investment has fallen short of the expectations of Chinese leaders, the fact remains that China has accounted for an increasing share of direct foreign investments made in developing countries, rising from over 3 percent in 1982 to an average of 20 percent in 1986–87.[11] The Soviet Union is much earlier in the process of reform and is still developing key aspects of its strategy, but clearly the potential for exporting manufactured goods is there, especially if the defense industries are mobilized for export.

But the changes so far are not fundamental. Rather, they have chipped away at the edges of a very thick protectionist wall. In both China and the USSR the genuine breakthrough in policy toward the world economy is yet to come; official thinking about these issues has a long way to go. Nonetheless, they have come as far as they have because of strong pressures to break out of isolation, and those pressures will grow. The ability of the USSR to sustain its status as a world power, now based primarily on its military might and its sheer size, rests on the success of efforts to bring the Soviet economy up to the standards of the world's

11. Calculated from Harding, *China's Second Revolution*, p. 154; Xinhua News Agency, February 23, 1988; and International Monetary Fund, *World Economic Outlook: A Survey by the Staff of the International Monetary Fund*, World Economic and Financial Surveys (Washington, D.C.: IMF, 1988), p. 160.

other industrialized economies. A reintegration into the world economy is the only effective route to that goal; however many false starts the leadership makes, eventually the logic of Soviet goals will point in that direction. Chinese leaders know that their modernization goals are not even remotely achievable without an opening to the outside world. Continued economic isolation would mean a continuation of backwardness in a poor country that can ill afford it.

Thus the transition to more open economies in China and the USSR will occur; the questions are when, how, and how far will they go? There is no easy answer to "when," except to say that the transition, though already started, will most likely take decades in both countries. China begins the process with the "advantage" of underdevelopment; relatively inexpensive technologies of the 1970s and early 1980s, now somewhat behind the front line, could do wonders in the Chinese economy. China also has a huge labor pool to support the production and exportation of that dwindling, but nevertheless still significant, pool of labor-intensive products moving in international trade. Chinese leaders are convinced that the rising labor costs and appreciating currencies in many of the newly industrialized economies, particularly Taiwan and South Korea, give China an important opportunity to replace them as a key manufacturer and exporter of labor-intensive goods. There is also some reason to believe that China's unusually large heavy industrial base—itself a legacy of China's experimentation with the Soviet model—will give it some comparative advantage in a few capital-intensive products, including certain kinds of machinery and spare parts for automobiles. Still, even with these advantages it will take, at a minimum, decades for China to begin to emerge as a serious economic force in the world economy.

The USSR is far more developed than China and technologically far closer to the frontier, though in a very uneven way, the strongest sectors being related to defense. Labor is scarce; the capital stock is huge, but in poor repair and generally outdated. To enter the world economy, the Soviets will have to take a more capital-intensive path than the Chinese, based in part on their tremendous raw material and fuel reserves. The problem is that raw materials and fuels are increasingly small proportions of product costs in Western economies, diminishing the importance of those factors in determining comparative advantage. A skillfully designed development policy and a good deal of foreign capital will be needed to make the transition successfully. Even then, it will take at least two to three decades for Soviet leaders committed to an opening to the world economy to achieve something.

The answer to "how" is clearer. Basically there are two ways in which Chinese and Soviet leaders could move toward a fuller integration with the world economy, and both involve exposing their economics to the rigors of competition. One is the straight and narrow path dictated by neoclassical economic theory; the second, based on Japan's postwar experience, is more gradual.

In theory, China and the USSR could eliminate all barriers to imports immediately. In practice, such a step would have extremely damaging short-run consequences: serious balance-of-payments problems, temporary unemployment, and severe reductions in the sales of many enterprises. After a lag, some domestic enterprises would start to reenter the market with products that were competitive with the foreign imports. Import substitution would begin, and imports would fall. In addition, some enterprises would begin to search out export markets in an effort to earn profits and retain their labor force. Eventually the economy would emerge as far stronger and probably with a much changed profile of production, imports, and exports. If economic policy were sufficiently strict macroeconomically, while accommodating those enterprises responding profitably to the new situation, the debts incurred in the transition would be serviced and eventually repaid as the country moves into export surplus.

But this idealized version of a transition to a leaner, internationally competitive socialist economy is an unlikely scenario. Most socialist countries simply do not have the large foreign exchange reserves that such a strategy would require. Moreover, it would mean a total turnabout in the Communist party's relationship to society, with the party moving from the role of protector against the vicissitudes of the world economy to that of a channel through which those forces buffet the domestic economy. Few parties would even contemplate such a new role; of those that might, the chances of political survival would be low. Historically, Western governments have sometimes been forced by political realities—despite economic realities—to protect small segments of society from import competition and avoid the political backlash from allowing foreigners to "steal" domestic jobs. In a socialist economic system a rapid reduction in protective barriers would be tantamount to an attack on almost the entire labor force, which would be political suicide.

But there is another way to accomplish much the same result, suggested by the Japanese model, which is particularly appropriate for China and the USSR because of their size.[12] Japan's postwar development occurred

12. See Laura D'Andrea Tyson and John Zysman, "Politics and Productivity: Devel-

behind strong barriers that protected domestic industry from import competition, an approach that would appeal to all socialist countries. But at the same time the Japanese government consciously strove to foster competition among domestic enterprises so as to use competitive pressures to drive down costs and stimulate technical change. Since a high saving rate limited the domestic market, Japanese enterprises' struggle for market share naturally spilled over into exports. Enterprises were authorized to borrow foreign technology and could acquire financial resources to do so, but the Ministry of International Trade and Industry (MITI) used its monopoly power to choose which technologies could be imported and to bargain down fees on those that were. A system of small enterprises contracting to the large Japanese firms provided the flexibility needed in that competition, along with the incentive for the small firms themselves to innovate constantly in order to retain their contracts. This skillful combination of protection from foreign competition and institutionalized domestic competition preserved Japanese markets for Japanese firms, while forcing those firms to learn to compete internationally.

Clearly the Japanese model is a more sensible choice politically for both China and the USSR than the scenario based on textbook economics. Both economies are huge, leaving ample room for large and small firms to compete with one another without sacrificing the advantages of scale economies. A government policy favoring domestic competition while retaining protective barriers against imports would pit domestic enterprises and workers against each other for social gain, without the politically deadly stigma of foreign-owned enterprises creating domestic unemployment. Such a policy would include not only an aggressive effort to maintain conditions of free entry and exit in domestic industry, but also tight monetary and fiscal policies to eliminate excess demand, thereby reducing the power of sellers and increasing competition among producers.

An indispensable component of this approach would be an unshakable commitment by the government to allow unprofitable enterprises to fail, while providing unemployment and retraining benefits for the dismissed workers on their way to new jobs in more efficient enterprises. If the

---

opmental Strategy and Production Innovation in Japan," BRIE Working Paper 45, November 1987; and Kenneth Flamm, *Targeting the Computer: Government Support and International Competition* (Brookings, 1987), pp. 125–72. See also Edward J. Lincoln, *Japan: Facing Economic Maturity* (Brookings, 1988), pp. 14–68, which provides a general discussion of the process of successful economic development in Japan.

government bows to political pressure to save a large number of enterprises as "exceptions," or forces profitable enterprises to "absorb" or "merge with" the insolvent ones, then the incentive to operate efficiently and to export is lost, and the entire strategy collapses.

In both China and the Soviet Union the government bureaucracy potentially has the mechanism, though possibly not yet the skill or inclination, to act like MITI in controlling access to the market and using that control to foster agreements which fit into an overall development strategy and benefit the system as a whole. In both countries the barriers to domestic competition are huge; eliminating those barriers would create a burst of innovation and cost cutting that could propel rapid economic development for some time to come. Then, as domestic industry strengthened, the introduction of import competition would be a useful continued spur to development without threatening the extinction of large portions of domestic industry.

Obviously, if this policy is to be effective, the price system will have to be flexible so that enterprises—through price changes—can see and react to changes in supply and demand. Some sort of capital market will also be necessary in the form of financial intermediaries that can quickly and efficiently move capital from where it accumulates to where it can most profitably be applied. The less bureaucracy in these areas, the quicker the pace of economic development. If the procompetitive policy is effectively pursued, prices will be controlled through competition, and administrative price controls will be unnecessary.

Although the policy prescription is the same for both countries— domestic free trade with controls on demand—the USSR and China would have to tailor it to their individual circumstances. In China there are strong interregional barriers to specialization and trade. Erected by regions, these import barriers to goods from other regions are taking an increasing toll as the economy grows in sophistication. To be sure, many provinces in China are larger than most of the world's countries, but they are all at relatively low levels of development, the southeast being the closest to an exception. A truly unified internal Chinese market would unleash tremendous energy in this system.

In the Soviet Union regional protectionism is not a great problem; rather, the issue is ministerial autarky. Ministries, representing economic sectors, and even individual enterprises, have responded to chronic supply uncertainties by vertical integration. As a result, most ministries are close to self-sufficient in many of their input needs. The obvious solution in the USSR would be to open up all markets to any entrant wishing to supply the products so as to draw out the efficient domestic producers, whatever their ministry.

Neither country has gone far in the direction of competition to date; of the two, China has outdistanced the USSR, at least in creating strong incentives to operate profitably on the domestic market while satisfying domestic demand. Both countries share critical weaknesses in their current approaches. Monetary policy is loose in both countries, creating tremendous inflationary pressures that are now—more often in the USSR than in China—poorly controlled by administrative price controls. Basically, new money is issued in these systems through excessively easy finance for investment projects—for which there is an insatiable demand—and through subsidizing enterprises that are experiencing heavy losses. Tight monetary policy is a euphemism for real bankruptcies, and neither country—or for that matter no socialist country—has yet been able to muster the courage to follow such a path.

The case for strong domestic competition is understood by some in each country, but as a rule is not accepted. The love affair with large enterprises, and the general conviction that economies of scale swamp any potential gains from competition among smaller enterprises, still reign supreme, particularly in the Soviet Union. In China the problem is that provincial leaders, who receive a large portion of local revenues from the industrial enterprises under their jurisdiction, are not eager to see local enterprises face competition from more efficient factories in other provinces.

In sum, though this Japanese-type strategy seems to be viable, both economically and politically, there is as yet little evidence that either China or the USSR has embraced it. Until they do, or until they discover yet another way to force domestic enterprises to compete on international markets, their roles in the world economy will remain modest.

IMPLICATIONS FOR THE WEST

Economic relations with socialist countries are now a quite minor consideration for the developed West. In the mid-1980s, when developed market economy (DME) exports were at about $1.3 trillion, exports to the centrally planned economies were about $60 billion, or 4.6 percent of the total. DME exports to the USSR and China were about $20 billion each, the same level as exports to Australia and New Zealand combined.[13] Imports by the DMEs from all centrally planned economies were slightly lower than exports during the same period, leading to a small, but inconsequential, trade surplus.[14]

If economic reforms were boldly pursued in the USSR and China, an aggressive borrowing strategy could result in a rapid increase in imports of machinery and equipment from the DMEs. But even so, the result would be equivalent to rapidly expanding imports by two Australias and New Zealands, a welcome but hardly momentous event for the world economy. Only under the most optimistic of scenarios, in which all goes well in these economic reforms and in which an economic opening to the West plays a prominent role in reform strategy, would there be a notable impact on the world economy in this century.

Moreover, there is no indication so far that either the USSR or China will be so bold, or move so quickly. To be sure, the desire to open to the global economy seems to enjoy wide acceptance in both reform programs. But the commitment to protectionism and financial conservatism is so strong in the two countries that it now appears likely they will continue to stress export promotion, giving only a modest role to new imports. This approach effectively eliminates the possibility that either China or the USSR will be a significant source of new demand for DME exports in the near future. In any case neither China nor the USSR is likely to make dramatic inroads into DME markets very soon, though China, with its more aggressive joint venture policy, will probably move somewhat faster than the USSR into that area.

Although actual changes in the Soviet and Chinese role in the world economy may be slow, both countries will aggressively pursue efforts to enhance their status and influence in the world economic system. The Soviet Union may, indeed probably will, seek to enter the GATT as a market economy with a two-column tariff system, granting most-favored-nation treatment to those members that reciprocate. China is already applying for full membership in the GATT as a "multiformed economy" and has promised the gradual development of a foreign exchange market and greater transparency in its foreign trade and investment regulations. The USSR may "declare" some limited form of ruble convertibility as preparation for seeking membership in the International Monetary Fund,

13. United Nations, Department of International Economic and Social Affairs, Statistical Office, *1986 International Trade Statistics Yearbook*, vol. 1: *Trade by Country* (New York: UN, 1988), pp. 1084–85.

14. Ibid., pp. 1156–57.

which will mean little in terms of the economy but may have a significant effect on world opinion.

The problem for Western governments will be to separate wish from reality and to focus on real changes rather than merely on rhetoric. That will be hard. Because the socialist countries' desire for change may be genuine and the direction may be right, the temptation in the West will be to accept the combination of desire and change as a promise for the future, in part to encourage the process. There are no easy formulas to evaluate such issues; they will have to be addressed case by case.

Those interested in deeds not words in assessing the direction and magnitude of real change can watch certain indicators. Most important will be those that reflect the emergence of genuine competition within the socialist countries: enterprises suffering sales problems, or possibly even closing; frequent, and sometimes large, movements in relative prices; and a general rise in the quality and a decline in the cost of products. Another positive sign will be the increasing complexity of financial systems as they expand the number of instruments through which individuals and institutions can sell and buy claims to a part of the income stream of an enterprise. Such a change is obviously a sensitive subject for a socialist country, but there are ways to partly privatize property rights while retaining a significant role for the state. Some sort of formal or informal foreign exchange market will also be needed to ensure that, as with capital, foreign exchange is drawn to its most profitable use in the system.

If these processes begin to operate in the 1990s, the early part of the next century may see an expanding flow of competitive products across a wide spectrum of goods, moving from East to West. Simultaneously the opportunities for investment and, more gradually, exports to socialist countries should improve significantly.

As these economies integrate into world markets, it is impossible now to foresee exactly what products they will specialize in and what effects integration will have on the world system. Their products will most likely be competing with those from the newly industrialized economies, rather than with manufactured goods exported by developed Western countries. If the reforms go very well, the integration process will stimulate specialization, trade, and world growth in much the same way that the trade liberalizations of the 1960s and 1970s operated on the nonsocialist part of the system. The leaders of Western governments should therefore do all they can to understand the process, make sure they do nothing to hinder its development, and be prepared to take advantage of the new developments as they unfold.

Even if reform succeeds in China and the Soviet Union, the two countries will continue to view international issues differently from the United States; they may even work together in some ways that run counter to American interests. As suggested earlier, successful reform will not necessarily extinguish national ambition and may place more material and ideological resources at its disposal. Nonetheless, on balance the United States has a large interest in seeing reforms succeed in both the Soviet Union and China. If these countries are successful in their efforts to modernize and integrate into the world economy, they are more likely to serve as a force for stability than if they were to continue to develop in a halting, inefficient, and autarkic manner. Moreover, successful economic reforms would almost certainly require the domestic political and social reforms that Western countries have long hoped to see in the two countries.

Although the United States therefore has an interest in successful reform in both China and the Soviet Union, its policies toward the two countries cannot be identical. Economically, the Soviet Union is a relatively developed country that still conducts most of its trade with the socialist bloc, whereas China is a developing nation that is oriented more toward Japan and the West. Geopolitically, despite recent improvements in Soviet-American relations, the Soviet Union remains the principal adversary of the United States, whereas China, despite its insistence on an "independent" foreign policy, shares many common interests with America. These factors imply that American policy can be more forthcoming toward China than toward the Soviet Union.

China's status as a friendly developing country warrants some degree of technical and economic assistance from the United States. Given the budget constraints now confronting the American government, the United States will probably not be able to offer China large quantities of subsidized credits, as can Japan (and, to a lesser degree, Western Europe). But the United States can support capital increases for the Asian Development Bank and the World Bank, part of whose lending is directed toward China. And China's growing need for economic and technical information is a natural complement to the openness of American educational and commercial organizations. It is entirely appropriate not only that the United States make such information available to China through academic and technical exchange programs, but also that most of the cost of such activities be borne, as in the past, by the United States.

Beyond that, it would be desirable for the United States and China to work together to create the framework for an expanded economic relationship. For its part, America must continue to relax controls on the transfer of civilian technology to China, permanently extend most-favored-nation status to Peking, revise American trade legislation to reflect the fact that China is changing from a nonmarket to a regulated market economy, and, once China has entered the GATT, make China eligible for tariff reductions under the generalized system of preferences. In return, China must do more to open its economy to American trade and investment. Peking should further improve the climate for foreign investment, including the repatriation of profits earned on the domestic market; offer greater protection to intellectual property; and increase the transparency of both its domestic economic regulations and its economic policymaking processes. In addition, however, Chinese leaders must come to understand that American investment in and trade with their country will be guided primarily by commercial considerations, and that the U.S. government will have only limited ability to encourage those endeavors.

The underlying considerations in U.S. policy toward the Soviet Union differ from those for China in important ways. The legacy of years of tension in U.S.-Soviet relations cannot be quickly dissipated, even with the best of intentions on both sides. Nor can the two countries quickly eliminate the huge military arsenals that each has built up in its race to best the other. Furthermore, aside from this difficult history, it is a fact that the USSR, unlike China, is a developed country, which eliminates one of the motives behind U.S. willingness to aid China. Clearly reforms in the Soviet Union are moving in a direction favorable to U.S., indeed Western, interests. But Americans cannot, and do not want to, grant to the USSR its wish to become a major political and economic force in the world. It will have to earn that status. It would be equally foolish for the United States to attempt to sabotage that effort or to try to pave the way.

As a practical matter, therefore, the U.S. government should create a stable atmosphere within which cultural contacts and commercial relations between the United States and the Soviet Union can develop, giving full play to the basic economic and social forces in both societies. The U.S. government should not discourage businessmen to deal with the USSR, but it need not go overboard in encouraging them. In such areas as joint ventures, U.S. policy should emphasize that, within the constraints of legitimate national security concerns, the commercial merits of proposed agreements, not their ultimate effect on the U.S.-Soviet relationship or on Soviet society, should be the main consideration. If business executives are convinced these ventures are profitable, they should go ahead with them.

As the USSR continues its efforts to join in the work of major international economic organizations, the United States should take a general view that it is willing to talk, and willing to be convinced. The USSR will, for example, soon be applying again for membership in the GATT. The U.S. reply to the first Soviet overture to the GATT in August 1986 was a simple no. This time around we should agree to negotiations, the basic thrust of our position being that if, and when, the domestic reforms truly begin to take hold, Soviet membership in the GATT might well be workable—but not until then. In addition, we would want to be sure that the Soviet Union was genuinely interested in making the GATT work, rather than in using it solely to make points about the relations between developed and developing countries. Similarly, if and when Soviet leaders express more than modest interest in membership in the Asian Development Bank, the IMF, and the World Bank, we should at least be willing to listen to what they have in mind.

In both China and the Soviet Union, U.S. influence will be modest. The most important thing we can do is to make sure we understand, as best we can, the reform processes in the two countries. We must be able to sort out apparent from real changes if we are to calculate the effect of developments there on our interests. Then with all the skill we can muster, we must judiciously apply our limited resources and influence to support positive trends in the two societies.

CHAPTER SEVEN

The East Asian Laboratory

HARRY HARDING
EDWARD J. LINCOLN

The importance of East Asia to the United States has become part of the conventional wisdom of the late 1980s. Asia has long since surpassed Europe as America's largest trading partner and now accounts for fully 60 percent of the American trade deficit. The Pacific Basin joins the United States to Japan, China, and the Soviet Union, three of the world's other major powers, and to several increasingly significant regional actors. Asia houses not only a rich store of traditional art, literature, and philosophy, but also vital and original contemporary cultures, whose impact on the United States is being magnified by a new wave of Asian immigrants and by the expanding role that Asian-Americans play in U.S. politics and society. The American fascination with Asia is reflected in the ever more frequent references to a "Pacific century," an "East Asian edge," a "Pacific challenge," and other formulas suggesting that the center of world geopolitics and commerce is shifting from Europe to Asia.

Although the importance of Asia is now generally accepted by Americans interested in foreign affairs, the agenda facing the United States in the region is less well understood. One reason is the size and complexity of the Asia-Pacific region. Economically, Asia ranges from some of the poorest nations in the world, such as Burma and Laos, to some of the wealthiest, including Brunei and Japan. Geographically, the region includes the microstates of the South Pacific, the city-states of Singapore and Hong Kong, the island archipelagos of Japan and Indonesia, and the huge multi-ethnic empires of China and the Soviet Union. Politically, the states of Asia include colonies, Stalinist tyrannies, military dictatorships, liberalizing authoritarian systems, and pluralist democracies. And culturally, Asia is an amalgam of Confucian, Moslem, Hindu, Buddhist, and Christian influences, as well as of traditions indigenous to each country.

Given this complexity, it is understandable that governmental officials

185

and foreign policy analysts tend to define the U.S. agenda in Asia in terms of the problems and opportunities America faces in individual countries. This bilateral approach, however, sometimes obscures the broader issues in the region and fails to fit the particular pieces of the Asian agenda into a coherent pattern.

We believe that three broad trends characterize Asia as it enters the last decade of this century. One is a growing preoccupation with economic affairs in an increasingly interdependent and competitive environment. The second is the growing pressure for political liberalization in a region still dominated by various forms of authoritarianism. The third is a more diffuse pattern of geopolitical influence in Asia, featuring the gradual emergence of several regional and subregional powers alongside the Soviet Union and the United States. These three trends are closely related: economic dynamism fuels many of the pressures for liberalization, and, together, economic success and political awakening are creating new centers of national power and nationalistic sentiments in a more pluralistic Asia-Pacific region.

We believe, moreover, that these three broad trends are a foreglimpse of what is to come, not only in Asia, but in the rest of the world as well. A principal thesis of this chapter is that in Asia one can see many of the trends that together mark the end of the postwar era and herald the emergence of a new international system, in which the superpowers are less dominant and economic issues more central. If, as seems likely, the world as a whole is moving in this direction, then Asia can serve as a laboratory for American policymakers, in which they can develop concepts and strategies for coping with the more complex and competitive world of the next century.

Adjusting to the new Asian political economy will be a challenge for the United States, but not an insuperable one. Despite recent discussions of American decline, developments in Asia have not relegated the United States to isolation or passivity. America will continue to be the most important single market for Asian exports, a vitally important source of capital and technology, and an essential participant in the region's strategic balance. Nor do present trends in Asia require wrenching changes in American policy. The United States has, since the conclusion of the Vietnam War, forged strong and effective relations with most Asian nations, and has struck a sustainable balance between its resources and its commitments in the region. Moreover, most Asian countries hope for constancy, rather than convulsion, in American relations with their region.

But economic dynamism, political liberalization, and strategic complexity are inexorably changing the face of contemporary Asia. The United States can no longer expect to be as predominant in the region, economically or politically, as was the case in the early postwar era. Our Asian partners are increasingly competitive, nationalistic, and independent. These new realities call for adjustments in both our bilateral and regional relationships. Happily, if we respond creatively to the emerging trends in the region, we will discover that the new Asia provides great opportunities for building mutually beneficial economic relations, for promoting political liberalization, and for enhancing strategic stability.

THE ECONOMIC IMPERATIVE

Perhaps the most dramatic—and certainly the most widely discussed—feature of East Asia over the last several decades has been its remarkable economic success. First Japan, then the smaller economies now known as the "four little dragons" (South Korea, Taiwan, Hong Kong, and Singapore), and more recently some of the larger nations of Southeast Asia (particularly Malaysia and Thailand), all adopted export-oriented strategies that have allowed them to industrialize at an extraordinarily fast pace. These countries used the rapid expansion of world markets in the 1960s and 1970s as a principal source of domestic growth, with increases in exports accounting for as much as 80 percent of the growth in South Korea's GNP between 1979 and 1985, and nearly 53 percent of growth in Taiwan over the same period. They also developed the intellectual and social capability to absorb a rapid flow of technology from more advanced countries through direct foreign investment, licensing, academic exchange, and other devices.

The results are impressive. Japan's advanced industrial economy is now the second largest in the world, surpassing that of the Soviet Union. Hong Kong and Singapore have achieved GNPs per capita of around $7,000–$8,000, and Taiwan and South Korea have per capita incomes of around $4,000–$5,000, levels that place them above some of the poorer Western European countries. Malaysia and Thailand are experiencing bursts of growth that will probably soon propel them into the ranks of the newly industrialized economies. In Indonesia and the Philippines, attention is turning from the production of primary products to the task of industrialization, although inefficient government policies remain serious impediments to more rapid economic transformation. China's national output has grown at an average annual rate of 9 percent over the last decade, with substantial improvements in incomes and levels of consumption in both city and countryside.

Trade and financial flows in the Asia-Pacific region have also grown dramatically, largely focused on the United States and Japan. Over the twenty years between 1966 and 1986, the dollar value of exports from East Asian countries expanded at a remarkable average annual rate of 19 percent, far exceeding the annual increase in the value of total world trade. The region's share of American imports more than doubled over the same time period, from 17 percent of total imports to 37 percent, while American exports to the region also rose, from 13 percent of all U.S. exports to 24 percent.[1] Direct foreign investment by Japanese and U.S. firms in the rest of the region has far outweighed that by other sources. Although the predominant flows are between the developing countries and the United States and Japan, even among the developing countries trade ties have been gradually thickening, and investment from the newly industrialized economies to the less developed economies may soon follow.

The economic dynamism of Asia has had significant implications both for the United States and for the region as a whole. The first and most fundamental is a growing sense of international competition. This preoccupation with trade balances, market shares, productivity, and other measures of economic performance has supplemented and to some degree replaced the earlier focus on building political institutions and maintaining national security. It has also produced a growing willingness in many countries to adopt radically new policies in an effort to improve the productivity and competitiveness of their economies.

Nowhere is this preoccupation more striking than in the communist states of East Asia. The socialist countries have gradually become aware that their economic performance, particularly in qualitative terms, lags far behind the rest of the region. As early as 1978, Chinese leaders decided that their relatively self-sufficient, centrally planned economy would have to be fundamentally reformed if their country was to have any hope of competing with its more dynamic neighbors. Vietnam and Mongolia now appear to be coming to the same conclusion, judging from their tentative experiments with market mechanisms, private ownership, and expanded foreign economic relationships. Although

1. Here East Asia refers to Japan, China, South Korea, Taiwan, Hong Kong, Singapore, the Philippines, Thailand, Indonesia, and Malaysia. For trade figures, see International Monetary Fund, *Direction of Trade Statistics Yearbook, 1987* (Washington, D.C.: IMF, 1987), and *Annual, 1966–70*; and *Taiwan Statistical Data Book, 1987* (Taipei: Council for Economic Planning and Development, 1987).

Mikhail S. Gorbachev's effort at economic *perestroika* certainly has many causes, clearly one is the glaring contrast between the stagnation of the Soviet economy and the vitality of East Asia. It is not inconceivable that North Korea, the only remaining Stalinist state in the region, will also embark on a fundamentally different economic strategy after the death of Kim Il-sung.

Elsewhere in East Asia the newly industrialized economies, and the most successful of the developing nations, are concerned with identifying and maintaining their comparative advantage in an ever more heavily contested economic environment. Countries find it increasingly difficult to secure foreign markets and attract foreign investment, as foreign buyers shift their purchases from one country to another in pursuit of the highest quality at the lowest price, and as foreign investors seek the most profitable locations for their offshore operations. The rapid diffusion of technology throughout the region means that some countries must compete with rivals that once stood far below them on the ladder of technological sophistication. The growing anxiety over competitive positions has been heightened by the entry of a large new player—China—into the regional economy, with uncertain implications for flows of trade and investment.

Nor are the most advanced nations of the Asia-Pacific region—Japan and the United States—exempt from severe economic challenges. The rapid industrialization and productivity growth in other nations on the Pacific rim, combined with falling trade barriers over the past several decades, have allowed imports from the Asia-Pacific region to gain significant shares in some U.S. markets, forcing major structural adjustments. Because the yen has appreciated strongly against the dollar, Japan now faces comparable pressures for readjustment, and must find ways to stimulate domestic demand, open its markets to imports, and re- structure its export industries.[2]

In the United States also, the macroeconomic policies and trends of the last decade, outlined in chapter 2—a low rate of saving, a large government budget deficit, and so forth—have exacerbated these long- term developments by generating unprecedented American trade deficits with all major Asian countries (table 7-1). These deficits, in turn, have required large inflows of capital from Japan and other Asian economies, primarily in financial instruments and real estate and now increasingly in the form of direct investment.

---

2. Policy options available to Japan are discussed in Edward J. Lincoln, *Japan: Facing Economic Maturity* (Brookings, 1988), pp. 270–85.

Table 7-1. *U.S. Merchandise Trade Balance with Selected East Asian Nations, 1980, 1987*[a]
Millions of dollars

Region	1980	1987	Change
Japan	−12,183	−59,825	−47,642
Newly industrialized economies			
Hong Kong	−2,343	−6,507	−4,164
Singapore	1,049	−2,342	−3,391
South Korea	253	−9,892	−10,145
Taiwan	−3,030	−18,994	−15,964
China	2,591	−3,413	−6,004
Indonesia	−3,994	−2,952	1,043
Malaysia	−1,351	−1,157	194
Thailand[b]	447	−812	−1,259

Sources: U.S. Bureau of the Census, *Highlights of U.S. Export and Import Trade, FT990/December 1986* (Government Printing Office, 1986), pp. D-2, D-3; *December 1987*, pp. D-4, D-5; and *Statistical Abstract of the United States, 1988* (GPO, 1988), pp. 772–73.
  a. Exports f.a.s. value basis; imports c.i.f. value basis.
  b. Exports f.a.s. value basis; imports customs value basis for 1986 (1987 n.a.), f.a.s. value basis for 1980.

Because those American deficits must contract over the next several years, Asian countries cannot rely as heavily on the growth of American export markets as they did in the past. For the American current account deficit to shrink, American imports from Asia must either fall, or else rise much more slowly than in the past. To compensate for the loss of sales to the United States, the Asian economies must generate more demand at home, or find other nations willing to absorb their rising exports. Japan could potentially pick up much of the slack, and its imports from the rest of the region have in fact risen rapidly over the past two years. Although this is an encouraging sign, Japan retains the reputation of being a protectionist nation, and it is not yet clear how deeply manufactured imports from other Asian nations will be able to penetrate the Japanese market.

For all these reasons, most of the Asian economies foresee intensified competition within sluggish or changing international markets for this decade and beyond. As a result, government and industry leaders are seeking strategies for restructuring their economies, for maintaining economic growth, and for sustaining the prosperity that their societies have come to demand. In communist and noncommunist systems alike, less weight is being given to political ideology and more to economic performance. Nations that were once highly regulated, like China, Taiwan, South Korea, and New Zealand, are becoming more liberal, either as a response to American pressure or because they see their advantage as lying in a more market-oriented, less regulated economy. Even Japan is espousing liberal trade ideals and gradually opening some sectors of its economy to imports, although it continues to irritate its trading partners by retaining many highly protectionist nontariff barriers, including discriminating standards for product certification, explicit or implicit "buy-national" policies, and lax protection of intellectual property rights.

Conversely, the United States, once one of the most open economies on the Pacific rim, is becoming more protectionist as it attempts to cope with unprecedented trade imbalances and capital inflows. Protectionists in the United States have widened their demands from limits on imports by various tariff and nontariff barriers to restrictions on foreign investment in the United States, foreign acquisition of American real estate, and the export of advanced American technology to potential competitors. Some provisions of the U.S. Trade Act of 1988 could be used in a protectionist manner by an administration that so desired, and the textile bill passed by Congress but vetoed by the president was significantly more restrictive than the legislation it would have replaced. As noted later, the rise of protectionism in the United States is regrettable, since American consumers and American exporters both benefit from an open international economy. Nonetheless, it is an understandable response to the economic challenge that the United States now faces from its trading partners in Asia.

A second major consequence of the economic dynamism of the region is that economic issues have become paramount in most bilateral relationships, especially those linking the countries of the region with America and Japan. For the United States, the relatively stable strategic situation in Asia implies that many of the recent issues in its relations with the region have been economic. As the American mood changes in response to stiffer foreign competition, its foreign trade policy has become more assertive. American attempts to secure greater access to foreign markets, while to some extent protecting its own, have aroused resistance and resentment from a wide range of Asian nations. Economic problems are now at the top of the agenda of America's bilateral relations throughout the region: Americans want better protection of intellectual property throughout the region and seek to sell more beef, citrus fruit, and supercomputers to Japan, more insurance to Korea, and more poultry to Taiwan. As Taiwan develops closer economic and cultural ties with the mainland, the controversies in Sino-American relations center less on Taiwan and more on trade and investment issues.

Because of Japan's position as the world's second-largest industrial economy, much of the focus of American trade policy has been on the U.S.-Japan relationship. An insular nation with a strong domestic industrial policy, Japan has effectively restricted foreign penetration of its markets in many areas. It has also failed to play an active role in maintaining the openness of the international economic system. Japan's protectionist and nationalistic trade behavior was a major motive behind the Trade Act of 1988, and should its behavior fail to change, it could further undermine the American commitment to free trade and even jeopardize the strategic relationship between the two countries.

Moreover, as the relative economic role of the United States begins to contract, the rest of the region looks increasingly to Japan as a source of markets, capital, and technology. Although Japan has begun to liberalize its foreign economic relations, its continued commitment to a mercantilist strategy of maximizing exports and restricting imports has led to vocal demands from other nations in Asia for better access to the Japanese market, for greater Japanese investment, for more Japanese economic assistance, and for a more generous Japanese policy toward technology transfer. Thus economic tensions are ever more salient in Tokyo's relations with China, Korea, and Southeast Asia.

Although economics are therefore complicating some political rela-tionships, they are paradoxically ameliorating others. Commerce has been the solvent in melting several hitherto frozen political relationships, particularly those centered on China. Peking's post-Mao leadership has explicitly asserted that the first task of diplomacy should be to help the country to modernize by forging economic links with as many other nations as possible. The lure of the huge Chinese market has encouraged potential trading partners to respond favorably to Peking's overtures. Accordingly, the past several years have seen a dramatic increase in China's trade with South Korea and Taiwan, with a corresponding reduction in the tensions that once characterized those relationships. Similar progress toward a rapprochement between China and Indonesia, again motivated by economic considerations, is likely in the near future. And the recent improvements in China's relations with the Soviet Union are motivated in large part by Peking's desire for access to Soviet technology, markets, and ideas about economic reform.

China is not the only example of this significant trend. Other communist countries in Asia, including the Soviet Union, Vietnam, and even (to a more limited degree) North Korea, are circumventing stagnant political relations through economic ties. The Soviet Union is attempting to use economic relations as a way of easing tensions with the Association of Southeast Asian Nations (ASEAN) over Cambodia, and strains with

Japan over the Northern Territories. Vietnam seeks economic relations with South Korea, Japan, and even Taiwan, all of whose business executives seem eager to oblige. Throughout the region, in short, commercial interaction is building bridges across ideological divides.

Among the bridging mechanisms are proposals for new regional institutions to help defuse the tensions created by competition. This interest in regional organizations is a third major implication of the region's "economic imperative." A Pacific Free Trade Area was suggested by an influential Japanese economist in the late 1960s, and the even broader concept of a Pacific Community, initiated by Japanese government officials and academics in the late 1970s, has gained the support of some American and Australian specialists. But these proposals for a formal intergovernmental organization have never gotten off the ground and are actually attracting somewhat less attention today than they did several years ago.[3]

The obstacles to forming a Pacific Community concern both its sponsorship and its potential membership. Some smaller nations suspect that a formal intergovernmental organization would actually be a disguised device for institutionalizing Japanese or American dominance over regional economic relations. Less developed countries, from China to the members of ASEAN, have periodically expressed their insistence that a Pacific Community be committed to improving the terms of North-South economic relations, rather than simply preserving the status quo. Differences in economic system and political alignment also make it difficult to agree on the membership of such an organization. Should it include all nations in the region, or only those with market economies? Can it include both North and South Korea, and both China and Taiwan? At what point, if any, should the Soviet Union and Vietnam become eligible for membership? Thus, although there is widespread consensus on the need for greater economic consultation, at present no agreement exists on the goals or composition of a Pacific Community.

To date, therefore, the most fruitful approaches to the Pacific cooperation process have been smaller and more informal in character. At the subregional level, considerable successes have already been achieved by such organizations and programs as ASEAN, the South Pacific Forum, and the Australia–New Zealand Closer Economic Relations Agreement.

3. For a review of the evolution of the concept of a Pacific Community, see R. Sean Randolph, "Pacific Overtures," *Foreign Policy*, no. 57 (Winter 1984–85), pp. 128–42; and Palitha T. B. Kohona, "The Evolving Concept of a Pacific Basin Community," *Asian Survey*, vol. 26 (April 1986), pp. 399–419.

Even here, however, difficulties have arisen, notably in moving ASEAN in the direction of a customs union or a free trade area, suggesting the difficulties that would inevitably bedevil attempts at regional economic integration on a larger scale.

Unofficial organizations, such as the Pacific Trade and Development Conference (PAFTAD), the Pacific Basin Economic Council (PBEC), and the Pacific Economic Cooperation Conference (PECC), also promote informal consultation and dialogue among representatives of different sectors of various Asian countries, serving to build a network of personal ties across the region and to heighten awareness of the economic issues and problems confronting contemporary Asia. These are increasingly supplemented by a wide range of smaller forums, both multilateral and bilateral. The multifaceted character of the process is useful, in that each forum can involve a slightly different set of participants, so as to overcome some of the problems of membership described earlier.

Finally, the area's economic dynamism has fueled a debate over the very structure of the international economic order in the Asia-Pacific region. In essence, three alternative strategies compete for support. Some favor the continuation of the current liberal trading and investment system, based on the most-favored-nation principle by which nations use bilateral and multilateral negotiations to reduce or eliminate tariff and nontariff barriers to the flow of goods, services, and capital. Others espouse the need for more managed trade, in which market shares, trade volumes, or trade balances are the subject of negotiation among major trading nations, and in which governments compete to obtain the most advantageous terms for their societies. Still others call for regional or bilateral free trade agreements between nations willing to accept the principles of economic liberalization, with less advantageous treatment extended to others. As the United States—the past proponent of the liberal trade regime—loses its ability to define unilaterally the rules of the international economy, and as Japan—a nation comfortable with managed trade—rises as an international economic power, the issue of the basic rules and institutions that govern international commerce gains greater salience and urgency.

IMPLICATIONS FOR THE UNITED STATES. At a time of severe trade and budgetary imbalances in the United States, the dynamism of the East Asian economies poses a serious challenge to American policy. In the most general terms, the American goal should be to see a prosperous and competitive United States in as vibrant and open a regional political economy as possible. Although the United States can no longer dominate that economic system as completely as in the past, it can continue to play a major—indeed, indispensable—role in securing the benefits of economic openness. Our first priority, of course, must be to devise the most appropriate domestic and foreign economic policies for ourselves. But we must also help encourage Japan and the newly industrialized economies to bear a greater responsibility for the prosperity of the regional economy, to support the maintenance of an open international economic system, and to work with others to devise an effective framework for regional consultation and cooperation.

First and most important, the American trade and budget deficits need to be corrected through a combination of tax increases, expenditure reductions, and measures to bolster saving and productivity. Chapter 2 discusses this need primarily in terms of the direct economic impact of the deficits on the United States, but these economic imbalances have implications for foreign policy fully as important as their domestic economic ramifications. Continuing the deficits at high levels is virtually certain to trigger nationalistic outbursts on both sides of the Pacific. Conversely, reducing the deficits should ease bilateral tensions with Asian nations, both by lessening U.S. trade deficits with the region and by slowing the net increase in foreign capital flows into the United States.

Second, we should continue our efforts to maintain an open international trading system in Asia for flows of both goods and capital. The theoretical rationale for free trade—higher efficiency, better quality products, and lower prices for all—remains as true today as it has in the past. Moreover, the United States has an interest in seeing Asian countries absorb a higher level of American exports, so that the necessary readjustments in U.S. macroeconomic policy can occur with the smallest possible harm to the American standard of living. If Asian nations can sustain high rates of growth and can open their markets to American exports, then the United States can, in effect, grow its way out of its current trade deficit. If, in contrast, Asian nations are unable or unwilling to increase domestic demand, or if they retain tariff and nontariff barriers to imports, then the American adjustment is more likely to require a sharp recession, high levels of inflation, or a further devaluation of the dollar.

An open trading system is vastly preferable to managed trade, or even to regional and bilateral free trade arrangements. Negotiations aimed at determining the volume of trade between the United States and its trading partners, or at guaranteeing American exporters a certain market share abroad, are certain in the end to result in higher prices for American consumers and a less efficient American economy. Regional and bilateral free trade agreements are an intriguing idea, if they are intended as steps toward global liberalization rather than measures to divide the world into exclusive trading blocs. But not very many East Asian economies are plausible candidates for comprehensive trade pacts with the United States. Many governments in the region intervene substantially in their domestic economies and are not likely to curb the practice enough to warrant free trade arrangements. The one exception, of course, is Hong Kong; but the growing interdependence of Hong Kong's economy and that of China—itself highly regulated—makes a long-term trade arrangement with the territory rather doubtful. Furthermore, given the competition among Asian countries in American markets, special trade arrangements with one country would jeopardize relations with the others.

If an open trading system is in the best interests of the United States, how can we work most effectively to maintain it? One prerequisite is resistance to protectionist pressures in the United States. If the United States fails to lead the Asian trading system by its own example, then progress toward more open markets will be more difficult to achieve. Indeed, as the United States presses for more open markets abroad, it must anticipate that its trading partners will not only resist new protectionist measures but also insist that existing American nontariff trade barriers, such as "buy-American" regulations, be made subject to negotiations. Some restrictions on access to the American market may provide leverage in gaining access to other markets abroad. But the goal of such measures should also be to secure a more open international economy, rather than to erect protectionist barriers around the United States.

The other strategies by which the United States seeks to obtain open markets in Asia deserve careful reconsideration. In its negotiations with Japan and other trading partners, the United States has necessarily gone beyond general demands for broader market access and has engaged in extensive, detailed, and often contentious negotiations on specific commodities and services. A recent agreement with Japan to remove quotas on the import of American beef and citrus products suggests that such a strategy can be successful and must be continued. In some cases, however, the pursuit of this strategy has proceeded far beyond the point of diminishing returns. In Taiwan, for example, the first anti-American demonstrations in nearly ten years occurred in early 1988 over Washington's insistence on opening the island's markets to American poultry. The sales at stake probably amount to several million dollars a year—a fraction of our $19 billion trade deficit with Taiwan in 1987. But the damage to our political relationship with Taipei was considerable.

Elsewhere in the region, it is also easy to find situations in which the political cost of intense American pressure far exceeds the conceivable economic benefit.

A more desirable approach is continued reliance on exchange rate mechanisms and on multilateral negotiations. Although the adjustment has taken time, it is now clear that the sharp devaluation of the dollar, beginning with the Plaza accord of 1985, is beginning to have the desired effect. Although American imports are not shrinking in dollar terms, American exports—including exports to Asia—are increasing rapidly, indeed to the point where American industrial capacity is being strained to keep pace.[4] The United States should also join with other nations, through the current Uruguay Round of the General Agreement on Tariffs and Trade (GATT), to press for the liberalization of market restrictions in countries and in sectors or commodities where bilateral pressures might prove to be counterproductive. Inevitably, these multilateral approaches will be cumbersome, and they will probably not proceed as rapidly as the United States might like. Nonetheless, such an approach helps defuse anti-American sentiments in Asia and slowly builds consensus over the desirability of an open international trading system.

A further goal of American negotiation should be to persuade Tokyo to assume a larger, but less mercantilist, role in the region. It is necessary for Japan to open its markets to foreign manufactured goods, to stimulate imports, and to rely more heavily on its domestic market than on exports as a source of economic growth. The rapid and substantial appreciation of the yen since 1985 has provided an incentive for Japan to restructure its economy and accept more imports, but American pressure will be necessary to keep Japan moving in this promising direction. Japan must also consider other aspects of its role in the regional economy. Increasing its overseas investment, its foreign aid programs, and its contributions to multilateral lending agencies are all useful ways of recycling the capital generated by its trade surpluses.

Beyond this, Japan must also decide what kind of economic system is most in its interest. Japan's first inclination may be to support a form of managed trade, with bilateral economic disputes settled by government-to-government agreements on trade balances, trade volumes, or market shares. Tokyo may also promote a degree of hierarchy and exclusivity in economic ties, in which foreign aid, investment, and trade are all

4. The U.S. trade deficit with the newly industrialized economies shrank from $25.3 billion in January–August 1987 to $19.9 billion in the same period in 1988 on the strength of rapidly rising exports to these countries (a 59% increase over this time). Data from the U.S. Department of Commerce.

bundled in ways that tend to exclude other countries. There have recently been reports, for example, that Japan is considering an East Asian regional trading arrangement, from which the European Community and the United States would presumably be excluded.[5] The United States should resist these policies and attempt to convince Japan to join the United States, in the current GATT round and elsewhere, in actively supporting a more open international system.

Just as Japan must play a more positive role in managing the Asian regional economy, so too must the newly industrialized economies "graduate" from their previous status as developing countries by assuming a more prominent part in regional economic affairs. Despite protests in some of these countries, the end of generalized system of preferences status for South Korea, Taiwan, Hong Kong, and Singapore is appropriate, given their dynamic economies and their relatively high levels of per capita income. For the same reasons, these areas should lose the special privileges and exemptions granted to developing countries under the present GATT arrangements.

At the same time as the newly industrialized economies graduate out of their roles as developing countries, however, they should graduate into new roles befitting their prosperity and dynamism. One promising option is admitting more Asian nations to the Organization for Economic Cooperation and Development (OECD), a goal that already has the active support of the Japanese government. South Korea, Taiwan, Hong Kong, and Singapore all now have levels of per capita GNP that exceed those of Turkey and Portugal, the least developed members of the OECD. Similarly, the levels of political pluralism in the four societies—although not yet comparable to those in the United States, Japan, or contemporary Western Europe—arguably equal those in Greece, Turkey, and Spain at the time that they joined the OECD. To be sure, admitting Hong Kong and Taiwan to the OECD will require setting aside the sensitive issues of national sovereignty. But OECD rules extend membership to "governments," not to "nations" or "states."[6] There is every reason to believe that China could be persuaded to tolerate OECD membership for both Hong Kong and Taiwan, as long as its claims of sovereignty over these two territories were not openly challenged.

Admitting the newly industrialized economies to the OECD has several

5. Anthony Rowley, "Raising a Low Profile: The West Risks Overlooking Japan's Growing Status and Influence," *Far Eastern Economic Review,* July 7, 1988, pp. 14–15.
6. Convention on the Organization for Economic Cooperation and Development, article 16 (signed at Paris, December 14, 1960).

advantages for the Asia-Pacific economy as well as for the nations themselves. One of the main features of the OECD is the Development Assistance Committee, which promotes higher levels of foreign aid and attempts to coordinate the aid programs of its members. Although the effectiveness of the committee in coordinating national aid programs should not be exaggerated, it does provide a forum for discussion with a wider mandate than the multilateral lending institutions. As income levels in Asia rise, some governments (such as Taiwan) are becoming aid donors whose inclusion in the Development Assistance Committee would be a natural development. Moreover, the need is increasing for a venue in which to discuss aid programs for some of the principal Asian recipients of foreign assistance—notably the Philippines, but also Indonesia, India, the South Pacific islands, China, and eventually Vietnam. A Development Assistance Committee enlarged to include representatives of the more prosperous Asian nations would be a useful arena for such deliberations.

Adding Asian members to the OECD might also prove to be a more effective mechanism for regional economic coordination and cooperation than creating a separate organization for Asia. Given the growing interdependence of the world economy, there is little justification for conducting the highest level of policy coordination on a regional rather than a global basis. Because many of the most important members of the Asia-Pacific economy, including the United States, Japan, Australia, New Zealand, and Canada, are already members of the OECD, considerable duplication of effort would result from a new regional organization. A separate Asian organization competing with the OECD would also be perceived by Europeans as a threatening development, intensifying their growing sense of isolation from Asia. Moreover, the goals of any Asian economic organization—liberalized trade and investment flows, assistance to the developing countries, and better coordination of national economic policies—are already the ideals of the OECD. Membership in the OECD might well place more pressure on the Asian newly industrialized economies to liberalize their trade policies, reduce controls on inward foreign investment, and improve their protection of intellectual property rights than would the formation of a regional organization.

Admittedly, the OECD cannot be the only forum for dialogue on regional economic issues. But what form should such a process take? In the distant future, it may be possible to create a formal intergovernmental organization spanning the entire region. But the preconditions for such an institution—consensus on its membership, agreement on its goals, and erosion of the ideological divisions that still exist in the region—are not yet present and will take some time to create. The formation of a Pacific Community can be a legitimate long-term goal of American policy, but one must recognize that it can evolve only gradually and naturally from the less ambitious forms of regional coordination and consultation that have already begun to emerge.

PRESSURE FOR POLITICAL LIBERALIZATION

Throughout the Asia-Pacific region—in South Korea and Southeast Asia, and on both sides of the Taiwan Straits—pressure for political liberalization is mounting. In some cases the pressure is forcing progress toward a more pluralistic and responsive political order. In other countries, the pressure is successfully being resisted by leaders and interest groups committed to more authoritarian politics. The challenge for the United States, of course, is to encourage the tendencies toward political liberalization, while coping with the rising nationalism that accompanies it.

The pressure for political reform is rooted, above all, in the authoritarian character of most of the political systems in the region. Only Japan, Australia, and New Zealand have fully democratic political systems; elsewhere in Asia, there has not generally been the pluralism of ideology and organization that is the hallmark of truly democratic societies. Rather, most governments are characterized by some variant of what might be called "personalistic authoritarianism." Political power in such systems is exercised by hierarchical political institutions; authority is focused on a single paramount leader; and opportunities for participation and opposition are limited. In some cases, the political order is justified by some kind of official ideology. And the communist states of China, North Korea, Mongolia, and Vietnam have created totalitarian political systems, with almost total state penetration of society and complete government control over economic affairs.

The economic miracle of East Asia is making personalistic authoritarian systems increasingly illegitimate in the eyes of important segments of their populations. The dramatic growth in national output over the past several decades has been accompanied in most cases by improvements in education and communication. Throughout much of the region the proportion of the population employed in agriculture is declining, and urbanization is rising. In the newly industrialized economies, the proportion of young people receiving a college education has risen to levels comparable to those in more advanced societies. As a result, the professional and managerial middle class is expanding in most countries of East Asia, with wider knowledge of and interest in developments elsewhere in the world. Particularly in capitalist countries, where it is independent of the government, this middle class forms a powerful constituency for political liberalization. These professionals, and especially the younger generations among them, increasingly find personalistic authoritarianism an inadequate system of governance and seek more effective opportunities for political participation.

The emergence of younger generations of better-educated East Asians is occurring at a time when perhaps the last group of Asian political strong men are passing from the political stage. Mao Zedong of China and Chiang Ching-kuo of Taiwan have died. Ferdinand Marcos of the Philippines was significantly weakened by disease before the "People Power" revolution swept him aside in 1986. The tenures of President Suharto of Indonesia, Deng Xiaoping of China, Kim Il-sung of North Korea, and Lee Kuan-yew of Singapore are similarly limited by age and ill health.

The process of succession intensifies the pressure for political liberalization in several respects. As leaders age in today's Asia, there is a growing consensus that their successors cannot, and should not, exercise as much personal authority as the men they replace. More and more people come to the conclusion that their future leaders should be selected through a more open and competitive process than in the past. And there is also a growing demand that the time of leadership transition be the occasion for a broader restructuring of political institutions, so as to make them more responsive to popular interests.

Finally, the virus of political liberalization has proven to be highly contagious. The overthrow of Ferdinand Marcos in the Philippines in 1986 intensified demands for political change in South Korea and in Taiwan. The resulting liberalization of Taiwanese and South Korean politics was then noted enthusiastically by young intellectuals in China, who used it to support their own demands for political reform. The political restructuring now under way in China may come to reverberate throughout the rest of communist Asia.

What is particularly promising is that far-sighted leaders in several countries have decided that political liberalization is inevitable and consequently have launched reforms themselves so as to maximize the chances that the process will be relatively smooth, and that they and their supporters can maintain a share of political power. The sponsorship of at least limited reform by the leaders of China, South Korea, and Taiwan is evidence of this trend. Elsewhere, the creation of more open and responsive political systems has been much less easy. But the fall of Ferdinand Marcos in the Philippines and the collapse of the government of Ne Win in Burma suggest that established regimes can be set aside rather quickly by a coalition of student and middle-class opposition.

The growing demand for political liberalization in East Asia does not imply that the process will be untroubled, or that full democratization in the region is in any sense inevitable. Alongside the factors promoting liberalization must also be set several severe obstacles to political reform.

First, it is extremely difficult to create—or even to sustain—democratic institutions in societies that are rent by deep ethnic or religious cleavages. Members of minority groups are loathe to submit to the will of the majority, and members of majority groups may be reluctant to guarantee rights or autonomy to those in the minority. Ethnic tensions, disguised or repressed by authoritarian institutions, may assume more visible and disruptive form when opportunities for political participation increase.

Throughout much of East Asia, particularly in Southeast Asia, ethnic and religious cleavages are being activated by political liberalization and economic change. These problems include the rise of Islamic fundamentalism in Malaysia and Indonesia, supplementing the longer-standing problem of Moslem minorities in the Philippines; the tensions between overseas Chinese and indigenous populations in much of Southeast Asia; the conflicts between Taiwanese and mainlanders on Taiwan; the divisions between Indians and Melanesians in Fiji; and the cleavages between Han Chinese and various ethnic groups in China. These ethnic tensions have been the cause for some of the limitations on political liberalization that have provided a counterpoint to the broader tendency toward political reform in the region: the suppression of dissent in Tibet, the Taiwan government's rejection of demands for independence or self-determination, the military coup against an Indian-dominated government in Fiji, and the arrest of opposition leaders and the suspension of publications in Singapore and Malaysia.

A second problem concerns the economic disparities that plague many Asian societies. To be sure, some countries in the region have done a remarkable job of limiting economic inequality during the process of modernization. Taiwan, China, and to a lesser degree South Korea all come to mind. But even in these countries, as well as in the less fortunate countries of the region, significant differences remain between rich and poor, and between city and countryside, that may be a destabilizing force or at least a constraint on liberalization. The impact of these inequalities can be seen in the regional cleavages that characterized the recent South Korean presidential elections, the glacial pace of land reform in the Philippines, and the opposition of many wealthy industrialists and merchants in Hong Kong to direct elections to the local legislature.

Finally, neither political culture nor political institutions are conducive to easy democratization in many East Asian countries. Politics is often regarded as a zero-sum game, in which neither the government nor the opposition acknowledges the legitimacy of the other. Just as frequently, politics is seen as a struggle for spoils among personal factions, rather than a dispute among broadly based parties and interest groups over major social and economic issues. In such circumstances, liberalization will probably be hampered by an elite reluctant to share power, by dissidents who are unwilling to settle for anything less than the complete overthrow or abdication of the current government, or by an opposition that fragments along personalistic lines.

Similarly, the institutions that could support the expansion of political participation are absent in much of Asia. In much of Western Europe and the United States, contestation preceded inclusion: a system of competitive elections to a powerful legislature was developed before the rights of suffrage were extended to the entire population. In East Asia, in contrast, the two processes are occurring in reverse order. There has already been substantial political mobilization of significant sectors of society, but the institutions to channel and absorb that participation are not universally present.[7] Thus in some cases there is no directly elected legislature while in others there is a legislature whose powers are more nominal than real. In most places, there is a lack of broadly based, responsible opposition political parties, or genuine freedom of the press. And, under conditions of personalistic authoritarianism, there are few regular, well-tested procedures for leadership transition.

Unhappily, these obstacles suggest that political liberalization in East Asia is more likely to be slow and halting than smooth and rapid. In the near term, one may well see recalcitrant elites attempting to repress dissent, divided oppositions unable to mount sustained challenges to governments in power, and chronic protest by those dissatisfied with the pace of change—all punctuated by episodes of military intervention.

Even over the longer term, the case of Japan suggests that political liberalization may take a specifically Asian cast. Japan has a stable democratic system, and yet a single political party—the Liberal Democratic party (LDP)—has maintained its majority position in national elections for more than thirty years. Although opposition parties are

7. The terms "contestation" and "inclusion" are drawn from Robert A. Dahl, *Polyarchy: Participation and Opposition* (Yale University Press, 1971).

able to compete for support in fair elections, they have never been able to challenge the LDP's stranglehold on national political power, even when they have held office in important prefectures and municipalities. To many Asians, the Japanese example in politics may be as compelling as in economics: Japan gains many of the benefits of electoral competition without experiencing the disruptions and instabilities attendant upon true rotation of power.

IMPLICATIONS FOR THE UNITED STATES. Throughout our 200-year history, American foreign policy has combined in various measure the twin elements of idealism and realism. Supporting the tide of political liberalization that is rising across Asia befits both these tendencies. On the one hand, the creation of more open, responsive, and pluralistic political institutions is in keeping with traditional American values. On the other, when it helps resolve tensions between unresponsive governments and their populations, liberalization fulfills our pragmatic desire for stable allies. Promoting political change in foreign countries cannot be the driving imperative of American policy, but it can and should be one element in the broader tapestry of U.S. foreign relations.

The United States can legitimately claim credit for some of the political liberalization that has taken place, even though it must also accept some of the blame for its slow pace. American intervention secured the release of the prominent Korean dissident Kim Dae-jung in 1981, and American policy encouraged the constitutional reforms that led to direct presidential elections in Korea in 1987. The United States was instrumental in moving Ferdinand Marcos into exile in 1986, and in supporting Corazon Aquino's efforts at political and economic reform. In Taiwan, too, the United States has endorsed the steps taken by Chiang Ching-kuo and Lee Teng-hui toward liberalizing the political structure and expanding economic and cultural contacts with the Chinese mainland. In all these countries the progress toward democracy is helping resolve the familiar dilemma between our support for human rights and our security relations with authoritarian governments.

These successes should not blind us, however, to the difficulties ahead. As noted earlier, political liberalization is likely to be slow and halting. The United States will have to determine whether particular incidents— such as the arrest of dissidents or the suspension of opposition publications—reflect simply the cyclical relaxation and tightening of control that often characterizes political liberalization, or whether they represent a more basic retreat from the goals of reform. Whatever it decides, the United States will have to tailor its strategy to the circumstances and be prepared for charges that its comments and actions involve interference in another country's internal affairs.

The course of political reform in China provides numerous examples of these dilemmas. The post-Mao era has experienced several cycles of political advance and retreat, from the "Democracy Wall" period of 1978–79 to the campaign against "spiritual pollution" in 1983–84, and from the relatively open discussion of political reform in 1986 to the criticisms of "bourgeois liberalization" in early 1987. Some Americans tend to exaggerate both phases in this recurring cycle: to exult that China is about to "adopt capitalism" or "repudiate Marxism" when the reforms seem to leap forward, and then to despair that China is about to launch another antirightist campaign or even another Cultural Revolution when the reforms suffer a setback. Moreover, the periodic congressional resolutions criticizing various shortcomings of the Chinese political system, whether the repression of dissent in Tibet or the implementation of a draconian birth control campaign, have been seen by the Chinese government as unwarranted interference in their internal affairs.

There is, of course, no single policy that can be universally and mechanically applied to resolve these dilemmas. The vagaries of political liberalization will have to be addressed case by case. In general, however, official condemnations of foreign societies, whether by presidential proclamation or by congressional resolution, are best restricted to clear instances of pronounced political retrogression. Punitive measures, such as a reduction of military or economic assistance, should also be left to extreme cases. In more ordinary circumstances, American concern with the promotion of political and civil rights in the Asia-Pacific region is better conveyed through regular congressional hearings, the annual reports issued by the Department of State, academic and journalistic reportage, and monitoring by various human rights organizations.

Dilemmas will arise when liberalization succeeds as well as when it stalls. Recent developments in South Korea, Taiwan, and the Philippines clearly suggest what may lie ahead. In South Korea, students and intellectuals are taking advantage of the more open political climate to demand a fuller accounting of the history of American policy toward their country, in an attempt to gauge American responsibility for the division of the Korean peninsula and for Chun Doo-hwan's accession to power. In Taiwan, poultry farmers, supported by members of the new opposition party, have protested pressure to open the local market to U.S. turkeys and chickens, and environmentalists have objected to a chemical plant proposed by a U.S. firm. In the Philippines, a rising tide of nationalism is greatly complicating negotiations to extend the agreement on U.S. military bases there. In short, more open political systems may well be more nationalistic, and less willing and able to make concessions to the United States on issues of economic liberalization and security cooperation.

THE DIFFUSION OF POWER

To a degree, the widespread preoccupation with economic competitiveness and political liberalization in East Asia has cast geopolitical and strategic issues into a secondary position. In contrast with the past, leaders across the region are interested in trade balances rather than force balances, political opponents at home rather than strategic adversaries abroad, and investment climates rather than military budgets.

Still, security issues have by no means become irrelevant. The Asia-Pacific region remains plagued by an ongoing conflict in Cambodia and a continuing face-off on the Korean peninsula. The United States and the Soviet Union are still, despite the recent Intermediate-Range Nuclear Forces Treaty, engaged in a conventional arms race in the Northwest Pacific. China's commitment to military modernization, and increases in Japan's military budget, are causing widespread suspicion throughout the region. A wide range of territorial issues, both on land and at sea, are potential flashpoints for military conflict. Partly as a result, the geopolitical relations between several pairs of regional powers—China and Japan, Japan and the Soviet Union, the Soviet Union and China, China and India, India and ASEAN, ASEAN and Vietnam, Vietnam and China—remain hostile, strained, or uncertain.

Moreover, the geopolitical contours of East Asia are changing in response to its economic dynamism. As the dominance of the two superpowers has declined, both the United States and the Soviet Union have tried to reduce their commitments by sharing burdens with their allies and by moderating the confrontation with their adversaries. Although no other country has the combination of material resources, military arsenal, and political independence to become the equal of the superpowers, growing prosperity, nationalism, and technological sophistication in the Asia-Pacific region are producing a diffusion of power with new centers increasingly independent of either the United States or the Soviet Union.

Consider first the evolution of Soviet policy toward the Asia-Pacific region. For most of the early postwar era, the Soviet Union had little direct involvement in East Asia, choosing instead to rely on its close political ties with North Korea, China, and North Vietnam. With the collapse of the Sino-Soviet alliance and the withdrawal of the United States from Vietnam, however, Moscow saw both the necessity and the opportunity for more direct influence in Asian affairs. But in seeking a larger role in the Asia-Pacific region, the Soviet Union selected essentially military means. Throughout the 1970s and early 1980s, the Kremlin enlarged its naval, air, and ground forces in the region, enhanced their readiness, and equipped them with more modern and sophisticated weaponry. It supported the Vietnamese invasion of Cambodia in 1978 and intervened directly in Afghanistan the following year. Moscow increased its military cooperation with North Korea and India, secured the right to make naval port calls in a number of Asian countries, and took over the former American naval base at Cam Ranh Bay.[8]

After assuming the leadership of the Soviet Union in 1985, however, Mikhail S. Gorbachev concluded that these initiatives had proven both costly and counterproductive. The Soviet involvement in Afghanistan, increasingly unpopular at home, had failed to win a decisive victory over the *mujahideen*. Soviet assistance to Vietnam, estimated at about $3 million a day, had neither revitalized the Vietnamese economy nor consolidated Vietnamese influence over Cambodia.[9] Soviet military deployments in the Far East and elsewhere were placing an intolerable burden on the Soviet economy and had prompted a buildup of American naval and air power in the Northwest Pacific. Perhaps most important, the unrelenting growth of Soviet military forces in East Asia had produced an informal coalition of the United States, Japan, China, and ASEAN to resist what was widely regarded as Soviet expansionism in the region.

Beginning with a path-breaking speech on Asia delivered in Vladivostok in July 1986, Gorbachev has tried to recast Soviet policy to secure greater benefits at lower costs. Since then, he has begun to withdraw Soviet forces from Afghanistan, criticized the misuse of Soviet aid to Vietnam, removed at least one division of troops from Mongolia, reduced the readiness of Soviet forces along the Chinese border, and announced his preference for a negotiated solution to the Cambodian question. Moscow has also expressed interest in expanding its economic relations

8. On the Soviet military buildup and the American response, see Amitav Acharya, "The United States versus the USSR in the Pacific: Trends in the Military Balance," *Contemporary Southeast Asia,* vol. 9 (March 1988), pp. 282–99.

9. International Institute for Strategic Studies, *The Military Balance, 1987–88* (London: IISS, 1987), pp. 175–76.

with the Asia-Pacific region, and in joining some of the international organizations that form the cornerstones of the regional economic system. Many of these same themes were reiterated in Gorbachev's subsequent address in Krasnoyarsk in September 1988. On that basis, Soviet relations with China and ASEAN—but, significantly, not yet Japan—have noticeably improved.

The role of the United States in Asia has also been shaped by Soviet-American competition. As noted earlier, the United States responded to the increase of Soviet military deployments in the region with a strengthening of its own naval and air forces: it stationed F-16s in Japan and South Korea, created a seventh carrier task force and two new battleship groups, and deployed Tomahawk cruise missiles, Trident submarines, and new frigates and destroyer escorts in the western Pacific. In part, these new forces were intended as a defensive counterweight against the Soviet buildup. But they were also organized to conduct horizontal escalation through what became known as the "maritime strategy": to attack vulnerable targets in the eastern part of the Soviet Union if a conventional war between the superpowers erupted in Europe or the Middle East. At the same time, the United States began to encourage both China and Japan to improve their military capabilities to cope with the threat from the Soviet Union.

Broadly speaking, American military involvement in East Asia is in reasonable balance with our economic resources. We devote only about a tenth of our nonnuclear military budget to this vitally important region. The American withdrawal from Vietnam, followed by the normalization of our relations with China, eliminated or reduced some of the heaviest burdens that the United States bore in the 1950s and 1960s. Most of America's allies in Asia enjoy stable political systems and vital economies. Few of the regional conflicts in which the United States is involved pose much risk of escalation, and the Soviet Union does not appear to have adopted an offensive strategy in East Asia.

Still, some features of American security policy in East Asia have proven to be expensive, both economically and politically. The projective forces envisioned by the maritime strategy may simply be unaffordable, given the likely constraints on the defense budget during the 1990s. Besides, some analysts seriously doubt whether such forces could successfully perform the missions assigned to them in the event of a global conventional conflict.[10] More immediately, the strategy of horizontal

---

10. For a critique of the maritime strategy, see Francis Fukuyama, "Asia in a Global

escalation has produced strains in American relations with many of its friends and allies in the Asia-Pacific region. Some allies have expressed concern that their security relationship with the United States exposes them to preemptive or retaliatory action from the Soviet Union and thus may lessen rather than enhance their security. Such sentiments have been most clearly expressed by New Zealand, whose government has banned nuclear-armed American ships from the country's ports. The debates over the future of the American bases in the Philippines and over American deployment of nuclear weapons in that country reflect the same fear. Similar views can be heard in the South Pacific, and even in some quarters in South Korea and Japan.

Others have complained that the United States, in its zeal to counterbalance the Soviet Union, has been too eager to encourage the growth of Chinese and Japanese military power. Talk of a "quasi alliance" or "united front" between China and the United States in the late 1970s, and the development of a strategic relationship between the two countries, aroused considerable concern in both Northeast and Southeast Asia that Washington was sponsoring the military modernization of a country that in the end might threaten the security of its neighbors. American pressure on Japan to raise its military spending and enlarge the responsibilities of its self-defense forces provoked a similar response from many Asian nations—from Korea to Singapore—that recall Japanese aggression in the 1930s and 1940s.

Moreover, how power and responsibility should be allocated within America's strategic partnerships is arousing great debate on both sides of the Pacific. Americans increasingly wonder why the most dynamic economies of the region—particularly Japan and South Korea—cannot bear more of the burden of their own conventional defense. At the same time, some Asians complain about the degree to which the United States dominates their security relationships. Koreans chafe under a situation in which an American general holds nominal command over the Korean armed forces, and Filipinos resent their lack of influence over the uses to which American forces stationed in their country might someday be put. These developments suggest that, given the changes in the relative power and prosperity of the United States and its Asian allies, the

---

War," *Comparative Strategy,* vol. 6, no. 4 (1987), pp. 387–413; and Rear Adm. Stanley S. Fine, "The Navy's Troubled Waters," in Stephen Daggett and others, *The Military Budget on a New Plateau: Strategic Choices for the 1990s* (Washington, D.C.: Committee for National Security, 1988), pp. 61–75. For a more positive assessment, see Stephen P. Gibert, "Great Power Naval Strategies in Northeast Asia and the Western Pacific," *Comparative Strategy,* vol. 6, no. 4 (1987), pp. 363–85.

strategic relationships forged in the late 1940s and early 1950s need to be reviewed.

As both the Soviet Union and the United States try to reduce the political and economic burdens of their strategic competition in the region, other nations increasingly affect the balance of power in East Asia. Some of these—particularly China and Japan—are already strong regional powers, with growing influence on global issues. Others—such as India, Vietnam, Indonesia, South Korea, and Thailand—are proving themselves significant subregional actors. Some of these nations are fully independent strategically, unconstrained by an alliance with either superpower. Others, such as Japan and South Korea, are playing more assertive roles within their traditional alliance relationships.

The emergence of these new regional and subregional powers introduces considerable uncertainties into the strategic equation in East Asia. Some of the most important center on Japan, China, Vietnam, and India:

—Japan, in large part because of pressure from the United States, is increasing its military spending, enlarging the responsibilities of its armed forces, and playing a more active role in regional and global political and economic issues. But these developments, accompanied as they are by a growing sense of nationalism among many younger Japanese, are arousing considerable suspicion and disquiet elsewhere in Asia, among those who remember the history of Japanese economic and military expansion.[11]

—China has adopted a much more flexible, pragmatic, and peaceable foreign policy in the post-Mao era. Even so, Peking is devoting considerable resources to the modernization of its armed forces, is selling large quantities of weapons to countries in the Middle East, and is candid in stating its intentions to become a major independent power in both the regional and global arenas. Mindful of China's past cultural supremacy over much of the rest of the region, many of Peking's neighbors, particularly in Southeast Asia, worry that China will again seek political dominance over the Asian mainland.[12]

—Vietnam, now possessing one of the largest standing armies in the

11. On Japan's future role, see, among others, Ronald A. Morse, "Japan's Drive to Pre-eminence," *Foreign Policy,* no. 69 (Winter 1987–88), pp. 3–21; and George R. Packard, "The Coming U.S.-Japan Crisis," *Foreign Affairs,* vol. 66 (Winter 1987–88), pp. 348–67.

12. On the future role of China, see Harry Harding, *China's Second Revolution: Reform after Mao* (Brookings, 1987), pp. 239–70, and *China and Northeast Asia: The Political Dimension* (Lanham, Md., and New York: University Press of America and the Asia Society, 1988); and Michel Oksenberg, "China's Confident Nationalism," *Foreign Affairs,* vol. 65, no. 3 (1986), pp. 501–23.

world, has sought since the unification of the country in 1975 to dominate the rest of Indochina. The Vietnamese invasion of Cambodia was firmly resisted by the noncommunist countries of ASEAN. If the Cambodian conflict can be resolved, however, there may well be a renewed debate in Southeast Asia over the proper role for Hanoi in the region. Should Vietnam be regarded as a potential bulwark against Chinese inroads into Southeast Asia? Or would a revival of the Vietnamese economy and a growth of Vietnamese national power remain in the first instance a threat to its neighbors in Indochina and Southeast Asia?

—India, with the second largest population in the world, and with the potential to manufacture nuclear weapons, has already established itself as the paramount power in South Asia. The fact that neither the United States, the Soviet Union, nor even China challenged the Indian intervention in Sri Lanka suggests that India's preeminence in the region is now accepted as legitimate, even desirable, by the major powers. And yet India is expanding its naval forces to a degree difficult to justify in terms of its South Asian security interests alone. Will India seek to extend its influence in Asia beyond the subcontinent? If so, what will be the impact on New Delhi's already-strained relations with Pakistan and China?

To be sure, these developments will probably be gradual and evolutionary, rather than sudden and dramatic. For now the fact remains that only the United States and the Soviet Union can project military power throughout the region. Nonetheless, the relative decline of the two superpowers in East Asia, coupled with the emergence of new regional and subregional powers, is gradually making the balance of power more complex. Increasingly, the rivalries in the region will involve not the superpowers themselves, but rather such second-echelon powers as China and Japan, China and India, Vietnam and ASEAN, and North and South Korea. These tensions, moreover, are in most cases beyond the ability of the superpowers, either individually or in tandem, to control. Although the present preoccupation with economic affairs is likely to dampen the tensions among the emerging regional powers for the foreseeable future, they remain grounds for concern.

IMPLICATIONS FOR THE UNITED STATES. From a strategic perspective, the fates of America and Asia remain closely intertwined. The United States is, by geography, a Pacific power and has chosen to participate in the geopolitics of the Asian continent as well. Moreover, the overwhelming majority of nations in the Asia-Pacific region consider the United States a necessary element in maintaining a stable balance of power in the Far East. If anything, as the strategic situation in Asia becomes more complex, the need for an active American geopolitical presence in the region will grow rather than decline.

As in the past, the principal goal of American policy should be to prevent any power from establishing hegemony in East Asia, and to discourage countries from challenging, through military, economic, or political pressure, the well-being or security of their neighbors. At the same time, the United States should also recast its posture to respond to the challenges and opportunities that stem from the diffusion of power in the region.

If the United States is to continue to be a meaningful military factor in East Asia, it must maintain bases in the region. Forward deployments are necessary to fulfill our present defense commitments and to address future contingencies. They are an important symbol of active American involvement in the region and, by obviating the need for others to increase their military forces, they help dampen regional arms races. Moreover, the American military base structure in the western Pacific is also essential to our ability to project force into the Indian Ocean and the Persian Gulf. Increasingly, however, the maintenance of American naval and air bases in Asia requires an active consensus by the nations of the region—and particularly those countries in which our bases are located—that our deployments are necessary and desirable.

At present, the cornerstones of the American base structure are in Japan and the Philippines. Bases elsewhere, such as in South Korea, either are for local purposes or else play a subsidiary role. Fortunately, there appears to be a consensus both in Japan and across East Asia about the wisdom of a continued American military presence in Japan. There is a growing recognition in Japan of the military threat posed by the Soviet Union. As a result, support for the alliance with the United States—as well as for the country's own self-defense forces—has risen substantially over the past decade and remains high. There is increasing recognition also that the United States would have to use its bases not only in the event of an attack against Japan, but also to defend South Korea against an assault from the North. At the same time, more and more Asian nations, including even the Soviet Union, realize that the withdrawal of American bases from Japan would probably prompt a level of Japanese rearmament that would have destabilizing consequences for the rest of the region.

The bases in the Philippines, in contrast, are a more problematic element in American military deployments in the region. The extension of the bases agreement after 1991 has become controversial in Manila. To a degree, the bases are being held hostage to the Filipinos' desire for more economic assistance from the United States. But the question also has important political elements. There is much less consensus in the Philippines than in Japan on the presence or the nature of an external threat to the country. The extensive American military presence in the Philippines has come into conflict with rising nationalism and antinuclear sentiment, with some Filipinos complaining about their lack of control over the bases, and others apprehensive about their country's vulnerability to a Soviet attack. More generally, few Filipinos are fully aware of the contribution that the bases make to regional stability.

The United States must continue to make all reasonable efforts to maintain its bases in the Philippines. But the bases are not simply a problem for Americans and Filipinos. If Japan and the countries of Southeast Asia believe an American military presence in the region is beneficial, they should make that belief known to Manila and should also assume some of the political inconvenience and economic expense of supporting the forward deployment of American forces. In the event that the Philippines decides not to extend the base agreement, attaches unacceptable conditions concerning the nature and deployment of American forces, or demands too high a financial price, then the United States should be prepared to relocate the bases elsewhere in the western Pacific.

Although America must maintain an effective military presence in Asia, the increasing economic vitality of many of our allies in the region makes it possible for them to share more of the burdens of collective security with the United States, and the domestic economic constraints on the United States make it necessary for them to do so. Both Japan and Korea should increase their contributions of the cost of maintaining American forces on their territory and should, over time, assume a greater share of the responsibility of their own conventional defense. It is completely appropriate that Japan continue to develop the military capability to defend its own territory and air space, and to control the sea lines of communication around Japan. Given the increasing economic and technological advantages that South Korea enjoys over the North, one can also contemplate the measured reduction of American ground forces on the Korean peninsula. But such adjustments should be gradual to avoid misunderstanding and instability. Reducing American forces in South Korea can occur only as Seoul develops confidence in its ability to defend itself against the North, and the growth of Japanese military forces should be designed and carried out in ways that do not arouse suspicions of Japanese militarism elsewhere in the region.

If the United States is to ask its allies to assume more of the burden for the common defense, it must also recognize the need to allow them to share more of the responsibility for determining a common security policy. In the past, as Sheldon Simon has put it, "Washington has unilaterally devised strategies [and] defined each partner's role."[13] Such an approach is no longer adequate. The United States will have to engage in fuller consultation with its major allies—including Japan, South Korea, Australia, and the Philippines—over a common strategy toward the Soviet Union, particularly at a time when *glasnost* and *perestroika* are calling into question long-standing assumptions about Soviet foreign and military policy. A more consultative relationship will require a shift in attitudes on both sides. The United States will have to become more open to criticism from its allies, and its partners will have to become more constructive in their advice, if such a relationship is to succeed.

The need for consultation extends to regional conflicts as well. In several important regional disputes, the United States is already emphasizing the need for solutions to come from those countries directly involved. In Indochina, for example, the United States has followed the lead of ASEAN in seeking a resolution of the Cambodian question; on the Korean peninsula, Washington has increasingly stressed the development of a direct dialogue between North and South; and in the Taiwan Straits, the United States favors the development of economic and cultural contacts between Taiwan and the Chinese mainland.

Sharing with its partners in Asia the responsibilities for defense and conflict resolution does not obviate the need for American leadership. On the contrary, the United States may need to play an active role in resolving differences over the role of the Khmer Rouge in a successor Cambodian government, and it can usefully supplement a developing North-South dialogue on the Korean peninsula with its own opening to Pyongyang. Clearly, too, American dialogue with the Soviet Union and China can create a superpower environment conducive to resolving regional issues, from Afghanistan to Cambodia, and from Korea to Taiwan. Increasingly, however, the solutions to those regional problems will have to come from the inside out, with the United States playing a facilitating, catalytic, and supportive role, rather than attempting to define and impose its own solutions.

On the basis of a renewed relationship with its allies, the United States can then proceed to address the new possibilities suggested by recent developments in Soviet foreign relations. The new policy toward Asia announced by Mikhail Gorbachev in Vladivostok in 1986 presents

13. Sheldon W. Simon, "Is There a Japanese Regional Security Role?" *Journal of Northeast Asian Studies*, vol. 5 (Summer 1986), p. 32.

both opportunities and challenges for the United States. The Soviet Union has advanced several proposals for arms control in East Asia, featuring the creation of nuclear-free zones throughout the region, the withdrawal of American bases and forces from South Korea and the Philippines, and limits on the deployments of naval forces. Most of these proposals are so one-sided that they hold little interest for the United States. They appear designed to limit American deployments more than their own and to elicit fears of retaliatory Soviet strikes against American bases in the western Pacific in order to drive wedges between the United States and its allies. But there may be opportunities for creating confidence-building measures for naval exercises and maneuvers in the Asian region that would be comparable to those applied to air and ground deployments in Europe. There may also be some possibility for using American naval deployments in the Pacific as a bargaining chip in the search for asymmetrical reductions of conventional forces in central Europe.

It would also be desirable to engage the Soviet Union in serious dialogue about various regional disputes in Asia. Although Soviet leverage over Vietnam may well be limited, and although no outside power can completely control the situation in Cambodia, it is still promising that Moscow appears eager to find a negotiated solution to the Cambodian question that would involve the withdrawal of Vietnamese troops, the creation of a four-party coalition government, and the institution of international guarantees. The Soviet Union should also be urged to condemn North Korean terrorism, to expand its unofficial and informal contacts with Seoul, and to support the resumption of a North-South dialogue on the Korean peninsula. Above all, Moscow's willingness to refrain from intervening in the still delicate political situation in the Philippines—as well as any comparable instances of political unrest elsewhere in Southeast Asia or the South Pacific—will be an important measure of the content of the "new thinking" in its foreign policy.

A final subject for Soviet-American dialogue should be the Soviet Union's role in the Asia-Pacific regional economy. Beginning with Gorbachev's speech in Vladivostok in 1986, Moscow has expressed its determination to expand its economic relations with East Asia, and its interest in joining some of the key institutions of the emerging Pacific Community. The United States should be prepared to acknowledge the simple geographic fact that the Soviet Union is both an Asian and a Pacific power, even though it has not yet become closely integrated economically with the Asia-Pacific region. It should also welcome Moscow's interest in closer economic ties with its Asian neighbors, on the grounds that such economic interdependence may well serve as a significant restraining factor on Soviet foreign policy. If the Soviet Union is able to adopt a more conciliatory policy toward neighboring countries, help resolve outstanding regional issues, and reform its economic system so as to spur its foreign economic relations, then it might well be possible to see Moscow enter such regional economic institutions as the Asian Development Bank and the Pacific Economic Cooperation Conference in the near future.

One can also hope that, stimulated by the increasingly competitive economic environment in East Asia, Vietnam and North Korea can emulate some of the changes that have taken place in China and the Soviet Union: economic reform, political liberalization, a more conciliatory policy toward their neighbors, and fuller integration into the regional economy. Already, there are signs that Vietnam would be interested in such an accommodation, although it remains to be seen what price Hanoi is willing to pay for its policy in Cambodia. The situation in Pyongyang is much less promising: it may be necessary to wait until both Kim Il-sung and his son Kim Jong-il are out of power before there can be any such reorientation of North Korean policy. Still, the United States should be alert to signs of reform in both countries and be prepared to take the appropriate steps to encourage it.

Paradoxically, the prospects for a less expansionist Soviet policy in Asia pose challenges as well as opportunities for the United States. Common resistance to Soviet hegemony may no longer be as compelling a basis for our partnerships and alliances in the region as it was in the late 1970s and early 1980s. Accordingly, a new foundation will have to be found for American relations with China, Japan, and some of the smaller countries in the region. American relationships will increasingly be rooted in economic, cultural, and environmental issues, as well as a wider range of geopolitical questions. Although the emergence of the Soviet Union as a major Asian power will necessarily continue to be a serious concern for the United States and its allies, it can no longer be the sole focus of American policy.

There is the possibility, then, of a significant reduction of Soviet-American tensions in East Asia—perhaps even the end of the cold war in the region. If so, the challenge for the future will be to manage the relations among the other regional powers, to moderate their military competition and to prevent their rivalries from deteriorating into confrontation or even open conflict. Playing a constructive role in the emerging balance of power in Asia will require, first of all, that the United States establish channels for effective dialogue with all the major actors in the region. Fortunately, our relations with Japan, Australia, South Korea, and ASEAN are already close and extensive. We also have an increasingly rich geopolitical dialogue with China, have made considerable improvements in our relations with India, and have established diplomatic relations and academic exchanges with Mongolia. The suspension of military cooperation with New Zealand should provide the incentive for an expansion—rather than a contraction—of our official and informal consultations with Wellington. Dialogue with the island states of the South Pacific should also be expanded. And, as noted earlier, we should be ready to develop broader contacts with Vietnam and North Korea as the situation warrants.

Consultation is a key to reducing misunderstanding and narrowing differences of perspective, but it does not always result in consensus. We should acknowledge the fact that an increasing number of Asian nations will wish to maintain an independent foreign policy, rather than close or automatic association with the United States. At present, there are clear differences between China and the United States over Peking's policy of arms sales to the Middle East, and there are potential divergences over the best formula for a negotiated solution to the Cambodian question. Even Japan, our closest ally, may well hold somewhat different opinions from the United States on such issues as the future of Korea, the modernization of China, and policy toward the Soviet Union. While working for consensus and mutual accommodation whenever possible, we should acknowledge a degree of diversity as an inevitable feature of the growing strategic complexity in the region, rather than as a sign of hostility or unfriendliness to the United States.

These bilateral consultations between Americans and Asians should be supplemented by multilateral forums for discussing the increasingly complex security issues of East Asia. The United States is ideally suited to sponsor various forms of unofficial and informal dialogue among the leaders—and especially the emerging leaders—of East Asia, with an eye to minimizing the misunderstandings and misperceptions that can lead to miscalculation and conflict. Given the strained relations among many of these emerging regional powers, it is imperative that the development of regional dialogue keep pace with—and hopefully outstrip—the intensification of regional rivalries. If necessary, such consultations can form the basis for coordinated diplomatic, economic, and even military pressure against those nations that threaten the security of their neighbors.

Finally, the United States should take new distribution of power in Asia into account when shaping its policies of burden sharing, arms sales, and technology transfer. In an earlier, bipolar world, it may have been reasonable to assume that strengthening all the members of a potential anti-Soviet coalition could only be for the good. Today such thinking is no longer appropriate. In the more complex strategic environment of contemporary Asia, sudden increases in the power of any nation could well be destabilizing. Therefore, the United States should not encourage Japan to raise its defense spending more rapidly than at present or to develop a significant projective capability. Nor should it promote the rapid military development of China, India, or any other emerging regional power.

CONCLUSION

As we approach the beginning of the twenty-first century, we are also nearing the end of the postwar era of American economic hegemony and strategic bipolarity. This transformation should come as no surprise. The degree of economic and political influence that the United States has enjoyed since 1945 was, in large part, the artificial result of the devastation of Europe and Japan during the Second World War. The revival of those economies, and the growth of China and the Soviet Union, should be regarded as inevitable developments, even though they have meant a decline in the relative position of the United States.

Nor is it surprising that the postwar era seems to be ending first in Asia. The enormous human and material resources of that vast region have been harnessed by increasingly effective strategies of economic development. The pace of economic, technological, and political change has thus been more rapid in East Asia than in Latin America, Africa, the Middle East, Europe, or any other region of the world. The economic miracle of the Asia-Pacific region has provided the material basis for a more diverse regional economy, while the persistence of historical, political, and cultural differences has fueled the tendencies toward a diffusion of power.

In the past, such transitions from one era to another were usually catalyzed by major military conflicts, as rising and falling powers sought to clarify and redefine their relationships through war. Today, with nuclear conflict unthinkable, a new international system is being created not by a single cataclysmic shock, but by a series of lesser tremors: the American withdrawal from Vietnam, China's acceptance of the existence of a single world economy, Gorbachev's speech in Vladivostok announcing a new Soviet policy toward the Asia-Pacific region, the transformation of the United States from a net creditor to a net debtor, the growing trade surpluses and capital exports of Taiwan and Japan, Tokyo's decision to enlarge the roles and missions of its armed forces, India's emergence as the preeminent power in South Asia, and so forth. But although the shift to a new pattern of economic and strategic interaction may be undramatic and protracted, the cumulative changes will be revolutionary in their implications.

In the new strategic and economic environment in East Asia, the United States still bears many of the same responsibilities it has had since 1945. It should still strive to maintain a healthy and open domestic economy; to preserve a sound international currency system and a liberal international trading order; to contribute to a stable balance of military power in the Asia-Pacific region; and to find solutions to the ongoing regional disputes in Korea, Indochina, and the Taiwan Straits.

But if, in attempting to fulfill these obligations, we act in traditional ways only, we will find ourselves more and more isolated and overextended. If, for example, we continue to think of the strategic situation in Asia as bipolar, we will try unsuccessfully to build alliances with nations like China that see themselves as independent, and will encourage an expanded military role for other nations such as Japan that other friendly countries see as a threat to their own security. If we assume that strategic relations in the region are based solely on a military calculus, we will discount or overlook their critical economic dimensions. If we attempt to dominate our strategic relationships and alliances, we will continually collide with rising nationalism in the region, unable to persuade our partners to assume a larger burden of the common defense. And if we fail to control our budget and current account deficits, our credibility abroad will decline, protectionist sentiment at home will rise, tensions with our regional trading partners will increase, and our greater reliance on foreign capital will limit our room to maneuver in both economic and strategic matters.

The transition to this new era will create some economic and strategic uncertainties both for the United States and for the region as a whole. Geopolitically, the addition of new independent actors—China, Vietnam, Indonesia, and others—to the existing strategic equation may prove destabilizing at times. Given the historical, political, and cultural differences among these emerging powers, tensions are inevitable. Moreover, the greater complexity in the geopolitics of the region will make it harder for nations to calculate the balance of power and may increase the chances of sudden shifts of alignment that can destabilize the whole system. As Asia moves away from tight bipolarity toward a more fluid system, formal and permanent alliances may give way to more informal, temporary alignments. All this will be unfamiliar to the United States, which for historical reasons tends to feel more comfortable when the line between friend and foe, between ally and adversary, is clearly drawn. Unable to control developments in the region, Americans may feel increasingly frustrated and disappointed. That frustration may be vented in periodic displays of American nationalism, as a disgruntled public demands renewed efforts to bring to heel both uncowed adversaries and recalcitrant allies.

In the economic realm, all the actors face hard adjustments. The United States will have to restrict consumption if it is to control imports, expand exports, and service (let alone reduce) its burgeoning foreign debt. Japan must deal with serious problems of economic readjustment as it shifts production abroad to cope with an appreciating yen and faces growing competition from the newly industrialized economies. Those economies, in turn, must shift to larger-scale production and to higher value-added commodities if they are to maintain a comparative advantage against the less developed nations of the region. And the developing countries will have to compete with one another, and with China, to maintain their shares of export markets in the United States and Europe that will be growing slowly if not shrinking.

Despite these undeniable difficulties, there exists the strong possibility that the emerging system in Asia will be more stable and less costly than the one that preceded it. Strategically, the rivalries among the various powers in the region may be moderated by the continuing preoccupation with economics, and by the common interest of the Soviet Union and America in regional stability. Economically, a revitalized American economy in tandem with a more open Japan could spur economic growth and increase cooperative ventures throughout the region. Prosperity and cooperation in turn will promote liberalization and may attract those systems that have not yet chosen to participate (North Korea, Vietnam, Burma), while reinforcing the commitment of those countries that have.

The challenge facing the United States in Asia cannot be met by withdrawing from an active economic, cultural, or strategic role in the region. Rather, the task is to stay in the laboratory and develop new policy tools for a more complex and pluralistic world. The American role should be to revitalize its own economy, reenergize its bilateral relationships, and provide active leadership in designing a new set of regional economic institutions and security arrangements that can maintain prosperity and stability in one of the world's most dynamic regions.

CHAPTER EIGHT

The Arab-Israeli Conflict in a Global Perspective

HAROLD H. SAUNDERS

Each regional conflict has unique characteristics, but at the same time each dramatizes ways in which our whole world is changing. States alone do not initiate and shape change. Much of the change we see originates in the needs, hopes, fears, ambitions, anger, frustration, actions, and interactions of groups of people—not just in the economic or strategic interests of states. It begins at the bottom, not from state institutions at the top. Leaders increasingly recognize that the effectiveness—perhaps even the legitimacy—of states depends not on their own organization or power but on whether their institutions work constructively in the interactions among their peoples and with peoples of other nations.

Perhaps we see in regional conflicts more quickly than in big-power confrontations that familiar concepts of international relations often do not provide an accurate picture of how today's world works. Traditional tools of statecraft do not reliably produce the results normally expected of them. Other instruments of change are not used as creatively as they could be. Principles of international law and ethics do not probe deeply enough into the interaction among nations to provide useful guides for policy and conduct. Nowhere is that more true than in the Arab-Israeli conflict.

To step back from that conflict to see how relationships among nations are changing globally enables us to affirm our observations in a wider context and come back to the Middle East with new perspectives. No other situation will have exactly the character, complexity, or intensity of Israeli-Palestinian relationships within the Arab-Israeli conflict, but insights gained about them may in turn provide insight into other relationships.

I am *not* saying that states are obsolete or that force used by states has ceased to be a commonly used instrument of change. That would

221

be utopian and inaccurate. I am saying that other agents of change are also at work and that we need to learn to use them creatively. Failure to recognize them can paralyze states and deprive leaders of effective political—and therefore peaceful—means of reaching legitimate goals. Many scholars, analysts, and practitioners close their eyes to the implications of changes that are taking place. They point to evidence that the world continues to work as they believe it always did. They do not seem to understand the power that lies in understanding the sources of change and trying to harness them before they have to react to them.

POWER AND POLITICS IN THE ARAB-ISRAELI ARENA

In the summer of 1982 American television screens showed nightly pictures of men, women, and children living and dying under the Israeli bombardment of Beirut. Advanced combat aircraft and mechanized troops of the Israeli Defense Forces besieged the city. Beirut was mainly defended not by the armed forces of Lebanon—a state only in name, symbol, and geography—but by the armed men of the Palestine Liberation Organization (PLO) and local political organizations.

In the winter of 1987–88 American television screens again brought the Israeli-Palestinian conflict into American living rooms. This time, change came not from the armed power of a state but from the civil disobedience of an unarmed people. The screens pictured Palestinian youths in territories captured by Israel in the June 1967 war—the West Bank and Gaza—throwing stones at Israeli youths in the uniform of the Israeli Defense Forces. They also showed these Israeli soldiers not using planes and tanks but beating Palestinian youths on the ground with stones. The scenes dramatized the human scale and the fundamental intercommunal nature of the conflict between two peoples with claims in the same land.

In both instances Americans witnessed from their armchairs—as they had during the Vietnam War—a deadly conflict that was hardly the classic war between the armies of nation states. Military power did not produce decisive results. A state behaved as groupings of human beings with their own agendas, not as the cohesive rational actor international relations theorists often suppose. Politically organized groups militarily inferior to the Israeli Defense Forces demonstrated their ability to change the complexion of a conflict in the political arena.

The Israeli invasion of Lebanon in June 1982 was not the act of a cohesive nation state to protect or advance the security or territorial interests of its people. The full purposes of the invasion were set not by the decisionmaking mechanisms of the Israeli state but by a group of officials who seemed to circumvent the cabinet.

The declared reason for invading southern Lebanon had been to enhance national security by preventing Palestinian rocket attacks and cross-border infiltration into northern Israel. The undeclared purposes of advancing on Beirut were political. Those who planned the invasion seemed bent on redrawing the political map of Lebanon and destroying the leadership, structure, and armed capability of the PLO. They seemed to believe that by inflicting severe physical damage on the PLO, they would reduce the will of Palestinians in the West Bank and Gaza to resist continued Israeli military occupation and quasi annexation of those territories.

Israel's use of force in Lebanon did not decisively change the Arab-Israeli or the Israeli-Palestinian conflict. In the end Israeli forces withdrew without having achieved their undeclared political purposes. A modern military force with the most sophisticated equipment—presumably including nuclear warheads—which could defeat the combined forces of neighboring Arab states, could not end the Israeli-Palestinian conflict. It could not put Lebanon back together according to its leaders' wishes. For the moment it could prevent Arab armies from ending the conflict by force, but military force could not resolve the conflict in either direction.

In mid-August the firing in Lebanon formally ceased, but violent conflict continued. U.S. marines landed to provide protection for the evacuation of the leaders and armed men of the PLO, which reestablished headquarters in Tunisia. That mission accomplished, the marines withdrew. Many Palestinian refugees left behind were massacred by Lebanese militiamen, apparently before the closed eyes of some Israeli authorities. The marines returned. Israeli troops stayed on—face to face in some places with Syrian forces and in others with local guerrillas. U.S. marines began taking casualties in a guerrilla war they had not been sent to fight.

Eventually Israeli forces withdrew, not because they were militarily defeated but because the Israeli people would not sustain their government in pursuing its undeclared purposes at the cost of continuing losses. The shock of recognizing a possible—if indirect—Israeli role in the massacre in the Sabra and Shatilla refugee camps brought some 400,000 citizens—more than 10 percent of the Jewish population of Israel—into the streets of Tel Aviv one Saturday night in September 1982 to demand an investigation of the Israeli involvement. Then as Israeli casualties from small ambushes, sniping, and car bombs mounted, Israelis pressed their government to end a military venture for which the people saw no vital justification. The two leading political blocs—poles apart in their visions of the future of the Jewish state—agreed to cooperate on pulling Israeli troops back.

Eventually, the U.S. president withdrew the marines under pressure from a Congress that repeatedly demanded, but never received to its satisfaction, an explanation of their military mission. After a small organization and one man driving a vehicle full of explosives killed more than 240 U.S. marines with carrier air support, a president facing reelection decided that politically he could not sustain their deployment. The marines were not an ineffective fighting force; the problem they were sent to deal with could not be resolved by military force alone.

Recognizing the inadequacy of military force to resolve these conflicts, the new U.S. secretary of state, George P. Shultz, and President Ronald Reagan launched a diplomatic initiative to try to begin negotiation of a broad Arab-Israeli-Palestinian settlement. This approach, too, fell short of producing significant change because the Americans concentrated on trying to find terms of reference for a traditional negotiation that the bodies politic involved were too divided to accept.

For six years off and on, Secretary Shultz and his colleagues tried to organize a negotiation. Again and again their efforts fell short because they could not find a way to address the fundamental political obstacle— that neither the Israeli nor the Palestinian body politic had decided whether to negotiate at all. In fact, the objective of some in each camp could be served only by not negotiating. That issue, U.S. leaders did not seem to recognize, could be resolved only in the political arena, not by organizing a conference or crafting a formula for negotiation.

In the winter of 1987–88 the frustration of Palestinians living for more than two decades under Israeli occupation—now desperate in the loss of hope for help from either Arab states or the big powers—broke out in a campaign of civil disobedience. Their main weapons were not arms. They were political. Those Palestinians created the option of transforming a spontaneous expression of frustration into a political program by changing the picture of the problem both in Israel and in the Palestinian movement.

In short, familiar concepts and instruments of international relations do not adequately explain developments in the Arab-Israeli arena. The conflict is not just a state-to-state conflict; it is a conflict between two peoples who have asserted rights to the same territory. One people is organized as a state, but it is so deeply divided over its vision of that state's future that it is politically unable to make decisions and initiate actions to resolve the conflict and ensure the state's continuity. The other is not a state but a national movement also divided over its vision of the future and unable to take initiatives that might lead to political fulfillment. Military power cannot force a solution. Efforts at negotiation do not succeed, because they depend on change initiated in the political environment.

Experience in the Arab-Israeli peace process after the October 1973 war demonstrated that change begins in the political arena. The war itself was not launched to achieve traditional military objectives; it was a political act aimed at erasing the humiliation of the 1967 Arab defeat so that the Arabs could negotiate from a position of restored honor, at reinvolving the big powers, and at showing Israel it was not invincible. Between 1974 and 1979 the United States mediated five Arab-Israeli agreements. Each success in negotiation was preceded by an important political act: the October war, the unprecedented U.S. commitment by Presidents Richard M. Nixon and Gerald R. Ford through the shuttle diplomacy of Secretary of State Henry A. Kissinger, Egyptian President Anwar al-Sadat's historic visit to Jerusalem in 1977, President Jimmy Carter's invitation to Sadat and Israeli Prime Minister Menachem Begin to Camp David in 1978, and Carter's trip to the Middle East in 1979 to wrap up the Egyptian-Israeli peace treaty. Those acts by political leaders were essential.

The word *political* carries a heavy burden in these observations. To convey the full meaning intended, it is useful to move for a moment to the global sphere. Changes encountered in the Arab-Israeli peace process are reflected in experience there as well.

POWER AND POLITICS IN A CHANGING WORLD

Important changes that characterize today's world are described more fully elsewhere in this book. Six related propositions about the conduct of international relationships today are worth setting down briefly here because they widen our perspective on the Arab-Israeli conflict.

First, we see more and more problems that no one state can deal with alone. More centers of influence affect the course of events or block supposedly powerful states from doing so. In the past we have pictured nation states as rational institutions in which leaders amass power to pursue interests in a strategic chess game with other states. In that picture, states resolve problems by the use or threat of military or economic power and by formal negotiation. Today we must shift our focus beyond self-centered state institutions pursuing their interests to the relationships that states build together to address common problems. Protecting one nation's identity and security—the ultimate responsibility of states—may not be possible in a nuclear age without continuing interaction among both allies and adversaries who share a common security problem and its solution. Neither the Soviet Union nor the United States can reduce the threat of nuclear destruction by itself; they can only do so together. Neither Arabs nor Israelis can end their conflict alone; they can only do so together. These observations alone cause us to reflect on the limits of usable national power.

Second, in the relationships between nations today more attention is being given to the political energies and interaction of communities of people. Deepening global interdependence and the gradually increasing involvement of people in domestic and world politics demand new consideration of the human roots of international relationships. More people interact more immediately. What one leader says or does one day is heard, seen, and assessed within hours by another leader's constituencies. Beyond leaders, peoples in many nations are more aware of each other as human beings, not just as institutional abstractions. Fear, suspicion, rejection, mistrust, hatred, and misperception are often greater obstacles to peace between nations than the inability to resolve technically definable problems. This is just as true of Soviets and Americans as of Arabs and Israelis. These changing realities cause us to look beyond an abstract state system to question the proposition that states are different from the groups of human beings who influence, make, implement, and sustain their policies.

Third, traditional instruments of statecraft often do not accomplish what is expected of them. Nuclear weapons cannot be used, and non-nuclear weapons make war prohibitively costly as a way of pursuing interests or resolving disputes. Negotiation—traditionally thought of as the peaceful alternative to force—depends on the political environment. The following observation is as relevant to the summit talks between Soviet General Secretary Mikhail S. Gorbachev and U.S. President Reagan as it is to the Arab-Israeli peace process: Negotiation does not initiate change. Change is initiated and shaped in the political arena. Negotiation may define, capture, crystallize, and consolidate change already begun. But until political leaders have transformed the political environment, negotiators are unlikely to succeed. Or if they do reach a technically sound agreement, it may not be fully implemented or have the intended consequences.

Fourth, instead of seeing foreign relations as a contest between rational states, we more and more see a political process of continuous interaction among policymaking and policy-influencing communities. Change takes place through interaction on many levels at once rather than through a linear series of government actions and responses.

People have lived by the dictum that one nation should not meddle in another's politics. That is not possible now. Relationships among constituencies across borders are facts of life. Interaction—direct or empathetic—between Soviet dissidents and Americans has affected their governments' ability to ratify arms reduction agreements. Soviet and U.S. leaders operate in each other's political arenas day by day whether they choose to or not. An element of Israel's power is its ability through friends in the United States to manipulate the U.S. Congress. Nowhere is this continuous interaction more apparent than in the relationship between Israelis and Palestinians—though one is the occupier and the other the occupied.

Some of this cross-border interaction may be insidious, but some offers opportunities for guiding change peacefully and with respect for others. The sensible approach is not to pretend that this interaction does not take place, but to build relationships in which mutual respect keeps political interaction within limits that define the identity and integrity of each party. Understanding the process of interaction can suggest imaginative approaches to common problems.

Fifth, if power is the ability to influence the course of events, power today may emerge as much from the political ability to conduct that interactive process effectively as it does from wielding military or economic power or being an unyielding negotiator. Shifting focus to that political process incorporates two important dimensions of experience into our thinking about foreign affairs. First, we pay more attention to the larger political environment in which peoples reach fundamental judgments about peace, war, negotiation, and economic change. Second, when we turn to that political environment, we introduce ways of influencing those judgments and therefore the course of change by political action rather than only by contests of force.

To add this political dimension to thinking about power is to open the door to a range of political instruments alongside military and economic power. These instruments are not coercive but persuasive and sometimes even cooperative. The root of the word *political* leads to the citizen—the human being. Political instruments form ideas and perspectives that have organizing and directing power—organizing power as they become widely accepted ways of understanding events and directing power because of the actions that flow from them.[1] Politicians think this way because they understand the power of pictures in the mind to move people, but theories of international relations have not as commonly taken this perspective into account. Environment-changing political acts such as the Gorbachev-Reagan reconceptualization of the nuclear problem, Sadat's visit to Jerusalem, Carter's invitation to Camp David, or the Arias peace plan in Central America originated with politicians, not analysts.

Sixth, it is necessary to develop a concept that widens the focus of analysis to encompass that interactive political process itself. A concept is needed that includes but goes beyond analyzing the power, structures, decisionmaking, and formal positions of individual states and the instruments of force they use to get what they want from each other. In contrast to describing the international system in the metaphor of a chess game, I am suggesting that *relationship* is a concept that captures this dynamic interaction.

At first hearing, *relationship* is such a commonplace word that we hardly notice it. When we stop to think about relationships that sustain us as human beings, we begin to feel its power and depth. Like many commonplace but important words, it is sometimes confusing because we give it a different focus at different moments. At one moment, it may point to the comprehensive pattern of interactions that make up an overall relationship; at another, it may refer to a specific series of transactions or to just one facet of the overall relationship, as in a "working" as contrasted to a "personal" relationship. Relationships may be good and bad. We may interact creatively with some people and enjoy them; we may be locked by common needs and circumstances into a relationship with others whom we neither like nor trust. In international politics, it is necessary both to recognize the particular interactions that exist and to fashion them into overall relationships that can deal with common problems.

A relationship that permits two parties to deal with common problems combines four important characteristics: (1) a recognized mutuality of interests and needs, both practical and psychological; (2) limits that define, respect, and protect individual identity and needs; (3) the continuous process of interaction by which that interdependence of interests is defined, developed, and nurtured and which generates co-operative problem-solving action; and (4) eventually the evolution of a

---

1. I am indebted to John Steinbruner for the formulation in this sentence.

pattern of interaction and growth between the partners that acquires qualities and a life of its own that both partners value as an extension of themselves.

To apply the word *relationship* to nations is not simply to transfer personal qualities, values, and experience to them. We know nations have institutional characteristics beyond the sum of their citizens.

To use *relationship* in this context is to focus on what happens between nations or peoples when they interact. Cooperating, resolving conflict, or curbing confrontation requires understanding what grows in the space between leaders when they define a problem together as affecting common interests and work together over time on solutions. As they probe underlying needs that define what is vital to each party and what they can share without violating either's identity, a relationship begins to grow. As the relationship grows, the political environment changes. Nations can do more than they first thought possible. They need not surrender individual identities; to the contrary, the relationship may enlarge the potential of each. As time passes, the relationship itself acts as a brake against purely self-centered action. Focusing on relationship causes leaders to think and act differently from the way they would act if they were playing chess and tending balances of power. They concentrate less on sending signals, threatening, or negotiating and more on discussing, analyzing, and solving problems.

To focus on relationship is not to assume a utopian world in which nation states have faded away or conflict and power have become irrelevant. But two world wars in this century and nuclear weapons cause men and women to question a philosophy of nation states that use power unilaterally to pursue their interests. More and more, they refuse to accept that the world can work only through the clash of power. Most do not yet see a world federation. But an increasing number observe that all-out contests between states are no longer—if they ever were—effective, responsible, creative, or safe.

The transforming change that comes from building constructive relationships is one politically powerful experience we need to study and develop in practice. Scholars and analysts have studied governmental decisionmaking. They have studied how publics influence governments—even now in the Soviet Union. But they have not often studied how the many elements in one society interact with another society and in turn affect its actions. The transformation of relationships in Europe since World War II underscores the opportunity. The insights that may move Israelis and Palestinians toward resolution of their conflict will not come mainly from trying to initiate negotiation between state sovereignties.

They will come from focusing on the process of interaction between the two peoples.[2]

THE ARAB-ISRAELI CONFLICT AND PEACE PROCESS

Seeing international relationships as a continuous, interactive political process among policymaking and policy-influencing communities changes policy thinking. We ask a wider range of questions and seek answers beyond the usual analysis of state structures, power, interests, and capabilities. Those questions also probe the human roots of interests and conflict and help us to understand the politics of impasse and change.

Experience suggests that those who think about policy, whether in or out of government, usually work through three kinds of questions.

They first need to get their minds around a situation. They ask diagnostic questions. What kind of situation is this and how does it relate to others I know? What is really going on under the surface? Who is trying to achieve what and why? What are the identities and interests of those involved? Underlying this inquiry is the ultimate question: does the situation hurt my interests so badly that I have to do something about it?

If they then conclude they must take some action, they try to design a way of dealing with this hurting situation which could begin movement toward a preferable one. They envision possible alternatives. They try to understand the real obstacles to achieving those alternatives. They ask not just who is opposed to change but what fears, hopes, experiences, and misperceptions explain why they oppose it. Underlying this line of analysis is the policymaker's need to define the operational problem. In this case, the "problem" includes both recognizing the discrepancy between the present situation and a preferable one and determining the exact change needed to move from here to where one wants to be. This

2. These thoughts about shifting the lenses through which we look at our changing world are more fully developed in Harold H. Saunders, "Beyond 'Us and Them'—Building Mature International Relationships: The Role of Official and Supplemental Diplomacy," a draft monograph prepared in 1987–88 under a grant from the United States Institute of Peace and in collaboration with the Kettering Foundation. The more succinct statement of propositions describing our changing world was written under a specific grant from the Carnegie Corporation of New York with general support from the John D. and Catherine T. MacArthur and the Miriam and Ira D. Wallach Foundations. No foundation is responsible for the author's views.

dynamic definition of the problem identifies the key elements of policy design.

Finally, policymakers will set a direction and develop the instruments and scenarios for moving toward it. The essence of policy is a sense of direction—a judgment about destination and practical ways of getting there coupled with a readiness to try to create conditions and make mid-course corrections as new conditions permit.

Policymakers have long worked in these three areas. These are not stages in which one ends before the next begins. All questions are alive all the time. A policymaker will concentrate for a while in one area or another but protect the opportunity to circle back and rethink earlier conclusions in light of later insight or experience.

As the policymaker asks these questions in more probing ways and seeks broader answers, he or she enlarges the options. Here I apply this approach to the Arab-Israeli-Palestinian conflict. The purpose is to identify some of the difficult choices and opportunities that this perspective opens.[3]

Diagnosis: What Is the Situation?

How policymakers picture a situation influences what they will try to do about it. Political activists work hard to persuade policymakers to see a situation in one way rather than in another. The same is true in the public debate that surrounds policymakers. One way to change peoples' pictures of a situation is to change that situation physically. Another is to dramatize for people in other ways that an existing situation to which they have closed their eyes is already dangerous.

CHANGING PICTURES. As the "Palestinian revolt" went on in 1988, some people recognized that this campaign of sticks and stones was again changing their picture of the whole conflict. Since the Palestine question first came on the agenda of the new United Nations Organization in the 1940s, the picture of that problem has moved through at least three frames and may now be entering a fourth.

---

3. A fuller analysis of the state of the Arab-Israeli peace process appears in Harold H. Saunders, "Reconstituting the Arab-Israeli Peace Process," in William B. Quandt, ed., *The Middle East: Ten Years after Camp David* (Brookings, 1988), pp. 413–41. A full conceptualization of the peace process and approaches to it appear in Harold H. Saunders, *The Other Walls: The Politics of the Arab-Israeli Peace Process* (Washington, D.C.: American Enterprise Institute, 1985).

In the 1940s the world pictured the situation in the waning British mandate in Palestine as the Arab-Jewish conflict. The United Nations considered two choices—one state with human, civil, and political rights for each person or two states formed by dividing the land between the two peoples. The only viable solution seemed a partition of the land into an Arab state and a Jewish state. The Jewish population declared its independence as the State of Israel. Arab states surrounding Palestine rejected partition and attacked the new Jewish state.

The armistice agreements of 1949, which formally ended the fighting, transformed the conflict into the Arab-Israeli conflict—no longer a conflict between two peoples but now a conflict between the new State of Israel and surrounding Arab states. Between 1949 and the late 1960s the world saw a classic picture of nation states in conflict—increasingly massive collections of conventional and unconventional weapons, two further wars, regional power politics, and the intersection of more great power interests than in almost any other part of the developing world. The Palestinian people became refugees, stateless persons, and second-class citizens. They dropped from the picture, even in the Arab world.

By the late 1960s the picture began to change again. The PLO came under the new leadership of Yasser Arafat. The Palestinians reasserted themselves as a people. Israeli occupation of all the land west of the Jordan River in the 1967 war raised the possibility of single-state control in that land, and the Palestinians saw that their chance of creating their own state there was about to slip away. In 1974 the Arab states affirmed "the right of the Palestinian people to establish an independent national authority under the command of the Palestine Liberation Organization, the sole legitimate representative of the Palestinian people in any Palestinian territory that is liberated."[4]

In November 1975 the Ford administration authorized a statement before a congressional subcommittee that recognized the importance of dealing with the Palestinian dimension of the conflict: "We have also repeatedly stated that the legitimate interests of the Palestinian Arabs must be taken into account in the negotiation of an Arab-Israeli peace. In many ways, the Palestinian dimension of the Arab-Israeli conflict is the heart of that conflict. Final resolution of the problems arising from

---

4. *The Search for Peace in the Middle East: Documents and Statements, 1967–79,* Report Prepared for the Subcommittee on Europe and the Middle East of the House Committee on Foreign Affairs, by the Foreign Affairs and National Defense Division, Congressional Research Service, Library of Congress, 96 Cong. 1 sess. (Government Printing Office, 1979), p. 273.

the partition of Palestine, the establishment of the State of Israel, and Arab opposition to those events will not be possible until agreement is reached defining a just and permanent status for the Arab peoples who consider themselves Palestinians."[5] What had been pictured as a straight-forward state-to-state conflict now appeared as a conflict between two peoples embedded in that larger struggle.

In the late 1970s the picture began to change again. The new picture is not yet clear. Its exact focus is sharply debated. After 1977 the Begin government tightened Israel's grip on the West Bank and Gaza by implanting Israeli settlements to crisscross those territories, breaking up coherent Arab areas. Some Israeli analysts argue that the process is irreversible and that Israel has now internalized the Palestinian problem. They believe the destruction of the Zionist state has begun, because it cannot absorb a 40 percent or more Arab minority and remain a democratic Jewish nation. They foresee that this internal intercommunal conflict will plague Israel as Northern Ireland and South Africa have been plagued. For other Israelis, the die is not yet cast; they still hope to resolve the conflict by establishing a separate Palestinian political entity.

THE PARTIES AND THEIR INTERESTS. If one views the conflict in these terms, it is immediately obvious that this is not simply a traditional conflict between nation states. One needs to analyze more deeply the character of the parties to the conflict.

On one side, the Palestinian movement is a loose association of organizations and communities. The PLO is an umbrella group embracing widely divergent views about strategy and the future. Geographically, the Palestinians are divided between those living west of the Jordan River and those outside Israeli-controlled territories. Moreover, those outside are socially and economically diverse—from refugees to wealthy professionals and entrepreneurs—and are scattered. Although increasing national consciousness has given Palestinians common identity and purposes, one must take into account—without the intention of dimin-ishing that sense of peoplehood—the separate communities constituting the Palestinian people.

On the other side, though less apparent, Israel is itself made up of many communities. At the extreme, some orthodox religious groups

5. Statement by Harold H. Saunders, *The Palestinian Issue in Middle East Peace Efforts*, Hearings before the Special Subcommittee on Investigations of the House Committee on International Relations, 94 Cong. 1 sess. (GPO, 1976), p. 178.

deny the state's legitimacy. Even in the center, Israel is deeply divided between different philosophies about the foundational principles of a Jewish state. These diverse communities are kept together by the horrors of past persecution and the remarkable historic cohesion of the Jewish people. But deep differences are reflected in the government, even to the point of paralysis in taking decisions on peace with Israel's neighbors.

If the parties to the Arab-Israeli conflict are understood in this way, it becomes necessary to probe beneath the usual picture of state interests. Conventional statements of interests do not fully describe what is at stake in any move toward resolution of the conflict.

One common starting point is the undeniably and understandably deep Israeli interest in security. But that statement does not go far enough. To begin with, there is a serious debate among military specialists over just what is required to provide for Israel's physical security. Some think that to protect its Jordanian-Palestinian front Israel needs only early warning of attack and the capability to win the race to the Jordan River. Others believe Israeli must have control over the entire West Bank.

In that debate some statements of security interests are intertwined with the different views of the future of the Jewish state. Underlying both conceptions is a deep fear of annihilation that calls for the preservation of a Zionist state. But thinking diverges on what would constitute fulfillment of the Zionist dream. For one group, the strongest interest is to maintain control over the historic lands of the Bible. For another, the interest is to preserve in the state an embodiment of universal values in Judaism. In the late 1980s the first group sees its interests threatened by any arrangement with the Palestinians that would diminish Israel's grip on the land. The other group sees its interests threatened when Israel must use force to suppress another people.

That difference in defining Israel's interests leads to different judgments about whether those interests are being hurt by the present situation. Those who define interests in terms of maintaining Israeli control over all the land west of the Jordan River resist entering into negotiation, the only logical outcome of which would be giving up some of that land. Some of them would even expel much of the Palestinian population to preserve Israeli dominance. Those who define interests in terms of preserving a state built on universal Judaic values believe Israel should not violate the rights of the Palestinians and should withdraw from the territory where they predominantly live. This group would negotiate a new relationship between the two peoples.

In its most common statement, the prime Palestinian interest is to establish a state in the Palestinian homeland, but some Palestinians would word the statement of interest differently. They would say their first interest is to achieve practical recognition of a Palestinian identity tied to the land west of the Jordan. In response to a question about the primary Palestinian interest, PLO leaders focus on establishing a state, whereas Palestinians in the West Bank and Gaza are likely to say, "Getting rid of the Israeli occupation and beginning to build institutions of our own." All Palestinians have a common interest in the recognition of their peoplehood, but how they describe their interest as a precise guide to policy depends on where they live.

The Palestinian body politic, like the Israeli, is divided over the degree to which the present situation hurts long-term interests. Those who believe recognition of the PLO as the representative of the Palestinian people is necessary to fulfill their interest in a state resist negotiation that does not bring that recognition. Those who live under occupation feel the tightening Israeli grip and see the primary interest not in recognition of the whole Palestinian people and their right to a state but in more immediate recognition of Palestinians' right to self-government in that land. They would negotiate soon on limited practical issues to keep the door open for negotiation of larger issues later. In the absence of agreement within the Palestinian movement on the form a state might take, they seek recognition and expression of their identity in the land.

THE NEW RELATIONSHIPS. These differing pictures of the situation, the parties to the conflict, and their interests are not a matter of taste, theory, or fashion. They result from evolving patterns of human interaction— within each people and across the lines separating them. Any policymaker will need to know not just what formal relations exist between established institutions and what positions they take but also what relationships exist underneath the formal structures.

Since the Israelis took down the barbed wire along the 1949 armistice lines after the 1967 war, Israelis and Palestinians have interacted in many ways. This is one of the striking new realities in the Arab-Israeli confrontation. To quote the recent Brookings report of a study group: "Meanwhile, for a whole generation of Israelis and Palestinians, the 'green line' that had effectively separated their two societies from 1949 until 1967 has lost much of its earlier meaning, even though the political and cultural divide continues to be very real. Although in normal times some 100,000 Palestinians cross this line every day to work in Israel, there is still little real integration or cooperation between the two societies and peoples."[6]

Despite its limitations, that interaction has created an experience for the two peoples in dealing with each other that is unmatched even under the Egyptian-Israeli peace treaty. This interaction happens in many ways with different consequences.

Palestinian and Israeli intellectuals meet in dialogue all over the Western world and in their own institutions. A self-styled former assassin who fought in the pre-1947 Israeli underground against the British mandate hears a Palestinian doctor describe the frustrations of running a hospital when Israeli authorities harass the import of medicines. He decides to talk to the Israeli defense minister and later changes political parties. Palestinians listen to an Israeli describe how his wife was killed by a Palestinian bomb. Palestinians learn how deeply Israelis fear the Arabs and the threat of annihilation, and are frustrated at not being able to convince colleagues in Arab states of this reality. Israelis and Palestinians sitting together both speak of Palestine as their common homeland and of their needs to preserve separate identities. These Israelis and Palestinians visit each others' homes and, in limited numbers, meet each others' friends.

A few Palestinians have observed closely and learned how to move the Israeli system. At one end of the spectrum, they understand the need to take one small and minimally threatening step at a time to change Israeli occupation practices rather than demand a Palestinian state immediately, which they know the Israeli body politic cannot now accept. Some have learned how to get what they need from individual occupation bureaucrats; others have learned to lobby members of the Israeli parliament.

Person-to-person interactions affect the character of the relationship between Israelis and Palestinians in many different situations. Watching an Israeli soldier beat a young Palestinian who has thrown a rock at him raises questions about the impact of that scene on efforts to improve relations between Israeli Arabs and Jews essential to the long-term health of Israel as well as questions about whether those young people will ever be able to work together even if they recognize common interests. Does the interaction between the young Israeli woman and the Palestinian woman she strip searches at the border checkpoint perpetuate feelings of hatred and damaged self-esteem on both sides beyond remedy? What

6. *Toward Arab-Israeli Peace: Report of a Study Group* (Brookings, 1988), p. 20.

is the lingering effect of the glance that passes between them when the eight-year-old Palestinian boy looks into the eyes of the teenage Israeli soldier who is pointing a gun at him? What happens inside an Israeli employer or foreman and a Palestinian employee as they interact in the work place?

Patterns of continuous and extensive interaction have developed that are likely to shape long-term relationships between Israelis and Palestinians, whatever political arrangements may emerge. Even though the relationship is between occupier and occupied, the two peoples have interacted in ways that pose the Palestine question for both in a new form. Whereas establishing one secular state in Palestine seemed impractical in 1947, by the mid-1980s a one-state solution became a physical possibility, however unlikely politically. More important, small but significant numbers of thoughtful Israelis and Palestinians have become accustomed to discussing as a shared problem how to build a common future in the same land on the basis of mutual respect for separate political identities. Or they have learned harshly that, though they may be locked into a common future, they cannot share the same sovereign roof. While majorities on each side may choose to live with separate political identities, they will do so having experienced the challenge to human tolerance and moral principle of living in direct interaction under one political authority, albeit in a very unequal relationship.

In addition, two-thirds of the Jordanian population is Palestinian, and the underlying human interactions also extend east of the Jordan River. There is an intertwining of daily lives, a process of economic interaction and cultural abrasion that produces both conflict and accommodation at a personal and communal level. This process will influence the future character of the Hashemite Kingdom of Jordan as well as its relationship with Palestinians and Israelis. It imposes significant constraints on any attempt to define borders, to establish sovereignty, or to set policy in the region. It also provides the more promising opportunities for resolving historical conflict.

THE CHALLENGE. In short, the future of the area is evolving from below, not developing from the top down. The same is true of many other troubled regions of the world. The challenge for the policymaker or the mediator is to shape constructive change that builds from relationships already growing and reflects the real interests underlying them.

Adjusting to this observation and accepting its implications demands a sharp shift in the prevailing conceptions not only about the content of policy but even more about the means of defining or implementing it. Traditional conceptions of state power are less relevant and less effective in a world in which spontaneous human interactions are setting the context of events. Military power can be used much more readily against an opponent similarly organized than against an established society partly integrated into one's own. The calculating decisionmakers of one state can develop leverage, bargaining maneuvers, and other forms of direct influence to use on their counterparts in another state and can seek to secure advantage or "victory" in the outcome of specific actions. Spontaneous social actions, however, cannot be disaggregated into discrete episodic contests of this sort. They involve the formation of continuing relationships that are fabricated from principles of equity, mutual benefit, legitimated procedure, and shared interest.

If effective policy to deal with regional conflict depends more on creating and conducting political relationships than on wielding superior power, then it must be designed in new ways and given a new direction. In order to define the operational problem to be dealt with in moving from a present situation to a preferable one, policymakers must understand the alternatives that would meet the material and psychological needs of the participants as well as their resistance to change. They must identify direction and feasible routes of travel and have the starting conditions and local terrain in mind, not simply the location and characteristics of the ultimate destination. They must think of sequences and evolving interactions, not just of final outcomes.

Policy Design: What Is the Problem?

If a policymaker recognizes exactly how a present situation harms interests, he or she tries to envision alternatives and then to analyze the obstacles to moving from here to there. Defining the operational problem in dynamic terms of what obstacles must be overcome to produce an alternative situation provides the critical ingredient in policy design—a focus for efforts to move in a desired direction. Here the problem is not to devise a formula for negotiation between Israel and Arab states which would involve Palestinians. The problem is first to produce a commitment by Israelis and Palestinians to build a peaceful relationship with each other. To concentrate first on building a direct Israeli-Palestinian relationship is to give the peace process a focus it has not had.

ALTERNATIVES. One can define alternatives to the present Israeli-Palestinian relationship in either of two vocabularies. Each will lead to a different set of alternatives. If one defines alternatives in traditional terms of state institutions, one will think primarily about whether the Palestinians should have an independent state, or should have a moment of independent statehood followed by federation or confederation with Jordan or Israel, or both, or should be a clearly identified autonomous but subordinate unit in either Jordan or Israel. A less conventional way of looking at the alternatives is to think of what kinds of relationships among three peoples—Israelis, Jordanians, Palestinians—will meet their needs and serve their basic interests.

Taking the second approach, one might think first of economic relationships. To begin with, Palestinians have an interest in continuing to earn wages in the Israeli economy. Israeli manufacturers have an interest in the Palestinian and potentially the Jordanian markets. Establishing cooperative high-technology light industry both in Israel and in the West Bank and Gaza could benefit everyone. In the agricultural area, perhaps something could be learned from the European Community. Of course, security relationships would be needed that protect each party's identity from any threat by another, but the parties would also have common security concerns.

As political relationships evolve, important responsibilities will fall to local Palestinian authorities, but joint authorities may also be useful where interests such as water resources cut across the Israeli-Jordanian boundary and across Jewish and Palestinian communities in the West Bank. Agreements could further define the three peoples' rights to live, work, and own or rent property in each other's jurisdictions while voting at home. Security would require special arrangements. Other agreements might deal with the jurisdiction of courts.

By focusing on relationships that could be built, one might get a practical, evolving picture of alternatives that would involve growing Palestinian political authority as the three peoples learn to live together peacefully. New relationships may not be realizable in one step, so it may be necessary to move within a longer vision, as Europe has done for more than four decades.

OBSTACLES. Before trying to move toward an alternative situation, one must understand the obstacles. In the traditional view the obstacles to negotiating a settlement lie in the unwillingness of an Israeli prime minister or a Palestinian leader to accept terms of reference for a negotiation based on mutual recognition. In that view the issues to be dealt with in negotiation must resolve the question of sovereignty.

Israel takes the position that it will not negotiate with the PLO or agree to a Palestinian state. Within that government, the prime minister's coalition—the Likud—does not want to negotiate any diminution of Israeli control over the West Bank and Gaza. The other party to the national unity government in mid-1988—the Labor alignment—would negotiate some Israeli withdrawal and be willing to accept Jordanian, not Palestinian, sovereignty in the land given up.

The PLO now says it is ready to recognize and peacefully coexist with Israel if Israel will recognize the Palestinians' right to a state in land from which Israel withdraws. The PLO holds that Israel must withdraw to the borders that defined it before the 1967 war. PLO leaders say they cannot recognize Israel before they are sure that Israel will reciprocate. Unless they believe they can achieve their own goal of establishing a state through negotiation, they cannot persuade their constituents to recognize Israel by negotiating with it. Any pragmatic approach, such as the Camp David accords, that moves a step at a time through an open-ended political process seems to them to ignore the central issue of equal rights for Palestinians that would be symbolized in creation of a state.

At least conceptually, the main obstacle to Israeli-Palestinian settlement—the question of sovereignty—could be approached by thinking more broadly about what constitutes a people's exercise of sovereignty. In the later twentieth century, nations have learned that they must work together in ways that make sovereignty less than absolute. Even the Soviet Union and the United States are just beginning to accept as necessary the performance of such functions as inspection of arms production and discussion of human rights issues on each other's soil. Although Egypt was criticized on this point, the Egyptian-Israeli peace treaty includes provision for an international force stationed on both sides of the border to monitor treaty compliance. Syria in the 1974 disengagement agreement with Israel agreed to limitations on deployment of weapons in specified areas. If the designed relationships meet needs, each party exercises sovereignty by agreeing.

Other obstacles will often not appear on the usual list of arguments against particular terms of reference for negotiation. In 1977, for instance, Sadat recognized that the principal obstacle to negotiation was not the U.S. failure to produce terms of reference to which everyone could agree. It was deep Israeli suspicion that no Egyptian leader would make peace with Israel. Sadat visited Jerusalem to erode that suspicion. In the Israeli-

Palestinian conflict, each side fears deeply that the other plans its obliteration. That fear and the mutual dehumanization flowing from it may be the principal obstacle to negotiation. Such obstacles will be removed in the political arena, not in the negotiating room.

THE PROBLEM. What then is the problem for policymakers? Where should they focus their energies in tackling the Israeli-Palestinian impasse?

A traditional view would say that the problem is to write terms of reference that will bring the adversaries to an international conference. Such a document would try to come up with a formula for mutual recognition and would try to give each party a sense that its needs could be met in negotiation. It would have to square the circle created by Israel's refusal to negotiate with the PLO and the fact that only the PLO can speak authoritatively for the Palestinians in recognizing Israel.

A different view would say that the problem is to produce political commitments by Israelis and Palestinians, each to the other, to build new and mutually acceptable relationships, not just to begin a negotiation. If so, it is necessary to help precipitate commitments that clearly recognize each people's right to political expression in ways of its own choosing in their common homeland in Palestine. Defining the problem in this way changes the design requirements for policymaking. Talk about how to negotiate might be one way to shape the debate about whether to negotiate, but that by itself will probably not be enough. A policy to produce fundamental decisions about the futures of peoples will require a scenario of political steps designed to erode fear and suspicion and help Israelis and Palestinians explore commitment to new relationships.

Policy: What Should We Do?

Policy in the minds of statesmen is not so much a series of decisions as a sense of direction. When a direction is set, leaders begin to think about appropriate instruments and interacting steps to produce movement. The discussion that follows is written from a Washington perspective. A full analysis would also include the thought processes of leaders in other key capitals as well.

SETTING A DIRECTION. Telling a U.S. president that one of his options is to try to change the Israeli-Palestinian political environment reflects an unconventional approach to foreign policy thinking. Political leaders will understand the point from domestic political experience, but they do not often take this political perspective beyond the border. They have understood the principle that one state should not meddle in another's internal affairs. They often seem not to recognize, for instance, that the very existence of Palestinians whom Israelis fear makes the Palestinians' behavior a central factor in internal Israeli political life and policymaking. The example could be stated in reverse. In such situations trying to reshape behavior on one side or another may be a legitimate aim of policy.

If the problem is ultimately to develop a new Israeli-Palestinian relationship, it would be legitimate to try to reach inside the interaction between the two peoples to change the political environment and create the possibility of moving a step at a time to begin establishing the elements of that new relationship. As the political environment changes in the desired direction, attempts could eventually be made to define and advance those changes in negotiation. Beginning to move in a certain direction may offer a wider field of maneuver than trying to agree in negotiation on the exact description of the relationship at the outset. To move this way requires only agreement to move in one direction rather than in another. Setting the direction would include ending the isolation of the PLO in the process of developing a mutual Israeli-Palestinian commitment to build a peaceful relationship.

INSTRUMENTS. Traditionally, the instruments of statecraft have included the threat or use of military force, economic sanctions or inducements, diplomacy and negotiation, and steps to change opinion. Perhaps in the late 1980s only violent acts will cause the parties to see the present situation as intolerable. The challenge to leaders is to design peaceful, political acts that could refocus public debate, redefine the problem, and sharpen visions of alternative futures. If leaders view relationships as a political process of continuous interaction, they will need some concept to help them think about the conduct of the relationships that are the essence of that process. The concept introduced here for that purpose is the comprehensive political scenario.

Such a scenario combines political steps and steps to prepare for negotiation in ways designed to change the political environment. Political steps affect prospects for negotiation, and preparations for negotiation affect the political environment. Saying this sounds like stating the obvious, since leaders normally think about their political support. The fact is that those trying to advance the peace process have not always paid the necessary attention to the politics of the process; they have given disproportionate attention to trying to begin negotiations.

A comprehensive scenario of political steps can have three uses. First, it is an analytical tool for identifying deep-rooted political obstacles to progress and for matching those obstacles with acts that might erode them. Second, it establishes a time sequence for actions by each party and responses by other parties that can become mutually reinforcing. Specifically, one can construct a sequence that recognizes that no party can move immediately to a desired outcome, but that if one party were to take a step to which a second party responded and then the first party responded with the third step, it might be possible to move a step at a time toward the desired destination. Third, once a scenario has begun to take shape, a mediating party can use it in talking with each of the parties and then for establishing informally their agreement to play their respective roles.

This process of scenario-building sounds more technical than it is. During the Kissinger shuttles and the Camp David mediations of the 1970s, the United States, as the third party, talked through the other parties' views on the shape of an outcome for a particular negotiation and the steps that might help achieve their goal. Rarely were these ideas written down except for in-house working purposes. That in-house paper was simply a starting point for conversations with all parties until everyone was talking about the same goal and the same way of proceeding. Until each party was working from comparable interest in negotiating, from similar pictures of alternative futures and definitions of the problem of moving toward them, and from the same general scenario for proceeding, attempts to negotiate formally were futile.

The reason for introducing the idea of the political scenario is to lay out a broad menu of illustrative actions that in some combination could move the peace process forward. What is offered here is not a plan of action but a suggestion of the breadth of approach necessary to reconstitute the peace process. This approach could be used in other situations as well.

ELEMENTS OF A COMPREHENSIVE POLITICAL SCENARIO

The purpose of the scenario is to address the problem as it is defined; namely, to produce a mutual commitment to build a peaceful relationship. That will take time, but the political process must keep that objective explicitly in sight. There is no use in starting a negotiation without a substantive view of its purpose nor in setting in motion a political process with no clear objective.

Elements of a scenario might be organized for discussion under the six headings below. These headings do not represent stages. They are areas of activity. Some actions may have to be taken in sequence; others may need to proceed simultaneously on separate tracks.

Exploratory Exchanges

In periods of impasse, exploratory discussions that do not have the specific aim of producing complete agreement or action can provide different perspectives and approaches. They can be held in private, quasi-official, or official groups. Since critical substantive questions are often not adequately handled now in official dialogue, the purpose here is to broaden the ways of preparing a political scenario.

OFFICIAL AND NONOFFICIAL DIALOGUE. The format for exploratory exchanges can vary; the aim is to free participants to think creatively. Many nonofficial exchanges now take place informally between Israelis and Palestinians in the West Bank and Gaza and, less frequently, between Israelis and Jordanians. Some take place in international settings with third parties present. Going beyond completely nonofficial talks, governments could name a nonofficial group to explore ideas without the authority to negotiate but with the understanding that governments would take seriously the ideas produced. Those ideas might then be used in quiet, official dialogue. In addition to such informal meetings, governments could also arrange secret or open meetings among officials for dialogue, not negotiation.

Whatever the format, these exchanges need focus if they are to help change the political environment. The increased human contact itself conveys seriousness. But policy-relevant dialogue is distinguished from casual discussion by systematic probing for interests, needs, hopes, fears, pictures of the problem, and alternatives and by precise discussion of steps to erode the obstacles to peace. Sometimes it seems easier to talk about deep-rooted obstacles and needs in the informal setting of non-official dialogue, though there is no reason why officials could not be frank with one another.

In the move away from conventional state mechanisms to consultations among representatives of the peoples involved, the question of Palestinian equality might be dealt with in commonsense human terms. The recent Brookings report proposed the following:

> *We believe that Palestinians should be represented in any negotiations with Israel by spokesmen of their own choosing, whether in a joint Jordanian-Palestinian delegation or in some other configuration.* As a general guideline, the United States should have no objection to the participation of Palestinians who are on record as being prepared to coexist with the state of Israel, are committed to peaceful negotiations, can contribute to that objective, and agree to renounce the use of force. In practical terms, we recognize that Palestinians are unlikely to come forward to negotiate with Israel without having the implicit or explicit endorsement of the PLO.[7]

THE ISSUES. Dialogue short of official exchanges about negotiation allows freedom to use unconventional concepts in analysis and different ways of thinking about steps that might be taken. Among substantive questions to be explored is, for instance, a fundamental proposition arising from the analysis of the Arab-Israeli conflict in this chapter: a resolution must provide a satisfying mutual recognition and political expression of the identity of both the Jewish and the Palestinian peoples. The normal way that peoples have accomplished that objective is to create a state of their own. Israel has done just that. The Palestinians have not yet been able to do so, though now they are again considering creating a government-in-exile or some form of provisional government.

Since Israelis reject the creation of a Palestinian state and Palestinians have not yet designed their state, a first analytical question is whether there are ways to provide political expression and recognition of Palestinian identity other than by immediately establishing a Palestinian state or government. The Palestinians themselves may have given one clue when they say they want a passport and a flag as symbolic expressions of their nationality. More concretely, some authority over the use of land and water resources might tie transitional self-government to territory in Palestine. Discussing how to give political expression to Palestinian nationhood without infringing on Israeli and Jordanian rights to the same, rather than arguing over early creation of a Palestinian state or provisional government, could provide a different set of steps.

A first operational step may lie in recognizing the Palestinians as a

7. Ibid., p. 31.

people entitled to political expression of their identity in Palestine. One could speak functionally of their right to choose their own representatives to work as equal partners with Israel and Jordan in designing the relationship that is to be developed. One problem is that some Palestinians have confused recognition of the Palestinian people with recognition of the PLO. Without prejudice to the PLO's ultimate role, the distinction should be kept clear.

A supporting step may be to ask where sovereignty lies in a situation like this. After the end of the British mandate in 1948, sovereignty in Arab land west of the Jordan became uncertain. A U.S. legal answer has been that sovereignty lies in the people. If that is true, then the act of electing representatives to speak on their behalf is a practical expression of sovereignty. That, by itself, does not provide a symbolically important, definitive answer to the question of sovereignty over land. But electing people to exercise authority over concrete resources like land and water as well as to provide services and to regulate relationships may begin to define elements of sovereignty.

Looking at sovereignty in this way could arouse concern among Arabs that a distinction is being made to deprive them of sovereignty over the land. The point to be made is that, while jurisdictional borders need to be established, the right to exercise authority within those borders may not be absolute. Where three peoples are involved in a solution, there may need to be a recognition of rights that flow across those borders. If sovereignty resides in the people, they would have the right to negotiate a specific sharing of powers and responsibilities.

If people think seriously about negotiating functional cooperation across boundaries, they begin to generate new relationships in specific areas. Thinking in terms of developing new patterns of interaction is different from thinking in terms of two states negotiating a treaty. Gradually, new sets of interactions accumulate and the shape of a new overall relationship begins to emerge. In developing a new overall relationship, two peoples can sit and talk about what the specific elements of that relationship will be. If they start from that point instead of creating a state first and then bargaining between states, the result may be different. If the Israelis could accept the Palestinian people as equals and both could begin to share a common task of developing a constructive overall Israeli-Palestinian relationship, a different approach to solutions could evolve.

The concept of building a community of peoples, such as the European Community, may also offer some opportunity for defining practical relationships. A difference is that the EC began with the existence of states that gradually had to surrender some sovereignty to community organizations. In the Arab-Israeli arena, although Israel and the Hashemite Kingdom exist, the aim would be to create the community—the relationship—and then work back to precise political arrangements.

Changing the Political Environment

At some point the exploratory exchange of ideas could produce steps designed to develop in the political arena the belief that it is possible to build peaceful relationships and even to negotiate a settlement. One of the greatest obstacles to negotiation has been the sense on each side that the other does not seriously want a new relationship. In 1979 and 1980 the Egyptians suggested measures that Israel could take by itself in the West Bank and Gaza to show readiness to begin changing the status of those territories. Similar steps, such as a PLO moratorium on violence, would signal Palestinian seriousness. One purpose of exploratory dialogue would be to identify those steps that would have the most meaning to the people concerned.

As unilateral steps are identified and set in place, an effort could be made to arrange those steps and the responses to them in a scenario that would begin to establish a pattern of action and response which could make further action and response possible. If these steps emerged from quiet exploratory exchanges, messages could be sent through the same channels that the steps taken were intended to lay the groundwork for dialogue in a more open forum. The shared act of discussing steps and responses begins direct engagement in a common attempt to change the political environment, following on an informally understood effort to lay the political foundations for new relationships and negotiation. As this engagement develops, publics will start paying attention to the emerging pattern.

Shaping Constructive Debate

Parallel to a scenario of interacting steps to produce a political environment for negotiation would be a conscious effort to shape constructive debate within each body politic on the need for change and for negotiations to define and consolidate that change. That will require discussion of fundamental interests and how they are affected by the passage of time. As a scenario of foundation-laying steps proceeds, it can stimulate and shape domestic debate. Here may be the most difficult elements in the scenario: how to bring the Israeli body politic to a decision to make changes that could lead to less than complete Israeli control over the West Bank and Gaza and to a settlement that recognizes the Palestinians as equally entitled to a homeland in the land west of the Jordan River. On the other side: how to persuade Palestinians, especially those outside the West Bank and Gaza, that they could gain something worthwhile from negotiating with Israel.

Making Negotiation Happen

As a scenario of foundation-laying steps and public debate proceeds, the time will come when leaders can take politically significant steps to try to make a negotiation happen. These could include statements about readiness for peace; sharing a common homeland; willingness to negotiate on the basis of mutual recognition; recognition of each other's losses, dignity, and need for security; and even readiness to meet in a particular setting for negotiation. Such statements would convey the message that political leaders were ready to go beyond administrative steps and to test support or build support in the political arena for moving toward a negotiated settlement. It is one thing to talk about negotiation; it requires more serious steps to commit a body politic to negotiation.

As efforts to influence attitudes proceed, words and acts in one body politic influence attitudes in the other. At first, unspoken relationships begin to form among those on both sides who want to move toward talks. As those relationships become more explicit, they begin to form the political context that can eventually tackle issues through formal negotiation.

Precipitating Acts

As the scope of political measures broadens, the parties will approach actions that could precipitate change. Sadat's visit to Jerusalem in 1977 or Carter's invitation to Camp David are examples of dramatic, precipitating acts. To be effective, other such acts need not have the same high drama.

One example of a precipitating act, discussed since the late 1970s,

would be a unilateral Israeli move to provide greater Palestinian responsibility for self-government in the West Bank and Gaza, referred to as
"unilateral autonomy." This move would be a good example of how a
precipitating act might be taken either successfully or unsuccessfully.
Taken in a vacuum, steps toward greater Palestinian self-government
under Israeli occupation could be rejected by Palestinians as a move
toward autonomy in a final consolidation of Israeli control in the West
Bank and Gaza. Such steps taken in an understood context, which
included commitment to move toward negotiation of further steps, could
provide the stimulus that catalyzes a move toward negotiation.

Similarly, the Palestinian movement has stated its readiness to talk
about negotiation, but Israelis have been able to dismiss such statements
because they were often made equivocally and outside a political context
that could smooth the path toward negotiation. A clear-cut Palestinian
statement beamed into Israel in a way that could not be ignored, coupled
with a moratorium on violence, could be a precipitating act.

Not all such acts are peaceful. The purpose of precipitating acts is to
change attitudes and cause public debate that leads toward negotiation.
Some precipitating acts increase the pain of the present situation. The
1973 war had that effect. In the next decade heightened violence or a
sustained and mounting nonviolent campaign in the West Bank and
Gaza could cause Israeli repression that would arouse debate in Israel
and around the world. A political process offers alternatives to violence
if leaders will invest the energy in developing and sustaining them.

Organizing Negotiation

Alongside the evolution of dialogue about political steps to improve
the environment for negotiation, there must be talks about how to
organize the negotiation itself. When a precipitating political act is taken,
the mediators and negotiators must have woven into the political scenario
those steps that would also constitute first steps toward negotiation. For
instance, important political steps to signify mutual recognition and
acceptance would be critical elements in a scenario to change public
attitudes, but they could also be carefully stated so as to provide the
main elements in terms of reference for negotiation.

Also important in preparing for negotiation is a sense of the choices
about strategy in the negotiation. For instance, if a step-by-step approach
seems to offer the best prospect, can simultaneous political steps be

taken to ensure that all sides stay committed to the long-term objective of an overall settlement?

As part of moving toward negotiation, each party will need to make choices about the international environment in which it will attempt to develop a political process for achieving a settlement. There are essentially three possible courses to take.

First, a choice open to any party is direct negotiation, presumably secret, to try to work out a settlement with one other participant without broader international involvement. Experience suggests that doing so may be useful as a way of preparing for later understandings but that at some point the negotiation must be put into a larger political context. However, in the early stages each party has the option of beginning negotiations secretly and pressing them as far as is possible before making them public.

A second approach is to continue mediation by one major power—the role the United States served in the 1970s—and to direct that effort at a limited sphere of negotiation. In the 1970s, for instance, much of the mediation focused on the Egyptian-Israeli front. A fundamental question facing the parties in the mid-1980s has been whether to try to concentrate on an Israeli-Jordanian-Palestinian agreement that depends on U.S. mediation, leaving both the Soviet Union and Syria on the sidelines until a following round of negotiation between Israel and Syria.

A third option is to plan from the outset to develop and conduct a reconstituted peace process in a broad regional and international political setting. That does not necessarily mean specific negotiations cannot take place in separate arenas. It does mean that the preparations would include a broad understanding that separate negotiations will take place and that at some point there will be provision for incorporating their results into a larger settlement.

Within the Middle East, this question has important implications for building a political base both in Israel and in the Arab world. In Israel, opponents of negotiation use Soviet and Syrian involvement as an argument against a broad international effort, though that attitude has been changing with the gradual rapprochement between Israel and the Soviet Union. On the Arab side within the region, the fundamental question always asked is, can there be a peace process without Syria?

In the larger international environment, the question is whether the Soviet Union and the United States can work in parallel, if not jointly. The answer will depend partly on how Soviet and U.S. leaders conduct their overall relationship. The answer also depends on how fully the big powers support the United Nations' peacemaking efforts.

A CONCLUDING WORD

The purpose in laying out elements in a possible scenario for reconstituting the Arab-Israeli peace process is not to prescribe a plan of action. That is a task for those in authority. The purpose is to widen the angle of the lenses we use in looking at Arab-Israeli conflict.

Refocusing our picture of how nations relate—testing old assumptions against new realities—is not an abstract exercise. How leaders and citizens view what they are doing will influence how they will go about their tasks. We all need accurate concepts for understanding complicated situations that affect our interests.

Steadily we are changing our images of how the world works. We first noticed some of those changes in regions like the Middle East, but we find them affirmed by looking at relationships everywhere. Pictures in the mind—the essence of political environments—make a difference in how people act. As leaders around the world refocus their pictures of today's world, they will see the opportunity to give at least as much attention to political—and therefore peaceful—strategies for bringing about change as they do to preparations for using force.

Index